BIGGEST EVER BOOK OF
QUESTIONS & ANSWERS

BIGGEST EVER BOOK OF
QUESTIONS
& ANSWERS

p

This is a Parragon Publishing book
This edition published in 2006

Copyright © Parragon Books Ltd 2003

Written by John Farndon, Ian James,
Jinny Johnson, Fiona Macdonald, Angela Royston,
Philip Steele, and Martin Walters

Illustrated by David Ashby,
Mike Atkinson, Julian Baker, Andrew Farmer,
Rob Jakeway, John James, and Roger Kent

Consultant editor
Brian Williams

This edition created by
Starry Dog Books

ISBN: 1-40545-589-6

Printed in China

CONTENTS

UNIVERSE

How did the Earth begin?

Around 4.6 billion years ago, neither the Earth nor any of the other planets existed. There was just this vast, dark, very hot cloud of gas and dust swirling around the newly formed Sun. Gradually, the cloud cooled and the gas began to condense into billions of droplets. Slowly these droplets were pulled together into clumps by their own gravity—and they carried on clumping until all the planets, including the Earth, were formed. But it took another half a billion years before the Earth had cooled enough to form a solid crust with an atmosphere around it.

❓ HOW BIG IS THE EARTH?

Satellite measurements show it is 24,901 miles (40,075 km) around the equator and 7,927 miles (12,577 km) across. The diameter at the Poles is slightly less, by 26.7 miles (43 km).

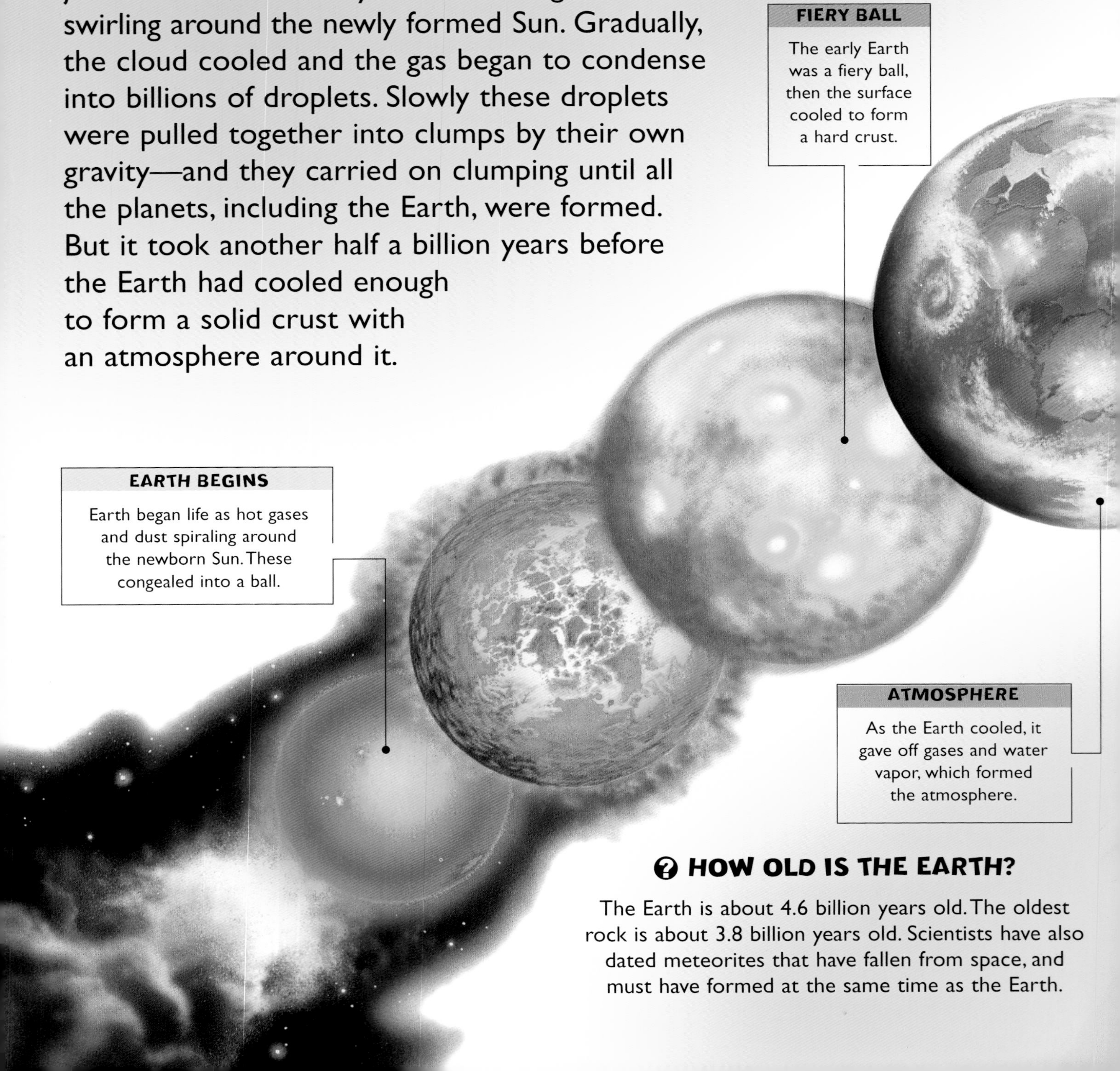

FIERY BALL

The early Earth was a fiery ball, then the surface cooled to form a hard crust.

EARTH BEGINS

Earth began life as hot gases and dust spiraling around the newborn Sun. These congealed into a ball.

ATMOSPHERE

As the Earth cooled, it gave off gases and water vapor, which formed the atmosphere.

❓ HOW OLD IS THE EARTH?

The Earth is about 4.6 billion years old. The oldest rock is about 3.8 billion years old. Scientists have also dated meteorites that have fallen from space, and must have formed at the same time as the Earth.

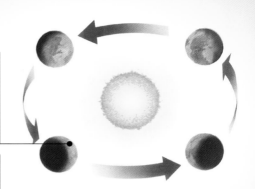

❓ WHAT IS THE EARTH MADE OF?

The Earth has a core of iron and nickel, and a rocky crust made mostly of oxygen and silicon. In between is the soft, hot mantle of metal silicates, sulphides, and oxides.

SUMMER AND WINTER

As the Earth orbits the Sun, the hemisphere of the planet that faces the Sun has its summer. The hemisphere facing away is in winter.

❓ EXACTLY HOW LONG IS A YEAR?

Every year the Earth travels once around the Sun. This epic journey covers a distance of 548,018,150 miles (938,886,400 km) and takes exactly 365.24 days, which gives us our calendar year of 365 days. To make up the extra 0.24 days, we add an extra day to our calendar at the end of February in every fourth year, which is called the leap year—and then we have to knock off a leap year every four centuries.

FORMATION OF OCEANS

The Earth cooled more, and the clouds of steam became water, creating vast oceans.

❓ HOW LONG IS A DAY?

A day is the time the Earth takes to turn once. The stars move to the same place in the sky every 23 hours, 56 minutes and 4.09 seconds (the sidereal day). Our day (the solar day) is 24 hours, because Earth is moving around the Sun, and must turn an extra 1° for the Sun to be in the same place in the sky.

METEOR CRATERS

By 4 million years ago, the Earth's crust was covered in meteor craters and huge volcanoes.

❓ WHAT'S SO SPECIAL ABOUT THE EARTH?

The Earth is the only planet with temperatures at which liquid can exist on the surface and is the only planet with an atmosphere containing oxygen. Water and oxygen are both needed for life.

❓ WHAT SHAPE IS THE EARTH?

The Earth is not quite a perfect sphere. Because it spins faster at the equator than at the Poles, the Earth bulges at the equator. Scientists describe Earth's shape as "geoid," which simply means Earth-shaped!

❓ WHY DOES THE EARTH SPIN?

Earth spins because there is nothing to stop it spinning. The Sun's gravity keeps it in orbit.

❓ WHO WAS COPERNICUS?

In the 1500s, most people thought the Earth was fixed in the center of the universe, with the Sun and the stars revolving around it. Nicolaus Copernicus (1473–1543) was the Polish astronomer who first suggested the Earth was moving around the Sun.

❓ WHAT ARE THE MOON'S SEAS?

The large, dark patches visible on the Moon's surface are called seas, but in fact they are not seas at all. They are huge plains formed by lava flowing from inside the Moon.

❓ WHAT IS MOONLIGHT?

The Moon is by far the brightest thing in the night sky. But it has no light of its own. Moonlight is simply the Sun's light reflected off the white dust on the Moon's surface.

❓ WHAT IS A LUNAR ECLIPSE?

As the Moon goes around the Earth, sometimes it passes right into Earth's shadow, where sunlight is blocked off. This is a lunar eclipse. If you look at the Moon during this time, you can see the dark disk of the Earth's shadow creeping across the Moon.

❓ WHO WERE THE FIRST MEN ON THE MOON?

The first men on the Moon were Neil Armstrong and Buzz Aldrin of the US *Apollo 11* mission. They landed on the Moon on July 20, 1969. As Armstrong set foot on the Moon, he said: "That's one small step for (a) man, one giant leap for mankind."

What is the Moon?

The Moon is the Earth's natural satellite. It has circled around the Earth for at least four billion years. It is a rocky ball about a quarter of the Earth's size and is held in its orbit by mutual gravitational attraction. Most scientists believe that the Moon formed when early in Earth's history a planet smashed into it. The impact was so tremendous that nothing was left of the planet, but a few hot splashes thrown back up into space. Within a day of the smash, these splashes had been drawn together by gravity to form the Moon.

THE MOON'S PHASES

The phases of the Moon, from left to right: new moon, half moon (waxing), gibbous moon (waxing), full moon, gibbous moon (waning), half moon (waning), old moon.

LUNAR MODULE

The lunar module from the *Apollo 15* mission was the astronauts' home during their brief stay on the Moon.

❓ WHAT IS A HARVEST MOON?

The harvest moon is the full moon nearest the autumnal equinox (when night and day are of equal length). This moon hangs bright above the eastern horizon for several evenings, providing a good light for harvesters.

❓ WHY DOES THE MOON LOOK LIKE CHEESE?

The Moon looks like Swiss cheese because it is full of holes and can appear yellowish. The holes are craters in the surface created when it was bombarded by huge rocks early on in its history.

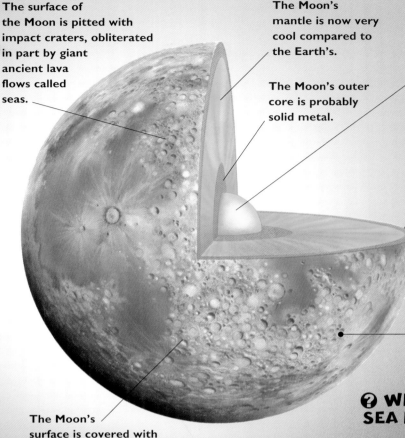

The surface of the Moon is pitted with impact craters, obliterated in part by giant ancient lava flows called seas.

The Moon's mantle is now very cool compared to the Earth's.

The Moon's outer core is probably solid metal.

The Moon has an inner core of metal, very much smaller in relation to its size than Earth's.

The Moon has a crust of solid rock thicker than Earth's. It is up to 90 miles (150 km) thick on the side away from Earth.

The Moon's surface is covered with a fine layer of dust.

MADE OF CHEESE?

The Moon is not made of cheese, but of rock, with metal at the very center.

❓ WHAT IS A NEW MOON?

The Moon appears to change shape during the month because, as it circles the Earth, we see its bright, sunny side from a different angle. At the new moon, the Moon is between the Earth and the Sun, and we catch only a crescent-shaped glimpse of its bright side. Over the first two weeks of the month, we see more and more of the bright side (waxing) until full moon, when we see all its sunny side. Over the next two weeks, we see less and less (waning), until we get back to just a sliver—the old moon.

❓ WHY DOES THE SEA HAVE TIDES?

The Moon's gravity draws the oceans into an oval around the Earth, creating a bulge of water on each side of the world. These bulges stay beneath the Moon as the Earth spins around and so seem to run around the world, making the tide rise and fall as they pass.

❓ HOW LONG IS A MONTH?

It takes the Moon 27.3 days to circle the Earth, but 29.53 days from one full moon to the next, because the Earth moves as well. A lunar month is the 29.53 days cycle. Calendar months are entirely artificial.

What is the Sun?

The Sun is an average star, just like countless others in the universe. It formed from gas left behind after an earlier, much larger star blew up and now, in middle-age, burns yellow and fairly steadily—giving the Earth daylight and remarkably constant temperatures. Besides heat and light, the Sun sends out deadly gamma rays, X-rays, and ultraviolet, as well as infrared and radio waves. Fortunately we are shielded from these by Earth's magnetic field and atmosphere.

❷ WHAT IS A SOLAR ECLIPSE?

A solar eclipse is when the Moon moves in between the Sun and the Earth, creating a shadow a few hundred miles wide on the Earth.

❷ HOW BIG IS THE SUN?

The Sun is a small-to-medium-sized star 0.86 million miles (1,392,000 km) in diameter. It weighs just under 2,000 trillion trillion tons.

❷ WHAT MAKES THE SUN BURN?

The Sun gets its heat from nuclear fusion. Huge pressures deep inside the Sun force the nuclei (cores) of hydrogen atoms to fuse together to make helium atoms, releasing huge amounts of nuclear energy.

❷ WHAT IS THE SUN'S CROWN?

The Sun's crown is its corona, its glowing white hot atmosphere seen only as a halo when the rest of the Sun's disk is blotted out by the Moon in a solar eclipse.

Beyond the chromosphere is the Sun's ultra-thin halo of boiled-off gases called the corona.

Sunspot

The photosphere is a sea of boiling gas. It gives the heat and light we experience on Earth.

The chromosphere is a tenuous layer through which dart tongues called spicules, making it look like a flaming forest.

THE SUN

Higher above the chromosphere are giant tongues of hot gases called prominences.

❓ WHAT IS THE SOLAR WIND?

The solar wind is the stream of radioactive particles constantly blowing out from the Sun at hundreds of miles per second. The Earth is protected from the solar wind by its magnetic field, but at the Poles the solar wind interacts with Earth's atmosphere to create the aurora borealis or northern lights.

❓ HOW OLD IS THE SUN?

The Sun is a middle-aged star. It probably formed about 4.6 billion years ago. It will probably burn for another five billion years and then die in a blaze so bright that the Earth will be scorched right out of existence.

❓ WHAT ARE SUNSPOTS?

Sunspots are dark blotches seen on the Sun's surface. They are thousands of miles across, and usually occur in pairs. They are dark because they are slightly less hot than the rest of the surface. As the Sun rotates, they slowly cross its face—in about 37 days at the equator and 26 days at the Poles. The average number of spots seems to reach a maximum every 11 years, and many scientists believe these sunspot maximums are linked to periods of stormier weather on Earth.

❓ HOW HOT IS THE SUN?

The surface of the Sun is a phenomenal 10,000°F (5,500°C), and would melt absolutely anything. But its core is thousands of times hotter at over 27 million°F (15 million°C)!

❓ WHAT ARE SOLAR FLARES?

Flares are eruptions from the Sun's surface that fountain into space with the energy of one million atom bombs for about five minutes. They are similar to solar prominences, the giant flamelike tongues of hot hydrogen that loop 20,000 miles (32,000 km) into space.

What are the inner planets?

The inner planets are the four planets in the solar system that are nearest to the Sun. These planets—Mercury, Venus, Earth, and Mars—are small planets made of rock, unlike the bigger planets farther out, which are made mostly of gas. Because they are made of rock, they have a hard surface a spaceship could land on, which is why they are sometimes called terrestrial (earth) planets. They all have a thin atmosphere, but each is very different.

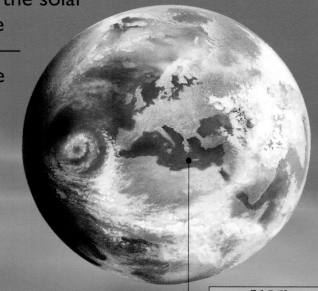

EARTH

Three quarters of Earth's surface is covered in water, which is why it looks blue.

MARS

Mars is reddish with shadows visible here and there on the surface of the planet.

❓ WHY IS MARS RED?

Mars is red because it is rusty. The surface contains a high proportion of iron dust, and this has been oxidized in the carbon dioxide atmosphere.

❓ WHAT'S FRIGHTENING ABOUT MARS'S MOONS?

One night American astronomer Asaph Hall got fed up with studying Mars and decided to go to bed. But his domineering wife bullied him into staying up—and that night he discovered Mars's two moons. Mocking his fear of his wife, he named the moons Phobos (fear) and Deimos (panic), after the attendants of the Roman war god, Mars.

MARTIAN CANYON

The dramatic landscape of Mars has not been worn down by rain or running water.

❓ LIFE ON MARS?

The Viking landers of the 1970s found no trace of life. Then, in 1996, microscopic fossils of what might be mini-viruses were found in a rock from Mars. These turned out not to be signs of life after all.

VENUS

Venus is a soft pinkish-white ball with no features visible on the surface through its thick atmosphere.

? COULD YOU BREATHE ON MERCURY?

Not without your own oxygen supply. Mercury has almost no atmosphere—just a few wisps of sodium—because gases are burned off by the nearby Sun.

? WHAT IS THE AIR ON VENUS?

Venus's atmosphere would be deadly for humans. It is very deep, so the pressure on the ground is huge. It is made mainly of poisonous carbon dioxide and is also filled with clouds of sulfuric acid.

MERCURY

Mercury has virtually no atmosphere and its surface is pitted with craters like the Moon.

? WHY IS VENUS CALLED THE EVENING STAR?

Venus reflects sunlight so well it shines like a star. But because it is quite close to the Sun, we can only see it in the evening, just after the Sun sets. We can also see it just before sunrise.

? WHAT ARE THE INNER PLANETS MADE OF?

Each of the inner planets is formed a little bit like an egg—with a hard "shell" or crust of rock, a "white" or mantle of soft, semi-molten rock, and a "yolk" or core of hot, often molten, iron and nickel.

? HOW HOT IS MERCURY?

Temperatures on Mercury veer from one extreme to the other because it has too thin an atmosphere to insulate it. In the day, temperatures soar to 755°F (400°C); at night they plunge to -280°F (-175°C).

? WHAT CANYON IS BIGGER THAN THE GRAND CANYON?

A canyon on Mars! The surface of Mars is more stable than the Earth's, and there is no rain or running water to wear down the landscape. It has a volcano named Olympus Mons which is 17 miles (27 km) high—three times higher than Mount Everest. It also has a great chasm, discovered by the *Mariner 9* space probe and named the Valles Marineris. This is over 25,000 miles (4,000 km) long and is four times as deep as the Grand Canyon.

HOW LONG?

Mars takes 687 days to orbit the Sun; Venus takes 225; and Mercury takes just 88.

What are Saturn's rings?

Saturn's rings are the planet's shining halo, first seen by Galileo Galilei (1564–1642), who invented the first simple telescope in 1608. The rings are made of countless billions of tiny chips of ice and dust, few bigger than a refrigerator and most the size of ice cubes. The rings are incredibly thin—no more than 164 ft (50 m) deep—yet they stretch way above Saturn's clouds, 4,350 miles (7,000 km) high, and over 46,000 miles (74,000 km) out into space.

❓ HOW HEAVY IS SATURN?

Saturn may be big, but because it is made largely of liquid hydrogen, it is also remarkably light, with a mass of 600 billion trillion tons. If you could find a big enough bath, it would float.

When it rains on Saturn, it rains drops of liquid helium.

Winds roar around Saturn's equator at 1,120 mph (1,800 km/h).

SATURN

Saturn's rings are made of billions of tiny chips of dust and ice.

❓ HOW WINDY IS SATURN?

Saturn's winds are even faster than Jupiter's and roar around the planet at up to 1,120 mph (1,800 km/h). But Neptune's are even faster!

❓ WHAT IS THE CASSINI DIVISION?

Saturn's rings occur in broad bands, referred to by the letters A to G. In 1675, the astronomer Cassini spotted a dark gap between rings A and B. This is now named the Cassini division, after him.

SATURN'S MOONS

Saturn's moons are all blocks of ice, made dirty with dust and organic compounds, and the surface is barren.

❓ HOW MANY MOONS HAS SATURN GOT?

Saturn has at least 18 moons, including Iapetus, which is black on one side and white on the other, and Enceladus, which is covered in shiny beads of ice and shimmers like a movie screen.

❓ WHAT IS JUPITER'S RED SPOT?

The Great Red Spot or GRS is a huge swirling storm in Jupiter's atmosphere. It is 16,200 miles (26,000 km) by 8,700 miles (14,000 km) across and has gone on in the same place for at least 330 years.

❓ HOW BIG IS JUPITER?

Even though Jupiter is largely gas, it weighs 320 times as much as the Earth and is 88,850 miles (142,984 km) in diameter.

❓ COULD YOU LAND ON JUPITER?

No. Even if your spaceship could withstand the enormous pressures, there is no surface to land on—the atmosphere merges unnoticeably into deep oceans of liquid hydrogen.

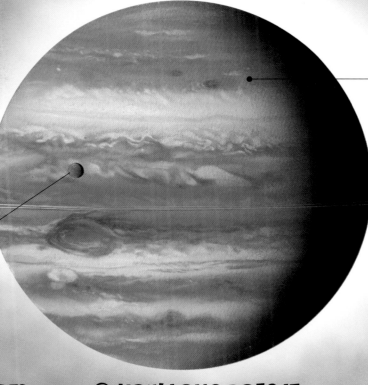

JUPITER
High-speed winds whirl around Jupiter's surface, creating bands of cloud in the atmosphere.

One of Jupiter's moons passing in front of the planet.

Jupiter has a ring system, like Saturn, but much, much smaller.

❓ WHAT ARE THE GIANT PLANETS MADE OF?

Jupiter and Saturn are made largely of hydrogen and helium. On Jupiter, internal pressures are so great that most of the hydrogen is turned to metal.

❓ HOW LONG DOES IT TAKE JUPITER TO ORBIT THE SUN?

Jupiter takes 11 years and 314 days (by our Earth calendar) to complete its journey around the Sun.

IO
Io is one of Jupiter's four big moons (it has at least 12 smaller ones as well). Volcanoes erupt sulfur on the surface.

❓ WHY ARE ASTRONOMERS EXCITED ABOUT TITAN?

Saturn's moon Titan is very special because it is the only moon in the solar system with a dense atmosphere.

❓ WHAT ARE THE GIANT PLANETS?

Jupiter and Saturn, the fifth and sixth planets out from the Sun, are the giants of the solar system. Jupiter is twice as heavy as all the planets put together. Saturn is almost as big. Unlike the inner planets, they are both made largely of gas, and only their very core is rocky. This does not mean they are vast cloud balls. The enormous pressure of gravity means the gas is squeezed until it becomes liquid, and even solid.

❓ HOW FAST DOES JUPITER SPIN?

Jupiter spins faster than any other planet. Despite its huge size, it turns right around in just 9 hours and 55 minutes, which means the surface is moving at 28,00 mph (45,00 km/h).

What are the outer planets?

The outer planets are Uranus, Neptune, and Pluto, and Pluto's companion Charon. Unlike the other planets, these were completely unknown to ancient astronomers. They are so far away, and so faint, that Uranus was discovered only in 1781, Neptune in 1846, Pluto in 1930, and Charon as recently as 1978. Uranus and Neptune are gas giants like Jupiter and Saturn.

❷ WHO FOUND NEPTUNE?

Two mathematicians, John Couch Adams in England and Urbain le Verrier in France, predicted where Neptune should be from the way its gravity disturbed Uranus's orbit. Johann Galle in Berlin spotted it on September 23, 1846.

❷ HOW LONG IS A YEAR ON NEPTUNE?

Neptune is so far from the Sun—over 2,8 billion miles (4.5 billion km) — that its orbit takes about 165 Earth years. So one year on Neptune lasts 165 Earth years.

❷ WHAT'S STRANGE ABOUT URANUS?

Unlike any of the other planets, Uranus does not spin on a slight tilt. Instead it is tilted right over and rolls around the Sun on its side, like a giant bowling ball.

❷ WHAT'S AN ASTEROID?

Asteroids are the thousands of rocky lumps that circle around the Sun in a big band between Mars and Jupiter. The biggest, Ceres, is 400 miles (640 km) across. Most are much smaller. Over 5,000 asteroids have been identified so far.

URANUS

Uranus rolls on its side and is the seventh planet out from the Sun.

NUCLEUS

At the heart of a comet is a nucleus of ice and dust, often shaped like a lumpy potato, just a few miles across.

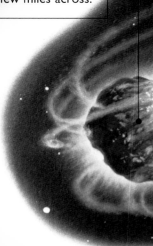

❷ WHAT IS A COMET?

Comets are really just dirty iceballs. Normally they circle the outer reaches of the solar system, but occasionally one of them is drawn in toward the Sun. As it hurtles toward the Sun, it melts and a vast tail of gas is blown behind it by the solar wind. We may see this spectacular tail in the night sky shining in the sunlight for a few weeks until it swings round the Sun and out of sight. The Hale-Bopp comet gave a spectacular display in 1997.

PLUTO AND CHARON
Pluto is visible from Earth only with a telescope. At about -346°F (-235°C), it is the coldest planet.

❷ WHY IS NEPTUNE GREEN?

Neptune appears greeny-blue because of the methane gas (a component of natural gas) in its atmosphere.

NEPTUNE
Neptune is the eighth planet from the sun, the outermost of the four 'gas giant' planets.

❷ HOW BIG IS PLUTO?

Pluto is very small, which is why it was so hard to spot. It is five times smaller than the Earth—just 1,485 miles (2,390 km) across—and 500 times lighter.

A tail of ionized atoms is blown out millions of miles behind the comet by the solar wind.

A comet in the night sky.

❷ WHAT IS A METEORITE?

Meteorites are lumps of rock from space big enough to penetrate the Earth's atmosphere and reach the ground without burning up.

❓ HOW ARE STARS BORN?

Stars are born when clumps of gas in space are drawn together by their own gravity, and the middle of the clump is squeezed so hard that temperatures reach 18 million°F (10 million°C), so a nuclear fusion reaction starts.

❓ HOW MANY STARS ARE THERE?

It is hard to know how many stars there are in the universe—most are much too far away to see. But astronomers guess there are about 200 billion billion.

❓ WHY DO SOME STARS THROB?

The light from variable stars flares up and down. "Cepheid" are big young stars that pulsate over a few days or a few weeks. "RR Lyrae" variables are old yellow stars that vary over a few hours.

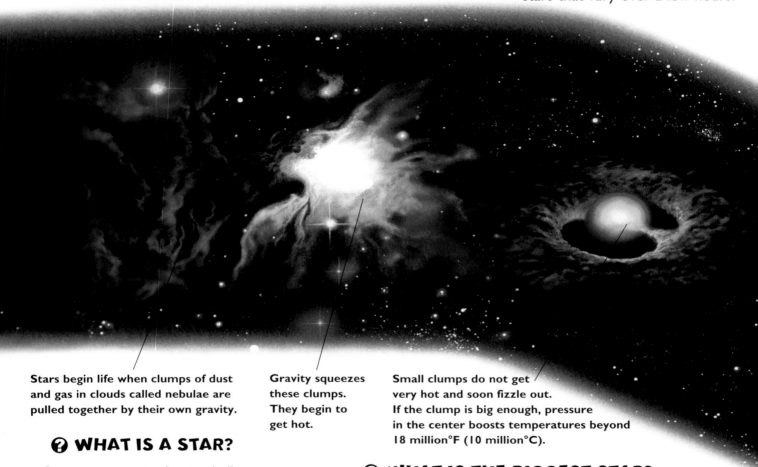

Stars begin life when clumps of dust and gas in clouds called nebulae are pulled together by their own gravity.

Gravity squeezes these clumps. They begin to get hot.

Small clumps do not get very hot and soon fizzle out. If the clump is big enough, pressure in the center boosts temperatures beyond 18 million°F (10 million°C).

❓ WHAT IS A STAR?

Stars are gigantic glowing balls of gas, scattered throughout space. They burn for anything from a few million to tens of billions of years. The nearest star, apart from the Sun, is over 25 trillion miles (40 trillion km) away. They are all so distant that we can see stars only as pinpoints of light in the night sky, even through the most powerful telescope. As far as we can see, there are no other large objects in the universe.

❓ WHAT IS THE BIGGEST STAR?

The biggest stars are the supergiants. Antares is 700 times as big as the Sun. There may be a star in the Epsilon system in the constellation of Auriga that is 1,860 million miles (3 billion km) across—4,000 times as big as the Sun!

❓ WHAT ARE CONSTELLATIONS?

Constellations are small patterns of stars in the sky, each with its own name. They help astronomers locate things in the night sky.

❓ HOW HOT IS A STAR?

The surface temperature of the coolest stars is below 6,300°F (3,500°C); that of the hottest, brightest stars is over 72,000°F (40,000°C).

Where are stars born?

Stretched throughout space are vast clouds of dust and gas called nebulae. These clouds are 99% hydrogen and helium with tiny amounts of other gases and minute quantities of icy, cosmic dust. Stars are born in the biggest of these nebulae, which are called giant molecular clouds. Here temperatures plunge to -441°F (-263°C). These nebulae are thin and cold, but contain all the materials needed to make a star.

❷ WHAT MAKES STARS GLOW?

Stars glow because the enormous pressure deep inside generates nuclear fusion reactions in which hydrogen atoms are fused together, releasing huge quantities of energy.

❷ WHAT COLOR ARE STARS?

It depends how hot they are. The color of medium-sized stars varies along a band on a graph called the main sequence—from hot and bright blue-white stars to cool and dim red stars.

STAR BIRTH
Stars are being born and they die all the time.

In medium-sized stars, like our Sun, the heat generated in the core pushes gas out as hard as gravity pulls it in, so the star burns steadily for billions of years.

Nuclear fusion begins as hydrogen atoms fuse together to make helium. The heat from the fusion makes the star shine.

❷ WHAT MAKES STARS TWINKLE?

Stars twinkle because the Earth's atmosphere is never still, and starlight twinkles as the air wavers. Light from the nearby planets is not distorted as much, so they don't twinkle.

After 10 billion years or so, all the hydrogen in the star's core is burned up, and the core shrinks as it begins to burn helium.

What happens when stars die?

Stars make energy by converting hydrogen into helium. When the hydrogen is used up they then use any other nuclear energy. Stars die when they exhaust these vast supplies of nuclear energy. They either blow up, shrink go cold, or become a black hole. Just how long it takes to reach this point depends on the star. The biggest stars have masses of nuclear fuel, but live fast and die young. The smallest stars have little nuclear fuel, but live slow and long. A star twice as big as the Sun lives a tenth as long.

❓ WHAT IS A SUPERNOVA?

A supernova is a gigantic explosion. It finishes off a supergiant star. For just a brief moment, the supernova flashes out with the brilliance of billions of suns. Supernovae are usually visible only through a telescope. But in 1987, for the first time in 400 years, a supernova (named Supernova 1987A) was visible to the naked eye for at least six months.

❓ WHAT IS A RED GIANT?

It is a huge, cool star, formed as surface gas on a medium-sized star near the end of its life swells up.

The outer layers cool off and swell so that the star grows into a cool red giant star.

The biggest stars go on swelling into supergiants. Pressure at the center becomes so immense that carbon and silicon fuse to make iron.

Once iron forms in its center, the star fails to give off energy, and suddenly and catastrophically collapses.

❓ WHAT IS A WHITE DWARF?

White dwarfs are the small white stars formed as stars smaller than our Sun lose their surface gas altogether and shrink.

❓ WHAT IS A PULSAR?

Pulsars, or neutrons, are stars that flash out intense radio pulses as they spin rapidly.

The remains of a supernova collapses to become a pulsar, a star made mostly of atomic nuclear particles called neutrons.

The collapse of a supergiant triggers an explosion like a huge nuclear bomb, called a supernova.

For a few weeks or months, the exploding supernova shines as brightly as billions of suns.

PULSAR

The pulsar spins rapidly, beaming out radiation in pulses, like light from a lighthouse.

❓ WHAT ARE THE OLDEST STARS?

The oldest stars we know of are not stars at all, but simply look like them because they are very bright and very far away. These are "quasi-stellar radio objects," or quasars. Some are so far away that the light we see left them 13 billion years ago.

❓ HOW OLD ARE THE STARS?

Stars are dying and being born all the time. Big, bright stars live for only 10 million years. Medium-sized stars like our Sun live for 10 billion years.

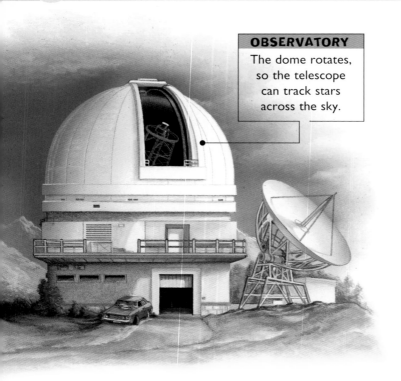

OBSERVATORY
The dome rotates, so the telescope can track stars across the sky.

❓ WHAT IS RED SHIFT?

When a galaxy is moving rapidly away from us, the waves of light become stretched out—that is, they become redder. The greater this red shift, the faster the galaxy is moving away from us.

❓ WHAT IS A LIGHT-YEAR?

A light year is 9,460,000,000,000 km. This is the distance light can travel in a year, at its constant rate of 186,300 miles (300,000 km) per second.

❓ HOW FAR IS IT TO THE NEAREST STAR?

The nearest star is Proxima Centauri, which is 4.3 light-years away, or 40 trillion km.

How far away is the Sun?

The distance of the Sun from Earth varies between 91 and 94 million miles (146 and 151 million km). Astronomers can measure the distance very accurately by bouncing radar waves off the planets.

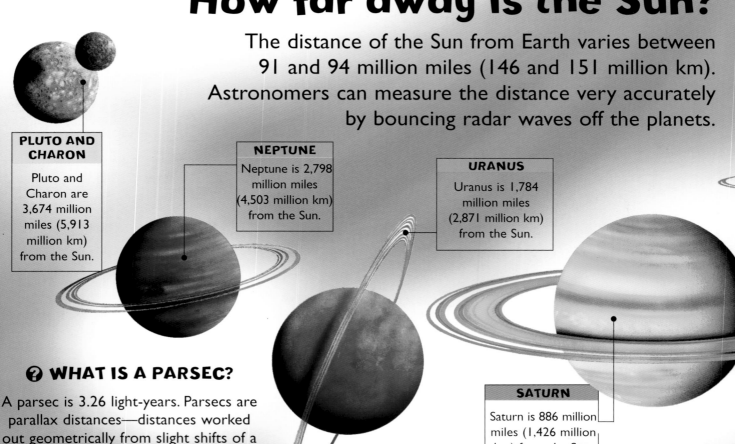

PLUTO AND CHARON
Pluto and Charon are 3,674 million miles (5,913 million km) from the Sun.

NEPTUNE
Neptune is 2,798 million miles (4,503 million km) from the Sun.

URANUS
Uranus is 1,784 million miles (2,871 million km) from the Sun.

SATURN
Saturn is 886 million miles (1,426 million km) from the Sun.

❓ WHAT IS A PARSEC?

A parsec is 3.26 light-years. Parsecs are parallax distances—distances worked out geometrically from slight shifts of a star's apparent position as the Earth moves around the Sun.

❓ HOW DID ASTRONOMERS FIRST ESTIMATE THE SUN'S DISTANCE?

In 1672, two astronomers, Cassini in France and Richer in Guiana, noted the exact position of Mars in the skies. They could work out how far away Mars was from the slight difference between their two measurements. Once they knew this, they could work out by simple geometry the distance from the Earth to the Sun. Cassini's estimate was only a few percent out.

❓ WHAT IS THE FARTHEST OBJECT WE CAN SEE?

The farthest objects we can see in space are quasars, which may be over 13 billion light-years away.

❓ ARE THE STARS GETTING FARTHER AWAY?

Analysis of red shifts has shown us that every single galaxy is moving away from us. The farther away the galaxy is, the faster it is moving away from us. The most distant galaxies are receding at almost the speed of light.

MERCURY
Mercury is 36 million miles (58 million km) from the Sun.

SUN

VENUS
Venus is 67 million miles (108 million km) from the Sun.

EARTH
Earth is about 93 million miles (150 million km) from the Sun (the distance varies).

MARS
Mars is 141 million miles (227 million km) from the Sun.

JUPITER
Jupiter is 484 million miles (779million km from the Sun.

❓ HOW DO ASTRONOMERS MEASURE DISTANCE?

For nearby stars, they use parallax (see What is a parsec?). With middle-distance stars, they look for "standard candles," which are stars whose brightness they know. The dimmer it looks, compared to how bright it should look, the farther away it is.

HOW FAR AWAY IS THE MOON?

At its nearest, the Moon is 221,529 miles (356,517 km) away from Earth; at its farthest, it is 252,718 miles (406,711 km) away. This is measured accurately by a laser beam bounced off mirrors left on the Moon's surface by *Apollo* astronauts and Soviet lunar probes. The distance is shown by how long it takes the beam to travel to the Moon and back.

What is a black hole?

If a small star is very dense, it may begin to shrink under the pull of its own gravity. As it shrinks, it becomes denser and denser and its gravity becomes more and more powerful—until it shrinks to a single tiny point of infinite density called singularity. The gravitational pull of a singularity is so immense that it pulls space into a "hole" like a funnel. This is the black hole, which sucks in everything that comes near it with its huge gravitational force—including light, which is why it is a "black" hole.

ORBITING EARTH

A craft orbiting Earth is effectively falling around it, pulled by the Earth's gravity. The craft shoots off into space if its forward momentum exceeds the acceleration due to Earth's gravity.

❓ WHAT IS GRAVITY?

Gravity is the mutual attraction between every single bit of matter in the universe. The more matter there is, and the closer it is, the stronger the attraction. A big, dense planet pulls much more than a small one, or one that is far away. The Sun is so big, it makes its pull felt over millions of miles of space. The Earth is smaller, but big enough to keep the Moon circling around it. The weight of an object is simply how hard gravity is pulling on it.

❓ HOW STRONG IS A PLANET'S GRAVITY?

The more massive the planet—that is the more matter it contains—the more powerful its gravity. Astronauts on the Moon could jump up high in heavy spacesuits, because the Moon is much smaller than the Earth and its gravity is weaker.

❓ HOW BIG IS A BLACK HOLE?

The singularity at the heart of a black hole is infinitely small. The size of the hole around it depends on how much matter went into forming it. The black hole at the heart of our galaxy may be about the size of the solar system.

❓ WHAT ARE ORBITS?

In space, many objects such as planets and moons continually circle around larger objects. An orbit is the path they take. This is usually elliptical rather than perfectly circular in shape.

BLACK HOLE

The black hole contains so much matter in such a small space that its gravitational pull even drags in light. We may be able to spot a black hole from the powerful radiation emitted by stars being ripped to shreds as they are sucked in. A giant black hole may exist at the center of our galaxy.

❓ WHAT HAPPENS INSIDE A BLACK HOLE?

Nothing that goes into a black hole comes out, and there is a point of no return called the event horizon. If you went beyond this, you would be "spaghettified"—stretched long and thin until you were torn apart by the immense gravity.

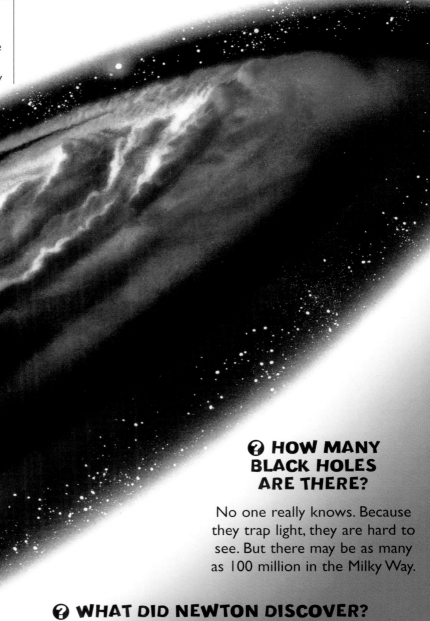

❓ HOW MANY BLACK HOLES ARE THERE?

No one really knows. Because they trap light, they are hard to see. But there may be as many as 100 million in the Milky Way.

❓ WHAT DID NEWTON DISCOVER?

The discoveries of Isaac Newton (1642–1727) include the three fundamental laws of motion. He also discovered the force called gravity, which holds the Moon in orbit around the Earth, and the planets in orbit around the Sun.

What is the universe made of?

The stars and clouds in space are made almost 100% of hydrogen and helium, the lightest and simplest elements of all. All the other elements are relatively rare. But some, such as carbon, oxygen, silicon, nitrogen, and iron can form important concentrations. This happens in the few rocky planets like Earth, where iron, oxygen, and magnesium are the most common elements. Carbon, a scarcer element, is the one on which all life forms are based.

FUSION
Some of these particles fused together to form the first atoms—hydrogen and helium.

QUARKS
First to form at the birth of the universe were countless particles much smaller than atoms, such as quarks.

HOT SPACE
In the first few moments of the universe's existence, there was no matter, only seething, incredibly hot space.

❓ WHAT WAS THE FIRST ELEMENT?
The first element to form was deuterium (a heavy form of hydrogen), which has the simplest and lightest atom of all. It formed within 1.5 minutes of the dawn of the universe.

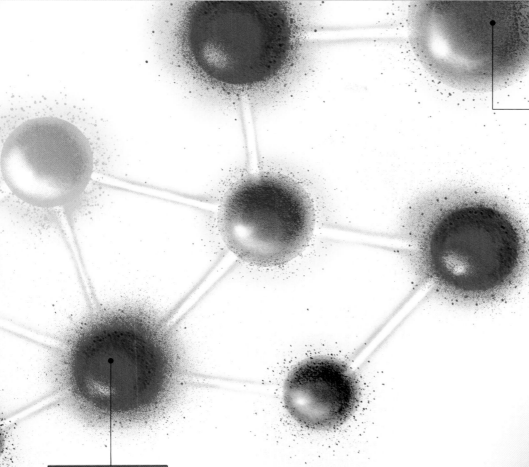

EVEN BIGGER ATOMS

The very large atoms of rare heavy elements such as tungsten and osmium are formed by the shock waves of supernovae (exploding stars).

❷ HOW WERE ATOMS MADE?

Atoms of hydrogen and helium were made in the early days of the universe when quarks in the matter soup joined together. All other atoms were made as atoms were fused together by the intense heat and pressure inside stars.

❷ WHAT ARE PARTICLES?

Particles are the tiny concentrations of energy from which all matter is made up, of which atoms are the largest. There are hundreds of kinds of particles, but all but atoms and molecules are too small to see, even with the most powerful microscope.

LARGE ATOMS

Larger atoms such as beryllium, carbon, and oxygen are made when nuclear reactions inside stars force the nuclei of helium atoms together.

❷ WHAT IS ANTI-MATTER?

Anti-matter is the mirror image of ordinary matter. If matter and anti-matter meet, they annihilate each other. Fortunately, there is no anti-matter on Earth.

❷ WHAT HOLDS EVERYTHING TOGETHER?

Everything in the universe is held together by four invisible forces. Two of them—gravity and electromagnetism—are familiar in everyday life. The other two—the strong and weak nuclear forces—are unfamiliar because they operate only inside the invisibly small nucleus of the atom, holding it all together.

❷ HOW WAS IRON MADE?

Iron was forged in the heart of supergiant stars near the ends of their lives, when the immense pressures there forced carbon atoms together.

❷ WHAT IS THE SMALLEST KNOWN PARTICLE?

The smallest particle inside the nucleus is the quark. However, there may be smaller particles as yet undiscovered.

What is a galaxy?

Our Sun is just one of a massive collection of two billion stars arranged in a shape like a fried egg, 100,000 light-years across. This collection is called the Galaxy, because we see it in the band of stars across the night sky called the Milky Way. ("Galaxy" comes from the Greek for milky.) But earlier this century it was realized that the Galaxy is just one of millions of similar giant star groups scattered throughout space, which we also call galaxies. The nearest is the Andromeda galaxy.

❓ WHAT ARE DOUBLE STARS?

Our Sun is alone in space, but many stars have one or more nearby companions. Double stars are called binaries.

❓ WHAT IS A SPIRAL GALAXY?

A spiral galaxy is a galaxy that has spiraling arms of stars like a gigantic Catherine wheel. They trail because the galaxy is rotating. Our Galaxy is a spiral galaxy.

❓ WHAT ARE STAR CLUSTERS?

Stars are rarely entirely alone within a galaxy. Most are concentrated in groups called clusters. Globular clusters are big and round. Galactic clusters are small and formless.

THE MILKY WAY

The Milky Way is over 100,000 light-years across, 1,000 light-years thick, and contains more than 100 billion stars. If we could see the Milky Way from above, we would see that it is a giant spiral galaxy.

❓ HOW MANY GALAXIES ARE THERE?

With the largest telescopes and most sensitive detectors, we could probably record about a billion galaxies—there may be many, many more beyond their limits.

❓ WHAT IS THE MILKY WAY?

The Milky Way is a pale, blotchy, white band that stretches right across the night sky. A powerful telescope shows it is made of thousands of stars, and is actually an edge-on view of our Galaxy.

❓ WHAT IS THE BIGGEST THING IN THE UNIVERSE?

The biggest structure in the universe is the Great Wall —a great sheet of galaxies 500 million light-years long and 16 million light-years thick.

SPIRAL GALAXY

Spiral galaxies are spinning Catherine wheel spirals like our Milky Way.

ELLIPTICAL GALAXY

Elliptical galaxies are shaped like rugby balls and are the oldest galaxies of all.

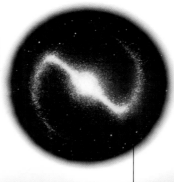

BARRED SPIRAL GALAXY

Barred spiral galaxies have a bar crossing the center with arms trailing from it.

IRREGULAR GALAXY

Irregular galaxies are galaxies that have no particular shape at all.

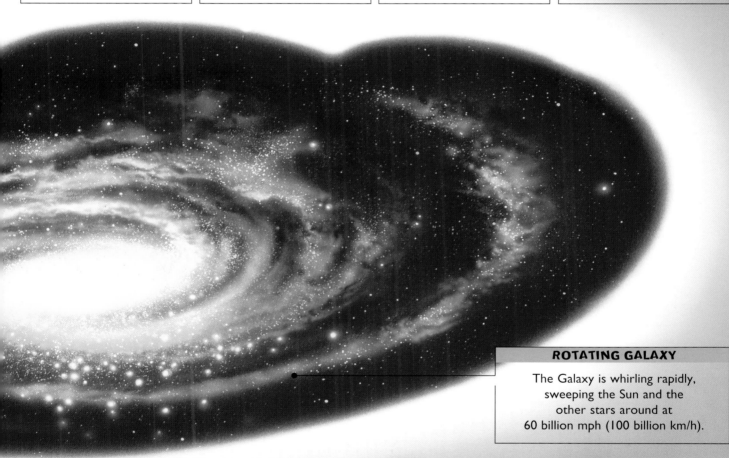

ROTATING GALAXY

The Galaxy is whirling rapidly, sweeping the Sun and the other stars around at 60 billion mph (100 billion km/h).

❓ WHERE IS THE EARTH?

The Earth is just over half way out along one of the spiral arms of the Galaxy, about 30,000 light-years from the center.

❓ WHAT EXACTLY ARE NEBULAE?

Nebulae are giant clouds of gas and dust spread throughout the galaxies. Some of them we see through telescopes because they shine faintly as they reflect starlight. With others, called dark nebulae, we see only inky black patches hiding the stars behind. This is where stars are born. A few, called glowing nebulae, glow faintly of their own accord as the gas within them is heated by nearby stars.

❓ HOW DO WE KNOW WHAT IT WAS LIKE?

We know partly by mathematical calculations, and partly by experiments in huge machines called colliders and particle accelerators. These recreate conditions in the early universe by using magnets to accelerate particles to astonishing speeds in a tunnel, and then crash them together.

HOTTER THAN HOT

In the beginning there was a ball smaller than an atom. It grew as big as a football as it cooled from infinity to ten billion billion billion°C

What was the universe like at the beginning?

The early universe was very small, but it contained all the matter and energy in the universe today. It was a dense and chaotic soup of tiny particles and forces, and instead of the four forces scientists know today, there was just one superforce. But this original universe lasted only a split second. After just three trillionths of a trillionth of a trillionth of a second, the superforce split up into separate forces.

❓ WHAT WAS THERE BEFORE THE UNIVERSE?

No one knows. Some people think there was an unimaginable ocean beyond space and time of potential universes continually bursting into life, or failing. Ours succeeded.

❓ WHAT WAS THE BIG BANG?

In the beginning, all the universe was squeezed into an unimaginably small, hot, dense ball. The Big Bang was when this suddenly began to swell explosively, allowing first energy and matter, then atoms, gas clouds, and galaxies to form. The universe has been swelling ever since.

❓ CAN WE SEE THE BIG BANG?

Astronomers can see the galaxies hurtling away in all directions. They can also see the afterglow—low level microwave radiation coming at us from all over the sky, called the background radiation.

❓ WHAT IS INFLATION?

Inflation was when dramatic expansion and cooling took place after the first second or so in the life of the universe, when space swelled up and cooled enormously.

❓ HOW DO WE KNOW THAT THE UNIVERSE IS GETTING BIGGER?

We can tell the universe is getting bigger because every galaxy is speeding away from us. Yet the galaxies themselves are not moving—the space in between them is stretching.

❓ HOW LONG WILL THE UNIVERSE LAST?

It depends how much matter it contains. If there is more than the "critical density," gravity will put a brake on its expansion, and it may soon begin to contract again to end in a Big Crunch. If there is much less, it may go on expanding forever.

❓ HOW DID THE FIRST GALAXIES AND STARS FORM?

They formed from lumps of clouds of hydrogen and helium, either as clumps broke up into smaller, more concentrated clumps, or as concentrations within the clumps drew together.

❓ HOW OLD IS THE UNIVERSE?

We know that the universe is getting bigger at a certain rate by observing how fast distant galaxies are moving. By working out how long it took everything to expand to where it is now, we can wind the clock back to the time when the universe was very, very small indeed. This suggests that the universe is between 10 and 20 billion years old. However, some stars may be older than this

UNIMAGINABLE!

After a split second, inflation began as space swelled a thousand billion billion billion times in less than a second—from the size of a football to something bigger than a galaxy.

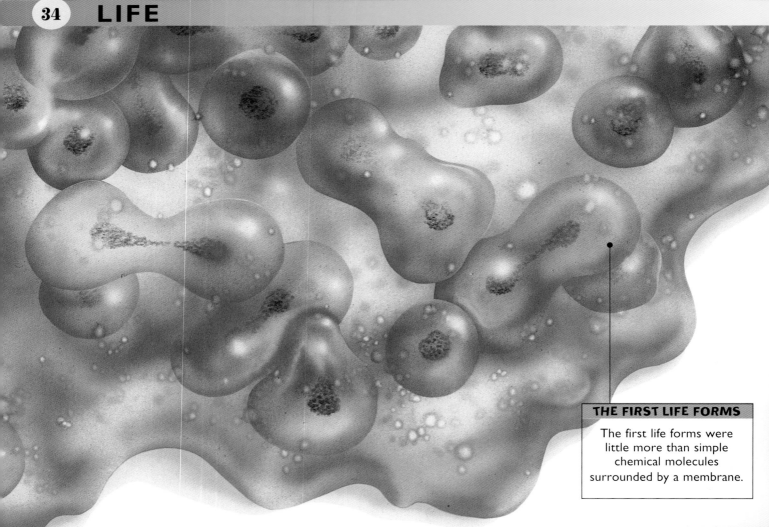

THE FIRST LIFE FORMS

The first life forms were little more than simple chemical molecules surrounded by a membrane.

How did life begin?

Scientific experiments in the 1950s showed how lightning flashes might create amino acids, the basic chemicals of life, from the waters and gases of the early Earth. But no one knows how these chemicals joined up to become "self-replicating"—that is, able to make copies of themselves. This is the key to life, which remains a mystery. However, the first life forms were probably tiny bacteria called Archebacteria, which thrive in very hot, chemically rich places.

❷ WHAT IS LIFE MADE OF?

Life is based on complex compounds of the element carbon, known as organic chemicals. Carbon compounds called amino acids link up to form proteins, and proteins form the complex chemicals that build and maintain living cells.

❷ WHERE DID THE MATERIALS OF LIFE COME FROM?

It used to be thought that organic chemicals all originated on Earth, but traces of all kinds of organic chemicals have been detected in giant molecular clouds, including formaldehyde, alcohol, and also acetaldehyde, one of the components of amino acids.

❓ WHERE DID LIFE COME FROM?

Most scientists think life on Earth began on Earth, in the oceans or in volcanic pools. But some think the Earth was seeded by micro-organisms from space.

❓ WHAT DOES AN ALIEN LOOK LIKE?

At the moment, the only aliens we are likely to encounter are very, very small and look like viruses.

❓ HOW ARE WE LOOKING FOR EXTRA-TERRESTRIAL LIFE?

Since possible fossils of microscopic life were found in Martian meteorite found on Earth in 1996, scientists have hunted for other signs of organisms in rocks from space. Robotic probes are currently searching for signs of life on Mars.

❓ ARE THERE ANY OTHER PLANETS LIKE EARTH?

There is no other planet like Earth anywhere in the solar system. Recently, though, planets have been detected circling other stars in neighboring galaxies. But they are much too far away for us to know anything about them at all.

❓ IS THERE LIFE ON OTHER PLANETS?

Organic chemicals are widespread, and the chances are that in such a large universe there are many planets, like Earth, suitable for nurturing life. But no one knows if life arose on Earth by a fantastic and unique chain of chance events, or whether it is fairly likely to happen given the right conditions.

ALIENS

No one knows what creatures from elsewhere in the universe would look like, but the chances are they would look pretty strange.

❓ WHY IS THE UNIVERSE LIKE IT IS?

The amazing chance that life exists on Earth has made some scientists wonder if only a universe like ours could contain intelligent life. This is called the weak anthropic principle. Some go further and say that the universe is constructed in such a way that intelligent life must develop at some stage. This is called the strong anthropic principle.

❓ WHAT IS DNA?

Deoxyribonucleic acid (DNA), the most remarkable chemical in the universe, is the tiny molecule on which all life is based. It is shaped a bit like a long rope ladder, with two strands twisted together in a spiral, linked by "rungs" of four different chemical bases. The order of these bases is a chemical code that provides all the instructions needed for life.

❓ WHAT IS SETI?

SETI is the Search for Extra-Terrestrial Intelligence project, designed continually to scan radio signals from space and pick up any signs of intelligence. It looks for signals that have a pattern, but are not completely regular, like those from pulsating stars.

LANDS AND PEOPLE

❓ HAVE HUMANS CHANGED OUR PLANET?

Over the ages, humans have changed the face of the world we live in. They have chopped down forests and dammed rivers. They have grown new plants and killed wild animals. They have built big cities and roads.

❓ HAVE PEOPLE ALWAYS LIVED WHERE THEY DO NOW?

During history many peoples have moved huge distances, or migrated. The Polynesians may have taken 2,500 years to sail across the Pacific Ocean and settle its islands. People are still on the move today.

❓ WHO ARE THE WORLD'S PEOPLES?

Human beings who share the same history or language make up "a people" or "ethnic group." Sometimes many different peoples share a country. Over 120 ethnic groups live in Tanzania, Africa.

HOW MANY PEOPLE?
By 2025 around 7.9 billion people will live on Earth.

❓ HOW MANY PEOPLE LIVE IN THE WORLD?

Billions! In 2000 there were about 6.1 billion human beings living on our planet. That's more than twice as many as 50 years ago.

ROOM FOR EVERYBODY?

Just about! But sometime in the future people may have to live in towns under the ocean or even on other planets, where they would need a special supply of air to stay alive.

How different are we from one another?

All human beings are basically the same, wherever they live. We may speak different languages and have different ideas. We may wear different clothes and eat different foods. Our parents may give us dark or pale skin, blue eyes or brown, or various colors of hair. But in the end we share the same needs, pleasures, hopes, and fears. We are all members of the same big family.

WHAT DO WE WEAR?
People wear different styles of clothing all around the world.

❓ WHERE ARE THE MOST CROWDED PLACES IN THE WORLD?

Tiny countries and large cities may house many millions of people. Bangladesh is one of the most crowded places in the world. There are over 1,450 people per square mile (900 per square km).

❓ WHAT IS A CONTINENT?

The big masses of land that make up the Earth's surface are called continents. The biggest continent of all is Asia, which is home to more than 3.5 billion people.

❓ WHICH COUNTRY HAS THE MOST PEOPLE?

More people live in China than anywhere else in the world. They number about 1,300,000,000 and most live in the big cities of the east and the south. In the far west of China there are empty deserts and lonely mountains.

ICY WILDERNESS
Some parts of the world are too harsh, too hot, or too cold for people to settle.

SKYSCRAPERS
Places where many people have chosen to settle have become big cities.

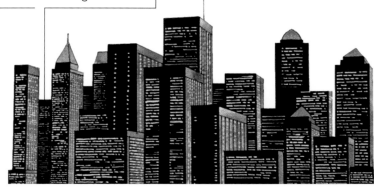

❓ WHY ARE SOME LANDS RICHER THAN OTHERS?

Some lands have good soil, where crops can grow. Some have oil, which is worth a lot of money. But other countries have poor soil, little rain, and no minerals. However hard people work there, they struggle to survive.

❓ WHERE DO PEOPLE LIVE?

Humans live wherever they can find food and water, which they need to stay alive. Nobody at all lives in Antarctica, the icy southern wilderness. Scientists do visit bases there, so that they can study rocks, icebergs, and penguins. The Sahara Desert in Africa is a land of burning hot sand and rocks. It has just a few places, called oases, where people can get the water they need to survive.

❓ ARE THERE MORE AND MORE PEOPLE?

Every minute, around 270 babies are born around the world. Imagine how they would cry if they were all put together! By the year 2050 there will probably be 9.3 billion people in the world.

NATIONAL FLAGS

These colorful flags are from countries around the world.

❓ WHY DO COUNTRIES HAVE FLAGS?

Flags can be seen flying from buildings and from boats. They show bold patterns and bright colors as they flutter in the wind. Many flags are badges or symbols of a nation, or its regions. The designs on flags sometimes tell us about a country or its history. The flag of Kenya includes a traditional shield and spears, while the flag of Lebanon includes a cedar tree, which were plentiful there in ancient times.

❓ WHERE CAN YOU SEE ALL THE FLAGS OF THE UN?

Rows and rows of flags fly outside the headquarters of the United Nations in New York City. Most of the world's countries belong to this organization, which tries to solve all kinds of problems around the world.

❓ DO ALL PEOPLES HAVE A COUNTRY THEY CAN CALL THEIR OWN?

No, the ancient homelands of some peoples are divided up between other countries. The lands of the Kurdish people are split between many countries.

KURDISH REFUGEES

Refugees are people who have fled their country because their lives are at risk.

❓ WHAT IS A COUNTRY?

A country is an area of land under the rule of a single government. A country may be vast, or very small. Its borders have to be agreed with neighboring countries, which sometimes leads to arguments. Countries that rule themselves are called independent. Countries that are ruled by other countries are called dependencies. Sometimes several countries join up to form a single new nation, but countries may also break up into smaller nations, too.

❓ WHICH COUNTRY FITS INSIDE A CITY?

The world's smallest nation is an area within the city of Rome, in Italy. It is called Vatican City and is the headquarters of the Roman Catholic Church. Less than one thousand people live there.

THE SWISS GUARD
Vatican City has been guarded by Swiss soldiers since the 16th century.

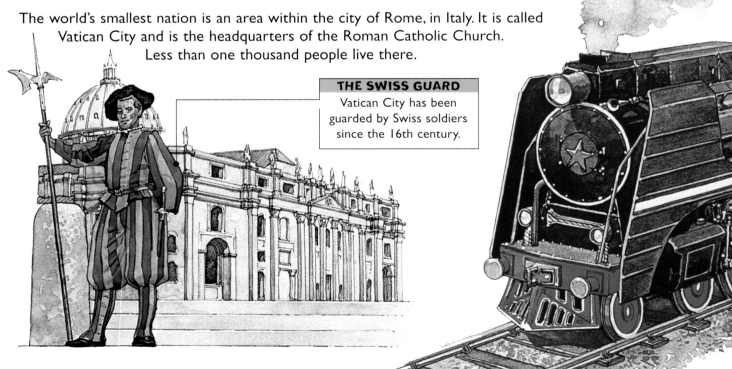

How long does it take to cross Russia?

It depends how you travel! These days, trains on the famous Trans-Siberian Railway take eight days to go from Moscow to the Pacific coast.

❓ HOW MANY INDEPENDENT COUNTRIES ARE THERE?

There are about 190 independent countries in the world—the number changes from one year to the next.

THE TRANS-SIBERIAN RAILWAY, 50 YEARS AGO

The Trans-Siberian Railway opened in 1904. It crosses most of Russia. Russia is so huge that when the Sun is setting over Moscow, it is rising over Vladivostock, on the Pacific coast.

❓ WHAT ARE COUNTIES AND STATES?

If you look at the map of a country, you will see that it is divided up into smaller regions. These often have their own local laws and are known as states, provinces, counties, or departments.

❓ WHICH IS THE BIGGEST COUNTRY IN THE WORLD?

The Russian Federation takes up over 6.5 million square miles (17 million sq km) of the Earth's surface. It spans two continents, Europe and Asia, and its clocks are set at 11 different times.

❓ HOW MANY DEPENDENCIES ARE THERE IN THE WORLD?

About 65 of the world's nations are still ruled by other countries. They include many tiny islands in the Caribbean Sea and in the Atlantic and Pacific Oceans.

How does anyone get to be a king or a queen?

Normally you have to be a prince or princess, born into a royal family with a king and queen for your dad and mum. In the past kings and queens were very powerful people. They could have their enemies thrown into some horrible dungeon and then throw away the key. Today, kings and queens do many charitable works. They visit hospitals and schools, open new bridges, and travel to meet other heads of state, as representatives of their own country.

FIT FOR A KING

Traditional robes worn by the Oba (king) of Akure, Nigeria.

❓ WHO RULES THE BIRDS?

Traditionally the king or queen of England owns all the swans on the River Thames, except for those marked in a special ceremony that takes place each summer.

❓ HOW DO YOU RECOGNIZE KINGS AND QUEENS?

For special ceremonies, rulers wear traditional robes, and some wear crowns and carry symbols of royal power, such as golden sceptres. The beaded crown and robes shown here were worn by traditional rulers of the Yoruba people, who live in Nigeria.

❓ WHAT IS A HEAD OF STATE?

The most important person in a country is the head of state. This may be a king or a queen or an elected president. The head of state often rides in a big car with a flag on it.

AN ENGLISH JUDGE

Governments make the law, but it is up to judges to decide who has broken it.

? WHAT IS A REPUBLIC?

It's a country that has no king or queen. France is a republic. Over 200 years ago the French king had his head chopped off, during a revolution.

? WHICH IS THE WORLD'S OLDEST PARLIAMENT?

A parliament is a meeting place where new laws are discussed and approved. The oldest parliament is in Iceland. Called the Althing, it was started by Viking settlers in AD 930.

? WHAT ARE 'JANA-GANA-MANA' AND 'THE STAR-SPANGLED BANNER'?

Both of them are national anthems or songs. The first tune is played to show respect to India, the second to the United States of America. National anthems are played at important occasions, such as the Olympic Games.

? WHERE DO JUDGES WEAR BIG WIGS?

In Great Britain judges wear wigs, which were in fashion 250 years ago. This old costume is meant to show that the judge is not in court as a private person, but as someone who stands for the law of the land.

? WHERE IS THE BIGGEST GENERAL ELECTION?

Over 275 million people are allowed to vote in general elections in India. They can cast their votes at any one of over a million Electronic Voting Machines set up all over the country.

? WHO INVENTED DEMOCRACY?

The people of ancient Athens, in Greece, started the first democratic assembly nearly 2,500 years ago. It wasn't completely fair, as women and slaves weren't given the right to vote.

? WHICH IS THE WORLD'S OLDEST ROYAL FAMILY?

The Japanese royal family has produced a long line of 125 reigning emperors over a period of thousands of years.

? WHAT IS A GOVERNMENT?

The members of the government run the country. They pass new laws on everything from schools to hospitals and businesses. Countries where the people can choose their government by voting for a political party are called democracies. Some countries do not hold elections or have a choice of political parties. The people who rule them are called dictators.

INDIA GOES TO THE POLLS

Over 340 million voters took part in India's 1996 general election.

How many languages are spoken today?

Somewhere around 6,000 languages are spoken in the world. Some are spoken by very few people. Less than 500 people in Latvia speak a language called Liv. One African language, Bikya, could have only one surviving speaker. The world's most spoken language is Chinese, which is used every day by 1,2 billion people. English is the world's most widespread language, spoken by 470 million people.

❓ DO WE ALL READ LEFT TO RIGHT?

The Arabic language is read right-to-left, and traditional Japanese top-to-bottom.

DIFFERENT CITIES, DIFFERENT SIGNS

Many languages are related to each other and have words that sound similar. Each language has its own culture and traditions. Methods of writing, such as alphabets, are called scripts. Different scripts are used in many parts of the world.

САНКТ ПЕТЕРОУРГ
ST PETERSBURG

አዲስ አበባ
ADDIS ABABA

❓ COULD WE INVENT ONE LANGUAGE FOR ALL THE WORLD?

It's already been done! A language called Esperanto was invented over 100 years ago. Around 100,000 have learned how to speak it.

❓ WHAT HAS MADE THE WORLD SHRINK?

The planet hasn't really got smaller, it just seems that way. Today, telephones, emails and faxes make it possible to send messages around the world instantly. Once, letters were sent by ship and took many months to arrive.

❓ HOW DO WE TALK THROUGH SPACE?

Satellites are machines sent into space to orbit the Earth. They can pick up telephone, radio, or television signals from one part of the world and beam them down to another.

INSTANT COMMUNICATION

Telephones use satellite links to flash messages around the world.

❓ DO WE USE DIFFERENT WAYS OF WRITING?

Many different kinds of writing have grown up around the world over the ages, using all sorts of lines and squiggles and little pictures. This book is printed in the Roman alphabet, which has 26 letters and is used for many of the world's languages. Chinese writers normally use about 4,000 different symbols, or characters, although ten times as many can be used. The Khmer alphabet, used in Cambodia, has 74 letters, while the Rotokas alphabet, used on the island of Bougainville, has only 11 letters.

❓ CAN WE TALK WITHOUT WORDS?

People who are unable to hear or speak can sign with their hands. Various sign languages have been developed around the world, from China to the USA.

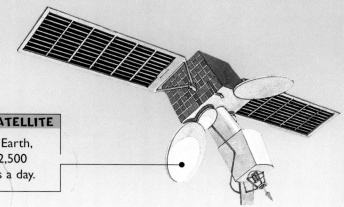

COMMUNICATIONS SATELLITE
In orbit high above the Earth, Intelsat 8 can relay 112,500 telephone conversations a day.

❓ DOES EVERYBODY IN ONE COUNTRY SPEAK THE SAME LANGUAGE?

Not often. For example, families from all over the world have made their homes in London, the capital city of England. Their children mostly speak English at school, but at home may speak any one of hundreds of other languages, from Turkish to Urdu.

❓ SHOULD I STAY OR SHOULD I GO?

Movements of the head and hands can be a kind of language. Be careful! In some countries, wagging the hand palm down means "come here," but in others it means "go away." Shaking the head can mean "yes" in some countries and "no" in others.

❓ WHAT'S IN A NAME?

In Norway there's a village called Å. In New Zealand there's a place called Taumatawhakatangihangakoa-uauotamateaturipukakapikim-aungahoronukupokaiwhenuaki-tanatahu.

❓ WHAT WAS THAT YOU WHISTLED?

In some parts of Central America, Turkey, and the Canary Islands, people worked out a way of communicating using whistles instead of words.

? WHY DO CHALETS HAVE BIG ROOFS?

In the mountains of Switzerland, the wooden houses have broad roofs, designed for heavy falls of snow each winter.

? WHAT ARE HOUSES MADE FROM?

Mud, stone, slate, boulders, bricks, branches, reeds, steel girders, sheets of iron, concrete, glass, timber, straw, turf, ice, bamboo, animal hides, cardboard boxes—you name it! All over the world people make use of whatever materials they can find or produce to build homes. Many modern buildings look much the same wherever they have been built, from Brasília to Singapore. However, all sorts of local types of houses can still be seen as well.

SHELTER

Houses must shelter people from cold and heat, rain and snow, storms and floods.

? WHY BUILD HOUSES WITH REEDS?

It makes sense to use the nearest building material to hand. Tall reeds grow around Lake Titicaca in Peru – so the Indians who live there use them to build their beautiful houses.

? WHY DO PEOPLE LIVE UNDERGROUND?

To stay cool! At Coober Pedy in Australia it is so hot that miners digging for opals built houses and even a church underground.

? WHAT ARE HOUSES LIKE IN THE ARCTIC?

Today the Inuit people of Canada live in houses, huts and tents. Traditionally, they lived in igloos made out of blocks of snow. Igloos are still used today by Inuits on the move.

LIGHT WORK

Reeds are used for building from South America to southwest Asia. They are also used to thatch cottages in England.

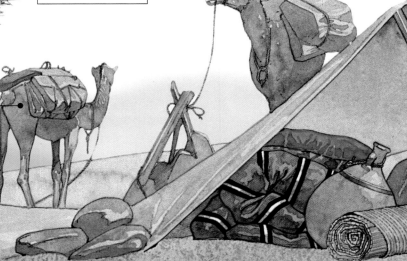

MOVING HOMES

Bedouin nomads use camels to travel across the desert. The camels carry their tents, which can be easily packed up when it is time to move on.

❓ WHERE DO THEY BUILD MUD HUTS?

Thatched huts with walls of dried mud can still be seen in parts of Africa, such as Mali. They are cheap to build, cool to live in, and often look beautiful too.

Why do people live in tents?

In many parts of the world, there are people who do not live in the same place all year round. Instead, they follow their herds of sheep and goats from one desert oasis to another, or from lowland to mountain pastures. Such people are called nomads. The Bedouin are nomads who live in the dry lands of North Africa. Their tents are woven from camel hair. Today some Bedouin have settled in towns.

A DOGON VILLAGE, MALI
Mud huts and grain stores are built on hillsides.

❓ WHICH PEOPLE LIVE IN CARAVANS?

Many of Europe's Gypsies live in caravans, moving from one campsite to another. The Gypsies, who are properly known as Roma, Sinti, or Manush, arrived in Europe from India about 500 years ago.

❓ WHY WERE SKYSCRAPERS INVENTED?

So that more people could fit into a small area of city. High-rise flats and offices were first built in Chicago about 120 years ago. By 1857 new lifts were saving people a very long climb upstairs!

Who built the first cities?

Towns first grew up when people stopped being hunter-gatherers and learned how to farm, which meant staying in one place. The first cities were built in southwest Asia. Çatal Hüyük in Turkey was begun about 9,000 years ago.

? WHO LIVES AT THE ENDS OF THE EARTH?

One of the world's most northerly settlements is Ny-Alesund, in the Arctic territory of Svalbard. The southernmost is Puerto Williams in Tierra del Fuego, Chile.

? WHY WAS LONDON BRIDGE FALLING DOWN?

Children today still sing a rhyme that says "London Bridge is falling down." It's a very old song. The ancient bridge over the River Thames may have been pulled down by a Viking named Olaf the Stout nearly a thousand years ago!

? WHICH IS THE WORLD'S OLDEST CAPITAL?

Damascus, capital of Syria, has been lived in for about 4,500 years.

? WHERE IS THE BIG APPLE?

This is a nickname for New York City. Take a bite!

? WHAT PROBLEMS DO CITIES CAUSE?

Cities can be exciting places to live in. They are full of hustle and bustle. But they often have big problems, too. Lots of people in one place need a lot of looking after. They need water and electricity, and proper drains, fire engines, ambulances, and police cars. Too much traffic often blocks up the roads and fills the air with fumes. In some countries people pour into the cities from the countryside. They cannot find work and have to live in poor conditions.

? WHICH CITY IS NAMED AFTER A GODDESS?

Athens, the capital of Greece, shares its name with an ancient goddess named Athena. Her beautiful temple, the Parthenon, still towers over the modern city. It was built in mid-5th century BC.

WHERE IS THE WORLD'S TALLEST BUILDING?

Until recently Petronas Towers in Kuala Lumpur, Malaysia, was the tallest building in the world at 1,483 feet (452 m). However, Taipei 101 in Taiwan is now the tallest at 1,671 feet (509 m).

WHERE ARE THE BIGGEST CITIES IN THE WORLD?

In Japan, where big cities have spread and joined up to make giant cities! Japan is made up of islands that have high mountains, so most people live on the flat strips of land around the coast. In order to grow, large cities have had to stretch out like ribbons until they merge into each other. Over 20 million people live in and around the capital, Tokyo, and it's still growing. The biggest city on the other side of the world is Sau Paulo in Brazil.

WHY ARE LANDMARKS USEFUL IN A CITY?

Each city has eye-catching buildings and monuments. These can be helpful if you are trying to find your way around a city. Paris, in France, has the Eiffel Tower. Berlin, in Germany, has the Brandenburg Gate.

WHICH FAMOUS BUILDING LOOKS LIKE A SAILING BOAT?

The Sydney Opera House dominates the harbor front of Sydney, Australia. Its roofs look like the sails of a big yacht.

SYDNEY, AUSTRALIA
The Sydney Opera House has become one of the best-known buildings in the world. Many tourists come from all over the world to see it.

WHICH COUNTRY HAS THREE CAPITALS?

The most important city in a country is called the capital. South Africa has three of them! Cape Town is the legislative capital. Pretoria is the executive capital. Bloemfontein is the judicial capital.

ANCIENT CATAL HÜYÜK, TURKEY
Çatal Hüyük had buildings of mud brick with flat roofs and narrow streets. Over 5,000 people lived there. This and other early cities became centers of trade, where people made pottery, baskets, food, tools, and clothes. How does this ancient town differ from a modern one?

WHICH IS THE HIGHEST CITY?

Lhasa stands 11,975 feet (3,650 m) above sea level. It is the capital city of Tibet, a mountainous region in the Himalayas that is governed by China. Tibet is sometimes called the "roof of the world."

❓ HOW DO YOU CROSS THE ARCTIC SNOW?

You could always ride on a sled pulled by a team of dogs, as in the old days. But most people today ride snowmobiles, which are a bit like motorcycles with runners instead of wheels.

CROSSING THE RUSSIAN ARCTIC

In Siberia, snowmobiles can use solid frozen rivers as roads during the long winter months.

❓ WHERE CAN YOU CATCH A TRAIN INTO THE SKY?

In the Andes mountains of South America. One track in Peru climbs to about 4,800 m above sea level. In Salta, Argentina, you can catch another high-rise locomotive, known as the "Train to the Clouds".

❓ WHO RIDES IN A CARAVAN?

No, not one pulled by a car! This kind of caravan is a group of traders who cross the desert by camel. Camels can carry people across the Sahara for more than six days without needing a drink of water.

❓ WHERE WAS A HOT-AIR BALLOON FIRST FLOWN?

The place was Paris, the capital of France, and the year was 1783. The passengers were, believe it or not, a sheep, a rooster and a duck! Later, people tried out the balloon for themselves.

❓ WHICH IS THE WORLD'S LONGEST ROAD?

The Pan-American Highway. It starts at the top of the world, in the chilly American state of Alaska. It then heads on through Canada and the USA to the steamy forests of Central America. There is still a bit missing in the middle, but the road starts up again and carries on all the way down through South America to Chile, looping round to Argentina and Brazil. The total distance? Well over 48,000 km!

❓ WHERE ARE THE LONGEST TRUCKS?

In the outback, the dusty back country of Australia, the roads are long and straight and pretty empty. Trucks can hitch on three or four giant trailers to form a "road train".

AUSTRALIAN ROAD TRAIN

A road train speeds across the Nullarbor Desert in southern Australia.

What is a junk?

It is a big wooden ship, traditionally built in China. Its big sails are strengthened by strips of wood. Junks aren't as common as they used to be, but they can still be seen on the South China coast.

❓ HOW CAN YOU TRAVEL UNDERNEATH THE ALPS?

The Alps are snowy mountains that run across France, Italy, Switzerland and Austria. They soar to 4,807 m above sea level at Mont Blanc. In the days of ancient Rome, a general named Hannibal tried to cross the Alps with a number of war elephants. Today, tunnels carry trains and cars through the mountains. The St Gotthard tunnel in Switzerland is 16 km long.

❓ WHERE IS THE WORLD'S BIGGEST AIRPORT?

Riyadh airport in Saudi Arabia is probably bigger than some countries. It covers 225 sq km of the Arabian desert.

❓ WHERE ARE BOATS USED AS BUSES?

In the beautiful Italian city of Venice, there are canals instead of roads. People travel from one part of the city to another by boat.

CHINESE JUNK

Many countries still use wooden boats. Traditional wooden junks sail along the Hong Kong waterfront. Dhows sail off Arabia and East Africa, and feluccas are used on the River Nile.

How do we keep warm and dry?

Since prehistoric times, people have used fur and animal skins to keep out the cold. In the Arctic today, the Inuit people still often wear traditional clothes made from fur, sealskin or caribou (reindeer) hide. The Saami people of northern Finland also use their reindeer herds to provide leather goods. Wool, woven into textiles or pressed into felt, is used wherever the weather is cold. It is a good warm fibre, and the natural oils in it keep out the rain.

MANY MATERIALS

Clothes today may be made from natural fibres such as wool, silk or cotton, or from artificial fibres such as nylon and plastic. Today it is not always easy to tell where people come from by the clothes they wear.

❓ WHICH LADIES WEAR TALL LACE HATS?

The Breton people of northwest France are proud of their costume, which they wear for special occasions. The men wear waistcoats and big black hats. The women wear lace caps, some of which are high and shaped like chimneys.

❓ WHERE IS THE CAPITAL OF FASHION?

Milan, London, New York and many other cities stage fantastic fashion shows each year. But Paris, in France, has been the centre of world fashion for hundreds of years.

❓ WHAT IS BATIK?

This is a way of making pretty patterns on cloth. Wax is put on the fibre so that the dye sinks in only in certain places. This method was invented in Southeast Asia.

❓ DO PEOPLE STILL WEAR NATIONAL COSTUME?

Most people today wear T-shirts and jeans, skirts or suits. Only on special occasions do they still put on traditional, regional costumes. In some countries, people still wear local dress every day.

❷ HOW DO PEOPLE DRESS IN HOT COUNTRIES?

In hot countries people protect their heads from the sun with all kinds of broad-brimmed hats, from the Mexican sombrero to the cone-shaped straw hats worn by farm workers in southern China and Vietnam. They may wear robes like the Arabs, or loose fitting cotton trousers. In desert lands people may cover their heads with cloths, to keep out the sand. The Tuareg men of the Sahara wrap scarves around the face so only the eyes can be seen. Their name means "the veiled people".

❷ WHO INVENTED SILK?

The Chinese were the first people to make silk, from the cocoons of silkworms, thousands of years ago. Today silk may be used to make beautiful Indian wraps called saris and Japanese robes called kimonos.

AFRICAN MASK
This mask is worn at special ceremonies in Baluba, Africa.

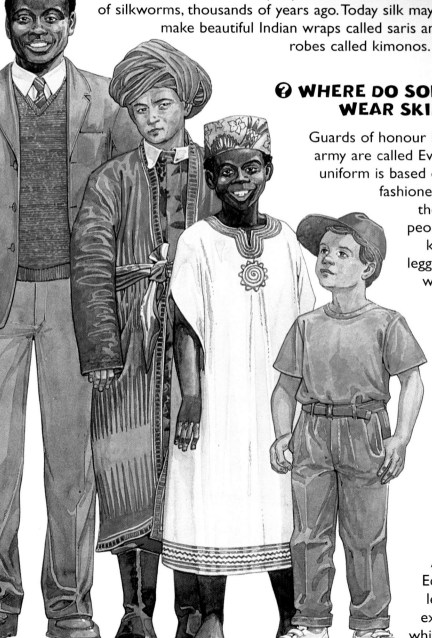

❷ WHERE DO SOLDIERS WEAR SKIRTS?

Guards of honour in the Greek army are called Evzónes. Their uniform is based on the old-fashioned costume of the mountain peoples – a white kilt, woollen leggings and a cap with a tassel.

❷ WHO ARE THE TRUE CLOGGIES?

A hundred years ago wooden shoes, or clogs, were worn in many parts of Europe. The most famous clogs were the Dutch ones, which are still often worn today by farmers and market traders in the Netherlands.

❷ WHO WEARS FEATHERS TO A SINGSING?

A singsing is a big festival in Papua New Guinea. Men paint their faces and wear ornaments of bone and shell and long bird-of-paradise feathers. Traditional dress may include skirts made of leaves and grass.

❷ WHERE DO PANAMA HATS COME FROM?

Actually, Panama hats were first made in Ecuador, where they were plaited from the leaves of the jipijapa palm. They were first exported, or shipped abroad, from Panama, which is why they are now called Panama hats.

❓ WHICH IS THE SWEETEST CROP OF ALL?

Sugar cane is grown on many islands in the Caribbean region. In Barbados, the end of the cane harvest is marked by Cropover, a grand celebration with music, dancing, and parades.

❓ WHO ARE THE GAUCHOS?

The cowboys of the Pampas—the grasslands of Argentina. Once the Gauchos were famous for their wild way of life. Today they still round up the cattle on big ranches called estancias.

Where are the world's bread baskets?

Important wheat-producing areas of the world are called "bread baskets", because they provide us with the bread we eat each day. Wheat is a kind of grass, and so it grows best in areas that were once natural grasslands. These include the prairies of Canada and the United States and the steppes of Ukraine and southern Russia. Combine harvesters move across the prairies for weeks on end, cutting the wheat and separating out the grain.

❓ HOW CAN BARREN DESERTS BE TURNED GREEN?

Water can be piped into desert areas so that crops will grow there, but this kind of irrigation is expensive, and the water can wash salts from the soil, making it difficult to grow plants.

❓ WHERE ARE THE WORLD'S BIGGEST RANCHES?

The world's biggest sheep and cattle stations are in the Australian outback. The best way to cross these lands is in a light aircraft.

❓ WHERE DO FARMERS GROW COCONUTS?

Coconut palms grow best on the shores of the Indian and Pacific Oceans. Coconut fruits are big and green. Inside are the large, brown nuts we buy in shops. The white flesh inside the nut may be dried and sold as copra.

❓ WHICH WERE THE FIRST ALL-AMERICAN CROPS?

About 500 years ago, nobody in Europe had ever seen potatoes, maize, or tomatoes. These important food crops were first developed by the peoples who lived in the Americas before European settlers arrived.

STAPLES

Basic foods such as wheat, shown here, and rice (opposite) are called staple crops.

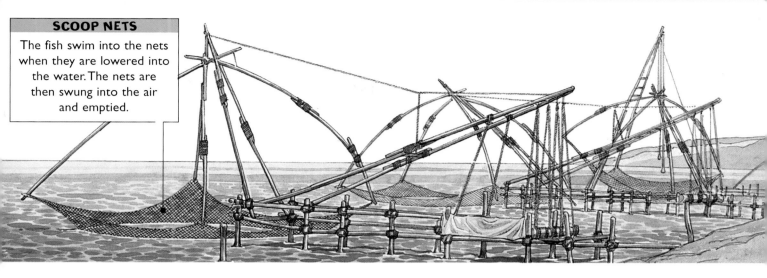

SCOOP NETS

The fish swim into the nets when they are lowered into the water. The nets are then swung into the air and emptied.

❓ WHERE DO FISHERMEN USE HOOPS AND SCOOPS?

Giant fishing nets like those above can be lowered from the shore into lakes and seas. They are often used in China and India.

❓ ARE THERE ENOUGH FISH IN THE SEA?

Modern boats catch so many fish that in many places fish have become scarce. Some of the richest fishing grounds were off Newfoundland, in the North Atlantic. Fishing there has now been restricted until fish numbers recover.

❓ WHAT IS A CASH CROP?

A cash crop is any crop that is sold for money. Not all crops are sold, however. Many small farmers around the world can grow only enough to feed themselves and their families—there is no surplus left to sell.

BY HAND OR MACHINE

Modern types of rice can produce several harvests a year. They can be planted by machines, but these are too expensive for many farmers.

❓ WHAT GROWS BEST IN FLOODS AND SOGGY WET MUD?

Rice keeps the world alive. Billions of people eat it every day, especially in Asia. Grains of rice are the seeds of a kind of grass that grows wild in wet river valleys. To cultivate it, farmers plant out the seedlings in flooded fields called paddies. In hilly lands, terraces are cut in the hillsides and the water flows down channels in the muddy soil.

ANCIENT TERRACES

Some rice terraces, like these in the Philippines, are thousands of years old.

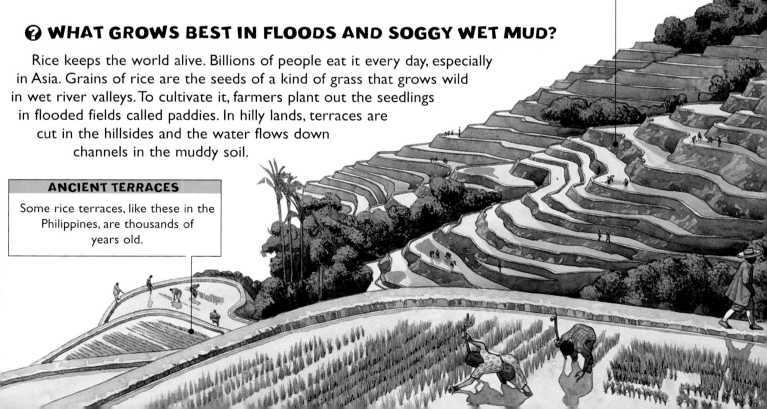

What is the most delicious food?

Haute cuisine is French, and it means high-quality cooking. People all over the world love French food. But is it really the most delicious food in the world? Chinese cooking is also considered a fine art. Really, which food we like or dislike is a question of personal taste. Sheeps' eyeballs, insect grubs, snakes, and pigs' ears can all be found on menus in one part of the world or another—and many people find them absolutely mouthwatering.

PREPARING AN AFRICAN MEAL

African dishes are often based on cornmeal, and served with spicy vegetables, fish, or meat.

❓ WHERE DO YOU BUY MILK BY WEIGHT?

In the Russian Arctic, it is so cold in winter that milk is sold in frozen chunks rather than by the pint.

❓ WHO MAKES THE WORLD'S HOTTEST CURRIES?

The people of southern India. A mouthwatering recipe might include fiery spices such as red chilli pepper, fresh hot green chillies, ginger, garlic, turmeric, and curry leaves.

❓ WHO WROTE A POEM TO HIS HAGGIS?

Robert Burns, Scotland's greatest poet, who lived in the 1700s. The haggis is a traditional dish from Scotland made of lamb's heart, liver, and lungs, suet, onions, and oatmeal, cooked inside—guess what—a sheep's stomach!

❓ HOW DO WE KEEP FOOD FRESH?

Today, butter can be sent to Europe all the way from New Zealand—kept cool by refrigeration. The first-ever refrigerator ship was invented in 1876 to carry beef from Argentina. But how did people keep food fresh before that? The old methods were simpler—pickling, smoking, or drying. Native Americans dried meat in the sun and mixed it with fruit to make pemmican for their travels. Traditional methods are still used today to produce some of the world's tastiest foods—for example, Indian pickles and chutneys, Irish smoked salmon, and Italian sun-dried tomatoes.

❓ WHO INVENTED NOODLES?

Which noodles came first—Italian spaghetti or Chinese chow mein? Some people say that the traveler Marco Polo brought the secret of noodle-making back to Italy from China in the Middle Ages. Others say the Romans were making pasta in Italy long before that. Maybe it was invented in both places.

❓ HOW DO YOU EAT WITH CHOPSTICKS?

Chopsticks are popular in China and Japan. One way of using them is to hold them between the thumb and fingers in one hand.

❓ WHAT IS YERBA MATÉ?

It is a bitter but refreshing hot drink, made from the leaves of the Paraguay holly. It is sipped from a gourd (a kind of pumpkin shell) through a silver straw, and is very popular in Argentina.

❓ CAN YOU EAT SEAWEED?

Various seaweeds are eaten in Japan, and in Wales, UK, seaweed is used to make laverbread. A seaweed called carrageen moss is often used to thicken ice cream and milk puddings.

❓ WHAT IS JAMBALAYA?

Rice, prawns, and peppers, all in an amazing hot spicy sauce. Where is this served up? New Orleans, in the steamy southern United States.

❓ WHAT IS CAVIAR?

Caviar is one of the most expensive foods in the world. It is the eggs of a fish called the sturgeon, which lives in lakes and rivers in Russia and other northern lands.

Where do people buy their food?

In India, many customers buy fresh produce at street markets. Among the goods sold are okra, tomatoes, beans, cauliflower, mooli, peppers, and lemons. Where do you buy your food— at a city store or in a traditional market?

❓ WHERE DO PEOPLE DO BUSINESS?

In Nigeria, money changes hands every day in the busy street markets, where goods are laid out on the ground. Customers haggle about the price of goods. In England, trading might take place in a big store, packed with shoppers. In Switzerland, bankers watch their computer screens to check their profits. In the New York stock exchange, traders grab their telephones as they buy and sell shares in companies. It's all in a day's work.

STREET MARKET, INDIA

Fresh produce is displayed by an Indian trader, who waits for customers. She will weigh the goods on scales.

❓ WHAT CAN PEOPLE USE AS MONEY?

Today, every country in the world uses coins and paper bank notes, although in many regions goods are swapped rather than bought. Through the ages, all kinds of other things have been used as money around the world—shells, stones, beads, and sharks' teeth. These had no value in themselves, but neither do the metal, paper, or plastic we use today. They are just tokens of exchange.

❓ WHAT ARE CURRENCIES?

A currency is a money system, such as the Japanese yen, the US dollar, the Mongolian tugrik, or the Bhutan ngultrum. The exchange rate is what it costs to buy or sell one currency for another.

❓ WHO MAKES THE MOST MONEY?

The mint—that's the place where coins and banknotes are made. The United States' treasury in Philadelphia produces billions of new coins each year.

❓ WHO CATCHES SMUGGLERS?

If you wish to take goods from one country to another, you may have to pay a tax to the government. Customs officers may check your luggage to see that you are not sneaking in—or smuggling—illegal goods.

❓ WHY SELL STAMPS ON PITCAIRN?

Although only 50 or so people live on Pitcairn Island, in the Pacific Ocean, the islanders print lots of stamps to sell to stamp collectors who will pay a lot of money because they are rare.

MONEY
All kinds of objects have been used as money.

❓ WHERE WERE BANKNOTES INVENTED?

Paper money was first used in China a thousand years ago.

❓ WHERE IN THE WORLD ARE THERE FLOATING MARKETS?

In Thailand and other parts of southeast Asia, traders often sell vegetables, fruit, flowers, and spices from small boats called sampans, moored along river banks and jetties.

❓ WHERE IS THE SILK ROAD?

This is an ancient trading route stretching all the way from China through Central Asia to the Mediterranean Sea. Hundreds of years ago, silk, tea, and spices were transported along this road to the west by camel and pony trains.

Where do pilgrims go?

Pilgrims are religious people who travel to holy places and shrines around the world. Muslims try to travel to the sacred city of Mecca, in Saudi Arabia, at least once in their lifetime. Hindus may travel to the city of Varanasi, in India, to wash in the holy waters of the River Ganges. Some Christians travel to Bethlehem, the birthplace of Jesus Christ, or to the great cathedrals of Europe, built during the Middle Ages, such as Santiago de Compostela in Spain.

❓ WHO WAS CONFUCIUS?

This is the English name given to the Chinese thinker Kong Fuzi. His beliefs in an ordered society and respect for ancestors became very popular in China.

❓ WHAT IS THE TAO?

Pronounced "dow," it means "the way." It is the name given to the beliefs of the Chinese thinker Lao Zi, who lived about 2,500 years ago. Taoists believe in the harmony of the universe.

❓ WHICH COUNTRY HAS THE MOST MUSLIMS?

Indonesia is the largest Islamic country in the world, although some parts of it, such as the island of Bali, are mostly Hindu.

❓ WHAT ARE THE FIVE K'S?

Sikh men honor five religious traditions. Kesh is uncut hair, worn in a turban. They carry a Kangha or comb, a Kara or metal bangle, and a Kirpan or dagger. They wear an under-garment called a Kaccha.

MUSLIM PRAYERS

Muslims pray to God (Allah) five times a day. The most important worship is at noon on Friday.

STAINED GLASS WINDOW

This round window in Lincoln Cathedral, England, is made of beautiful stained glass.

❷ WHY DO PEOPLE FAST?

In many religions, people fast, or go without food, as part of their worship. If you visit a Muslim city such as Cairo or Algiers during Ramadan, the ninth month of the Islamic year, you will find that no food is served during daylight hours. Many Christians also give up eating certain foods during Lent, the days leading up to Holy Week, when they think about the death of Jesus.

❷ WHICH CITY IS HOLY TO THREE FAITHS?

Jerusalem is a holy place for Jews, Muslims, and Christians. Sacred sites include the Western Wall, the Dome of the Rock, and the Church of the Holy Sepulcher.

❷ WHY IS MOUNT ATHOS IMPORTANT?

Mount Athos is a rocky headland in northern Greece, holy to Christians of the Eastern Orthodox faith. Monks have worshiped there since the Middle Ages. They wear beards, tall black hats, and robes.

❷ WHAT ARE PARSIS?

The Parsi religion began long ago in ancient Persia, now Iran. Many of its followers fled to India over a thousand years ago. They now live in India, Iran and Pakistan.

❷ WHERE DO YOUNG BOYS BECOME MONKS?

In Myanmar a four year-old boy learns about the life of Buddha at a special ceremony. He is dressed as a rich prince and is then given the simple robes of a Buddhist monk.

❷ WHAT IS SHINTO?

This is the ancient religion of Japan. At its holy shrines, people pray for happiness and to honor their ancestors. Many Japanese people also follow Buddhist beliefs.

❷ WHICH MONKS COVER THEIR MOUTHS?

Some monks of the Jain religion, in India, wear masks over their mouths. This is because they respect all living things and do not wish to harm or swallow even the tiniest insect that might fly into their mouths.

❷ WHAT IS HANUKKAH?

Hanukkah is a Jewish festival of light. It lasts eight days. Families light a new candle each day on a special candlestick called a menorah. Hanukkah celebrates the recapture of the temple in Jerusalem in ancient times.

❷ WHAT IS DIWALI?

This is the time in the fall when Hindus celebrate their new year and honor Lakshmi, goddess of good fortune. Candles are lit in windows and people give each other cards and presents.

THE LAMPS OF DIWALI

Lighted candles mark the feast of Diwali. The Hindu religion grew up in India many thousands of years ago. Light and fire are important symbols of the holy spirit in many religions.

Why do people love to dance?

Dancing is a dramatic way of expressing feelings of every kind. In Spain, passionate flamenco dancers stamp and click their fingers to guitar music. In England, morris dancers jingle bells tied to their legs and bang sticks together. In Africa, there are important dances for growing up and for funerals. The first dances of all were probably designed to bring good fortune to prehistoric hunters. A chief would wear the skins and horns of the type of animal his people wanted to kill.

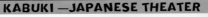

KABUKI — JAPANESE THEATER
In kabuki, all the parts are played by male actors, some dressed up as beautiful women.

❓ WHAT IS KABUKI?

Kabuki is an exciting type of drama that became popular in Japan in the 1600s and may still be seen today. The actors wear splendid make-up and costumes.

MBUTI DANCERS
Young Mbuti people from Congo decorate their bodies with white make-up for a dance to celebrate the beginning of adulthood.

❓ WHO DANCES A HAKA?

In New Zealand, young Maori people have kept alive many of their traditional dances. The haka was danced by warriors, to bring them strength to face the battles ahead.

❓ WHO MAKES PICTURES FROM SAND?

The Navaho people of the southwestern United States make beautiful patterns using many different colored sands.

? WHERE IS THE WORLD'S VERY OLDEST THEATER?

The oldest theater building still in use today is probably the Teatro Olimpico, in Vicenza, Italy. It opened over four hundred years ago. But people were going to see plays long, long before that. In ancient Greece people went to see masked actors appear in some of the funniest and saddest plays ever written, at open-air theaters made of stone. These can still be seen today all over Greece.

? WHERE IS STRATFORD?

There are two famous Stratfords. Four hundred years ago, Stratford-upon-Avon, in England, was the home of the most famous playwright who has ever lived, William Shakespeare. The other Stratford, in Ontario, Canada, holds a drama festival every year in his honor.

? WHO SINGS IN BEIJING?

Beijing opera is a spectacular performance. Musicians clash cymbals and actors sing in high voices. They take the parts of heroes and villains in ancient Chinese tales. Their faces are painted and they wear beautiful costumes decorated with pheasant feathers.

? WHO PLAYS THE "PANS"?

People in the Caribbean, at carnival time. The "pans" are steel drums, which can produce beautiful dance rhythms and melodies.

? WHERE ARE THERE 3 MILLION EXHIBITS OF ART?

In St Petersburg, in Russia. The gallery is made up of two great buildings, the Hermitage and the Winter Palace.

? WHERE DO DRUMS TALK?

The tama is nicknamed the "talking drum." Its tightness can be varied while it is being played, to make a strange throbbing sound. It is played in many places, including Senegal and the Gambia, in Africa.

? WHERE DO THEY DANCE LIKE THE GODS?

Kathakali is a kind of dance-drama performed in Kerala, southern India. Dancers wearing make-up that looks like a mask and gorgeous costumes act out ancient tales of gods and demons.

? WHO PAINTS THE DREAMTIME?

Australia's Aborigines look back to the Dreamtime, a magical age when the world was being formed, along with its animals and peoples. They paint wonderful pictures of it.

ABORIGINAL ART, AUSTRALIA

Like dance and theater, art often has its origins in religious and magical rituals.

Where do dragons dance?

Dragons dance wherever Chinese people get together to celebrate their New Year or Spring Festival. The lucky dragon weaves in and out of the streets, held up by people crouching underneath its long body. Firecrackers are set off to scare away evil spirits. Families give each other presents and wish each other good fortune for the year ahead.

❓ WHERE IS THE BUN FESTIVAL?

On the Chinese island of Cheung Chau, near Hong Kong, there is a big festival each May, with parades and religious ceremonies. During the celebrations people used to climb up huge towers made of buns.

❓ WHO REMEMBERS THE FIFTH OF NOVEMBER?

People in England. The date recalls the capture of Guy Fawkes, who plotted to blow up the Houses of Parliament in London in 1605. The night is marked by fireworks and blazing bonfires, on top of which a home-made "Guy" is burned.

FIREWORKS

Fireworks were invented long ago in China.

DRAGON DANCE

At the Chinese New Year people parade through the streets wearing the skin of a mighty model dragon.

❓ WHERE IS NEW YEAR'S DAY ALWAYS WET?

In Myanmar, people celebrate the Buddhist New Year by splashing and spraying water over their friends!

❓ WHAT IS CARNIVAL?

In ancient Rome there was a rowdy winter festival called *saturnalia*. People copied this idea in the Middle Ages. They feasted and had fun before the dark, cold days of Lent began, when Christians gave up eating meat. People still celebrate carnival today. In Germany there are wild parties and in Venice, Italy, people wear elegant masks and cloaks. In New Orleans, jazz bands parade in the streets. In Trinidad in the Caribbean and in Rio de Janeiro, Brazil, people dance in sparkling fancy dress and let off spectacular fireworks.

❓ WHO WEARS GREEN ON ST PATRICK'S DAY?

St Patrick's Day, on March 17, is the national day of Ireland. It is celebrated wherever Irish people have settled over the ages, from the United States to Australia. People wear green clothes or put green shamrock leaves in their buttonholes.

❓ WHO RIDES TO THE FERIA?

In April the people of Seville, in Spain, ride on horseback to a grand fair on the banks of the River Guadalquivir. They wear traditional costumes and dance all night.

THE FESTIVAL OF HOLI

Hindu children throw colored powder over each other at the spring festival of Holi.

❓ WHO GETS TO SIT IN THE LEADER'S CHAIR?

In Turkey, April 23 is Children's Day. There are puppet shows, dances, and a kite-flying competition. A child even gets the chance to sit at the desk of the country's prime minister!

❓ WHAT IS A POW-WOW?

It means "a get-together". The Native American peoples of the United States and the First Nations of Canada meet up at pow-wows each year to celebrate their traditions with dance and music.

HISTORY

Who walked to America?

The first Americans! For millions of years, North and South America were cut off from the world by deep, stormy oceans. No one lived there. Then, during the last Ice Age, the oceans froze and parts of the seabed were uncovered. A "land-bridge" of dry seabed linked America and northeast Asia. Many wild animals lived on the land-bridge, so groups of hunters roamed across it in search of food. Eventually, they reached America and settled there. Historians are not sure exactly when this happened, but it was probably about 18,000 years ago.

THE FIRST AMERICANS

Hungry nomads set out from Siberia on the long trek to America.

❓ WHAT DID THE FIRST AMERICANS CARRY WITH THEM?

Everything they needed to survive: spears and nets for hunting; seeds, berries, and dried meat to eat; furs to use as cloaks or blankets; and skin coverings for tents.

❓ WHO LIVED IN HUTS MADE OF BONES?

Groups of nomads who lived on the plains of eastern Europe about 15,000 years ago. They hunted wooly mammoths, ate the meat, and made shelters from the skin and bones.

❓ WHAT DID PREHISTORIC PEOPLE WEAR?

In cold countries, they wore leggings and tunics made from furs and skins, sewn together using bone needles and sinews for thread. In hot countries, they wore skin loincloths, or nothing at all!

❓ DID PEOPLE LIVE IN CAVES?

Yes, prehistoric people in cool climates lived in caves.

Ape: *Australopithecus*. This human ancestor lived between 5.3 to 1.6 million years ago.

Hominid: *Homo habilis*. The first tool-maker lived between 1.5 and 2 million years ago.

Human: *Homo sapiens*. Modern men and women developed about 250,000 to 10,000 years ago.

THE FIRST HUMANS

Our humanlike ancestors gradually learned to walk upright on two legs and use tools.

❓ HOW DO WE KNOW ABOUT APES WHO LIVED MILLIONS OF YEARS AGO?

From fossil remains. Fossils are the remains of once living organisms which have turned to stone over many, many years. They can include animal or plant life.

❓ WHEN DID PEOPLE START TO READ AND WRITE?

About 6,000 years ago. The Sumerians (who lived in present-day Iraq) were the first people to invent writing. They used little picture-symbols scratched on to tablets of soft clay. Only specially trained scribes could read them.

❓ HOW DID MODERN HUMANS DEVELOP?

Our distant ancestors are a group of animals known as primates. Primates first appeared on Earth about 50 million years ago, and looked rather like squirrels. Over millions of years they changed and grew as the environment changed around them, and they learned new skills. Slowly, they developed into apes, then into hominids (almost-humans), then into modern human beings.

WHEN DID PEOPLE START TO LIVE IN TOWNS?

Jericho in Jordan (built about 11,000 years ago) and Çatal Hüyük in Turkey (built about 9,000 years ago) were the world's first big towns. They were centers of trade and craftwork, protected by strong walls.

ICE AGE HOME

This tent is made with the skin and bones of the wooly mammoth.

❓ WHAT WERE THE FIRST HOUSES LIKE?

The first houses were probably small, single storey, and made of sun-dried mud. They were built in the Middle East about 11,000 years ago. The first villages grew up close to streams, which provided a steady water supply.

❓ WHO WERE THE NEANDERTHALS?

A type of human who lived in Europe and Asia from about 100,000 to 30,000 years ago. Neanderthals were short and stocky with low, ridged brows. They died out (no one knows why) and were replaced by modern humans, who originated in Africa.

Why were the pyramids built?

The pyramids were built as huge monumental tombs for Egypt's royalty. The Egyptians believed that dead people's spirits lived on after death if their bodies were carefully preserved. It was specially important to preserve the bodies of the pharaohs and nobles. Their spirits would help the kingdom of Egypt to survive. So the Egyptians preserved their dead bodies as mummies, and placed them in these splendid tombs, along with clothes, jewels, and models of everything they would need in the afterlife.

❓ WHERE ARE THE PYRAMIDS?

In Egypt, in North Africa. They stand on the west bank of the River Nile. The Egyptians believed this was the land of the dead, because the Sun set there. .

❓ HOW OLD ARE THE PYRAMIDS?

The first step pyramid was built between 2630 and 2611 BC. Before then, people were buried under flat-topped mounds called "mastabas," and in pyramids with stepped sides. The last pyramid was built about 1530 BC.

❓ WHY WAS THE RIVER NILE SO IMPORTANT?

Egypt received hardly any rain, but every year the River Nile flooded, covering the fields along its banks with fresh water and fertile black soil, excellent for growing crops. Farmers dug irrigation channels to carry water to more distant fields.

TOWARD THE SUN

A pyramid's shape was important. It represented the rays of the Sun. The Egyptians believed that a dead monarch's spirit travelled through the sky with the sun each day.

❓ HOW WERE CORPSES MUMMIFIED?

Making a mummy was a complicated and expensive process. First, a dead person's soft, internal organs were removed, then the body was packed with chemicals and left to dry out. Finally, it was wrapped in resin-soaked linen bandages and placed in a coffin.

❓ HOW WAS A PYRAMID BUILT?

By man-power! Thousands of laborers worked in the hot sun to clear the site, lay the foundations, drag building stones from the quarry, and lift them into place. Most of the laborers were ordinary farmers, who worked as builders to pay their taxes. Expert craftsmen cut the stone into blocks and fitted them together.

❓ WHAT WERE EGYPTIAN HOUSES LIKE?

Small and simple, with flat roofs that served as extra rooms and courtyards where people worked. Rich people's homes were large and richly decorated, with fine furniture, gardens, and pools.

❓ HOW MANY KINDS OF BOAT WERE USED ON THE RIVER NILE?

Many kinds: rafts made from papyrus reed, flat-bottomed punts, big, heavy cargo boats, splendid royal barges, and funeral boats carrying bodies across the river to the pyramid tombs.

CARVED SCARAB
The ancient Egyptians put green stone scarab beetles into the coffins of important people, along with the mummified bodies.

❓ WHY DID EGYPTIANS TREASURE SCARABS?

Scarabs (beetles) collect animal dung and roll it into little balls. To the Egyptians, these balls looked like the life-giving Sun, so they hoped that scarabs would bring them long life. Scarabs have been found in tombs and graves.

❓ WHAT ARE THE PYRAMIDS MADE OF?

Of hard, smooth limestone. Good-quality stone was used for the outer casing, and poor-quality stone and rubble for the inner core.

EGYPTIAN COFFIN
Beautifully decorated coffins protected the fragile mummy inside. Often, coffins were decorated with portraits of the dead person they contained.

Why did the Greeks build so many temples?

Because they worshiped so many different goddesses and gods! The Greeks believed each god and goddess needed a home where their spirit could live. So they built splendid temples to house them, with beautiful statues inside. Each god and goddess had special powers. Zeus was the god of the sky, Ares the god of war, and Aphrodite the goddess of love.

THE PARTHENON, ATHENS

The Parthenon (built in the mid 5th century BC) was one of the finest temples in ancient Greece. It was dedicated to the goddess Athena.

❓ WHY DID GREEK TEMPLES HAVE SO MANY COLUMNS?

Their design may have been copied from ancient Greek royal palaces, which had lots of wooden pillars to hold up the roof.

❓ WHAT WERE THE ORIGINAL OLYMPIC SPORTS?

At first, running was the only sport. Later, boxing, wrestling, chariot races, horse races, and pentathlon (running, wrestling, long-jump, discus, and javelin) were added.

❓ WHAT WERE GREEK WARSHIPS LIKE?

Long, narrow and fast. Galleys, called Triremes, were powered by 170 oarsmen and huge sails. Sea battles were fought by ships smashing into one another, or by sailing close enough for men to jump across and fight on deck with swords and spears.

❓ DID THE GREEKS INVENT MONEY?

No. The first coins were made in Lydia (part of present-day Turkey) about 600 BC. But the Greeks soon copied the Lydians and made coins of their own.

GREEK COINS
The owl was the symbol of the city of Athens.

❓ COULD WOMEN TAKE PART IN THE OLYMPIC GAMES?

No. And only the priestess of Demeter was allowed to attend. But once every four years, there were special games for women only. They were held in honour of Hera, wife of the god Zeus.

❓ DID THE GREEKS GO TO WAR?

In 490 BC and 479 BC, the Greeks defeated Persian invaders, on land and at sea. From 431 BC to 362 BC, there were many civil wars. In 338 BC, Greece was conquered by the Macedonians, and Greek power ended.

THE ORIGINAL OLYMPIC GAMES
The athletes wore little or no clothes when they competed. The prize, an olive branch, was a great honor.

❓ WHAT TOOK PLACE OUTSIDE TEMPLES?

Outside temples, animals and birds were killed and burnt on altars as offerings to the gods. People also made offerings of wine, called "libations."

❓ WHO WERE THE BARBARIANS?

Foreigners—people who did not speak Greek. The Greeks thought their words sounded like "baa, baa."

❓ WERE THERE GAMES IN OTHER GREEK CITIES?

There were over 200 different sports festivals in Greece and the lands around the Mediterranean Sea.

❓ WHAT WERE GREEK COINS MADE OF?

Greek coins were made of silver and gold. They were decorated with symbols of the cities where they were made, or with portraits of heroes and gods.

Why did Hadrian build a wall?

To mark the frontiers of the Roman Empire and guard them from attack. It ran from coast to coast across the north of Britain. Roman emperor Hadrian (ruled AD 117–138) made many visits to frontier provinces, such as England, to inspect the defences and to encourage the Roman troops stationed there.

OLIVE OIL JAR AND STRIGILS

Romans rubbed oil on to their skin, then scraped the oil and the dirt off with metal strigils (scrapers) before getting into the bath.

❷ WHY DID THE ROMANS SPEND SO LONG IN THE BATH?

Roman baths were great places to relax and meet friends. Most big towns had public bath-houses, with steam baths, hot and cold swimming pools, sports facilities, and well-trained slaves giving massages and beauty treatments.

❷ HOW ELSE DID THE ROMANS RELAX?

The Romans ate and drank in taverns, gambled, went to the theater, and watched chariot races and gladiator fights.

❷ HOW LONG DID ROMAN POWER LAST?

The Romans Empire lasted from 31 BC to AD 476, when the last Emperor, Romulus Augustulus, was deposed.

❷ WERE THE ROMANS EXPERT ENGINEERS?

Yes, among the best in the world! They built roads, bridges, aqueducts (raised channels to carry water), long networks of drains and sewers, and the first-ever blocks of flats.

❷ WHO WANTED TO RULE THE WORLD?

About 400 BC the Romans set out to conquer their Italian neighbors. By 272 BC they controlled all of Italy, but they didn't stop there! After defeating their rivals in Carthage (a city in northwest Africa), they invaded lands all around the Mediterranean Sea. In 31 BC they conquered the ancient kingdom of Egypt. They invaded Britain in AD 43. By AD 117, at the end of Emperor Trajan's reign, the mighty Roman Empire stretched from Scotland to Syria and to Iraq.

❷ WHO ATTACKED ROME WITH ELEPHANTS?

Hannibal, a Carthaginian general, who lived in North Africa. In 218 BC he led a large army, including war-elephants, through Spain and across the Alps to attack Rome.

❷ DID THE ROMANS HAVE CENTRAL HEATING?

Yes, they invented a system called the "hypocaust." Hot air, heated by a wood-burning furnace, was circulated through brick-lined pipes underneath the floor.

❷ WHO JOINED THE ROMAN ARMY?

By 200 BC all able-bodied men between the ages of 17 and 46 were conscripted to join the Roman army. Roman citizens became legionary (regular) soldiers. Men from other nations enrolled as auxiliary (helper) troops.

ROMAN LEGIONARY

Legionaries were Roman soldiers belonging to a legion, or unit. They wore a metal shirt over a short tunic, and a helmet topped with a crest of horsehair.

❷ WHAT DID ROMAN CENTURIONS WEAR?

Centurions were army officers. They dressed for parade in a decorated metal breastplate, and a helmet topped with a crest of horsehair. They also wore shin guards, called greaves.

❷ WHERE DID ROMAN SOLDIERS LIVE?

In goatskin tents, while on the march, or in big barrack blocks inside strongly built forts. Groups of ten ordinary soldiers shared a single room, fitted with bunk beds. Centurions (officers) had a room of their own, or shared with their wife and family.

❷ HOW LONG DID ROMAN SOLDIERS SERVE?

For about 25 years. After that, they retired. They were given a lump sum of money, or a pension, and a certificate recording their service.

HADRIAN'S WALL

Hadrian's Wall in the north of England is 73 miles (117 km) long. Roman soldiers patrolled the wall, looking out for Celtic raiders. The wall was up to 15 feet (4.5 m) high in places and had the additional protection of a defensive ditch.

Who were the raiders from the sea?

Vikings from Norway, Denmark and Sweden! Warriors who terrorized the people of Europe. The Vikings made raids from Scotland to Italy, killing, burning and carrying away all they could. It was hard to make a living in the cold Viking homelands, so Viking men raided wealthier lands. However, not all Vikings were raiders. Some travelled to new places to settle, and many were hunters and farmers, who never left home.

❓ DID THE VIKINGS REACH AMERICA?

Yes, around 1000 AD. A bold adventurer named Leif Ericsson sailed westward from Greenland until he reached "Vinland" (present-day Newfoundland). He built a farmstead there, but quarrelled with the local people, and decided to return home.

❓ WHAT WERE VIKING SHIPS MADE OF?

Narrow, flexible strips of wood, fixed to a solid wooden backbone, or keel. Viking warships were long and narrow, and could sail very fast. They were powered by men rowing, or by the wind—the ships had big, square sails.

❓ WHY DID THE VIKINGS COMB THEIR BEARDS?

They wanted to look good enough to attract girlfriends! At home, all Viking people liked to look good and keep clean. They combed their hair and took sauna baths in steam, produced by pouring water over red-hot stones. Viking men and women proudly wore the best clothes they could afford. Both sexes liked to wear fine jewelry and eye make-up, and they painted their cheeks a glowing red.

❓ WERE THE VIKINGS GOOD SAILORS?

Yes. They sailed for thousands of miles across the icy northern oceans in open wooden boats, known as longboats. They learned how to navigate by observing the sun and the stars.

❓ WHAT DID THE VIKINGS SEIZE ON THEIR RAIDS?

All kinds of treasure. Churches were a favorite target for attack, because they contained gold crosses and holy books covered with jewels. The Vikings also attacked farms and villages, and kidnapped people to sell as slaves.

VIKING BROOCH

This beautifully crafted brooch was used to fasten a man's cloak at the shoulder.

❓ WHEN WERE THE VIKINGS POWERFUL?

Viking raiders first sailed south to attack the rest of Europe about AD 800. They continued raiding until about AD 1100.

❓ WHO LED THE VIKINGS ON THEIR RAIDS?

Usually, the most powerful people in Viking society. Sometimes Viking raiders were led by wild law-breakers, who had been expelled from their local community for fighting and causing trouble.

❓ WHO HELPED VIKING RAIDERS AND SETTLERS?

The Vikings prayed to many different gods. Thor sent thunder and protected craftsmen. Odin was the god of wisdom and war. Kindly goddess Freya gave peace and fruitful crops.

VIKING RAIDERS

Viking raiders leap from their longboats and rush up the beach to make a surprise attack.

VIKING COMB

The handle of this Viking comb is made from an elk antler.

❓ WHERE WERE THE VIKING HOMELANDS?

The countries we call Scandinavia today: Norway, Sweden, and Denmark. The word "Viking" comes from the old Scandinavian word "vik," which means a narrow bay beside the sea. That's where the Vikings lived, ready to set off on raids.

Who climbed up stairways to gaze at the stars?

Priests of the Maya civilization, which was powerful in Central America between 200 and 900 AD. They built huge, stepped pyramids, with temples and observatories at the top. The Mayans were expert astronomers and mathematicians. They worked out very accurate calendars, and invented a system of numbers using just three symbols: shells, bars, and dots.

INCA GOLD

Incas gave gold offerings, like this model of a llama, to their gods.

❓ WHY WERE LLAMAS SO IMPORTANT?

Llamas could survive in the Incas' mountain homeland, over 10,000 feet (3,000 m) above sea level. It is cold and windy there, and few plants grow. The Incas wove cloth and blankets from llama wool, and used llamas to carry heavy loads up steep mountain paths.

❓ WHO WERE THE INCAS?

A people who lived in the Andes mountains of South America (part of present-day Peru). They ruled a mighty empire from early 15th century to early 16th century AD.

❓ WHAT WERE MAYAN PALACES MADE OF?

Great slabs of stone covered with a layer of plaster, then decorated with pictures of gods and kings. Mayan temples were built in the same way, but were painted bright red.

❓ WHAT WAS A HUACA?

An Inca holy object or place, or the spirit embodied in that object or place. Inca people made regular offerings to huacas, to bring good luck. Rich nobles left food or clothes. Poor people left blades of grass, drops of water, or just an eyelash.

❓ WHO WERE THE AZTECS?

The Aztecs were wandering hunters who arrived in Mexico about AD 1200. They fought against the people already living there, built a huge city on an island in a marshy lake, and soon grew rich and strong.

❓ WHO WROTE IN PICTURES?

Mayan and Aztec scribes. The Mayans used a system of picture symbols called glyphs. Mayans and Aztecs both wrote in stitched books, called codexes, using paper made from fig-tree bark.

❓ WHO FOUGHT THE FLOWERY WARS?

Fierce Aztec soldiers, armed with bows and arrows, knives, and clubs. During the 15th and early 16th centuries, they fought against other tribes who lived in Mexico, in battles called the Flowery Wars. The Aztecs believed that the blood of their enemies fertilized the land and enabled flowers and crops to grow. They sacrificed prisoners of war and offered their hearts to the gods.

❓ WHO WAS THE GREAT FEATHERED SERPENT?

An important Aztec god, whose name was Quetzalcoatl. The Aztecs believed that one day, he would visit their homeland and bring the world to an end. Quetzalcoatl was portrayed in many Aztec drawings and sculptures, and was worshiped by many other South American peoples, too.

FEATHERED GOD
Quetzalcoatl, drawn by an Aztec scribe.

❓ HOW DID THE INCAS RECORD EVENTS?

On bundles of knotted string, called quipus. The pattern of knots formed a secret code, which no one today knows how to read.

❓ WHO INVENTED CHOCOLATE?

Aztec cooks. They made a bitter, frothy chocolate drink from ground-up cocoa beans and honey, flavored with spices. The Aztec name for this drink was "xocolatl."

❓ WHO WAS THE "SON OF THE SUN"?

Inca rulers were kings, worshiped and feared. The Inca people believed they were descended from Inti, the Sun god. The greatest Inca leader was Puchacuti Yupanqui (ruled 1438–1471), who conquered many neighboring lands.

❓ HOW DID THE MAYAS, AZTECS, AND INCAS LOSE THEIR POWER?

They were conquered by soldiers from Spain, who arrived in America in the early 16th century, looking for treasure, especially gold.

MAYAN PALACE, PALENQUE
The splendid Mayan royal palace at Palenque was topped by a tall tower, built about AD 600 to 900, where scribes and priests studied the stars.

What were ships of the desert?

Camels belonging to traveling merchants who lived in Arabia. They were the only animals that could survive long enough without food and water to make exhausting journeys across the hot, dry desert, laden with valuable goods to sell. They stored enough nourishment in their humps to last several days. Although smelly and bad-tempered, camels were highly prized.

❓ WHAT IS ISLAM?

The religious faith taught by the Prophet Muhammad. People who follow the faith of Islam are called Muslims.

CROSSING THE DESERT

Muslim merchants led camel trains laden with valuable goods across the deserts of Arabia. They carried frankincense (a perfumed gum from an Arabian tree), pearls, and fine glassware.

❓ WHO LIVED IN A CIRCULAR CITY?

The citizens of Baghdad, which was founded in AD 762 by the caliph (ruler) al-Mansur. He employed the builders and architects to create a huge circular city, surrounded by strong walls. His royal palace was at the center, with government offices and army barracks nearby. There were mosques, hospitals, schools, libraries, markets, fountains, and gardens.

ASTROLABE
This instrument was used by navigators at sea.

❓ WHERE WAS THE MUSLIM WORLD?

From about AD 700 to 1200, the Muslim world included southern Spain, North Africa, northwest India, Central Asia, and almost all the Middle East. It was ruled by Muslim princes and governed by Muslim laws. The scientists and scholars of the Muslim world wrote books in Arabic, and all across this vast area the ordinary people shared many traditions and beliefs.

❓ WHERE DID MUSLIM TRADERS SAIL?

All around the Mediterranean, down the east coast of Africa, across the Indian Ocean, and on to Indonesia. They traded silver, glass, and perfumes for cloth, slaves, herbs, and spices.

❓ WHO WERE THE MONGOLS?

Nomads who roamed over the vast plains of Central Asia, tending their horses, sheep, and goats. They lived in felt tents, called yurts.

SAMARRA'S SPIRAL TOWER
Five times a day a muezzin climbed to the top to summon Muslim people to prayer.

❓ WHO WAS THE PROPHET MUHAMMAD?

A religious leader who lived in Arabia from AD 570 to 632. He taught people to worship Allah (God). Muhammad reported that he had received many revelations (messages) from God about how to lead a good life. These were written down in a holy book, the Qur'an.

❓ WHO INVENTED THE ASTROLABE?

Muslim scientists who lived and worked in the Middle East probably about AD 800. An astrolabe was a scientific instrument that helped sailors find their position when they were out of sight of land. It measured the height of the Sun above the horizon.

❓ WHEN DID THE MONGOLS ATTACK?

In AD 1206, all the separate Mongol tribes united under a warlike leader, called Temujin. He took the title Genghis Khan (supreme ruler) and set out to conquer the world. His grandson, Hulegu, destroyed Baghdad in 1258. The Mongol Empire reached its height between AD 1260 and 1294..

❓ WHERE IS THIS SPIRAL TOWER?

At Samarra, in present-day Iraq. It is part of a mosque built for the caliphs of Baghdad in about AD 848. By this time, there were Islamic mosques from Afghanistan in the east to Spain in the west.

❓ WHAT WERE THE CRUSADES?

A series of wars fought between Christian and Muslim soldiers for control of the area around Jerusalem (in present-day Israel), which was holy to Muslims, Christians, and Jews. The Crusades began in 1095, when a Christian army attacked. They ended in 1291, when Muslim soldiers forced the Christians to leave.

What made China so prosperous?

The inventions of Chinese farmers and engineers made the land productive, and this made China wealthy. In the Middle Ages, the Chinese made spectacular strides in agriculture. They dug networks of irrigation channels to bring water to the rice fields. They built machines like the foot-powered pump (below) to lift water to the fields from canals. They also worked out ways of fertilizing fruit and vegetable plots with human manure.

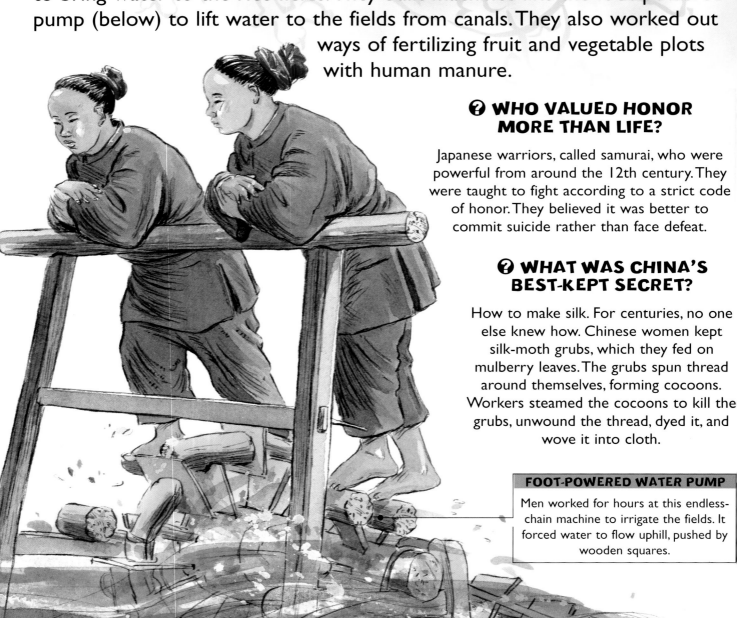

❷ WHO VALUED HONOR MORE THAN LIFE?

Japanese warriors, called samurai, who were powerful from around the 12th century. They were taught to fight according to a strict code of honor. They believed it was better to commit suicide rather than face defeat.

❷ WHAT WAS CHINA'S BEST-KEPT SECRET?

How to make silk. For centuries, no one else knew how. Chinese women kept silk-moth grubs, which they fed on mulberry leaves. The grubs spun thread around themselves, forming cocoons. Workers steamed the cocoons to kill the grubs, unwound the thread, dyed it, and wove it into cloth.

FOOT-POWERED WATER PUMP

Men worked for hours at this endless-chain machine to irrigate the fields. It forced water to flow uphill, pushed by wooden squares.

MING VASE

Chinese potters left clay to weather for up to 40 years before firing (baking) it at very high temperatures, until it was smooth as glass.

❓ HOW DID CHINA GET ITS NAME?

From the Qin (pronounced Chin) dynasty, the first dynasty to rule over a united China. Founded by Qin Shi Huangd, it lasted from 221 to 206 BC. It was responsible for the standardization of Chinese script, weights and measures and the construction of the Great Wall.

❓ WHERE DID THE SILK ROAD GO?

From rich Chinese cities, through the mountains of Central Asia to trading ports in the Middle East and around the Mediterranean Sea. European merchants traveled for years along the Silk Road, bringing back silk, porcelain, and other valuable goods.

❓ WHERE WAS THE MIDDLE KINGDOM?

The Chinese believed their country to be at the very center of the world, which is why they called it the Middle Kingdom. Certainly, for many centuries, China was one of the largest, richest, and most advanced civilizations anywhere on Earth. Under the Tang and Song dynasties (ruled AD 618–1279), for example, Chinese cities like Chang'an (present-day Xi'an) and Kinsai (present-day Huangzhou) were the biggest in the world, and very prosperous.

❓ WHEN WAS THE WORLD'S FIRST BOOK PRINTED?

No one knows for certain, but it was probably between AD 600 and 800, in China. The world's oldest surviving book is "The Diamond Sutra," a collection of religious texts printed in China in AD 868.

❓ WHO WROTE ONE OF THE WORLD'S FIRST NOVELS?

Shikibu Murasaki, who lived at the elegant, cultured Japanese court between AD 978 and 1014. Japanese nobles loved music, poetry, painting, graceful buildings, and exquisite gardens. They lived shut away from ordinary people, who had harsh, rough lives.

❓ WHICH RULERS CLAIMED DESCENT FROM THE SUN GODDESS?

The emperors of Japan. The first Japanese emperor lived about 660 BC; his descendants ruled until AD 1192. After that, shoguns (army generals) ran the government, leaving the emperors with only religious and ceremonial powers.

BULLOCK CART

A pottery model of a bullock cart on the Silk Road. Carts were made of wood and woven bamboo, with strong wooden wheels.

❓ WHO MADE LAWS ABOUT CART WHEELS?

Qin Shi Huangdi, the first Chinese emperor, who united the country. He made strict new laws, reformed the coinage, and burned all books he disagreed with. He ruled from 221 to 206 BC, and was buried with 6,000 terracotta warriors guarding his tomb. He wanted to stop carts crashing on rutted roads, so gave orders that they should all have wheels the same distance apart. That way, they could follow the same track.

Who did battle in metal suits?

Kings, lords, and knights who lived in Europe during the Middle Ages. In those days, men from noble families were brought up to fight and lead soldiers into battle. It was their duty, according to law. About AD 1000, knights wore simple chain-mail tunics, but by about 1450, armor was made of shaped metal plates, carefully fitted together. The most expensive suits of armor were decorated with engraved patterns or polished gold.

❓ WHEN WERE THE MIDDLE AGES?

From the collapse of the Roman Empire, around AD 500, to the Renaissance in about AD 1500.

❓ WHAT WAS A KNIGHT'S MOST VALUABLE POSSESSION?

Probably a war horse. Keeping a war horse demanded a lot of money and time.

❓ WHAT JOB WAS FIT FOR A LADY?

When knights went into battle, their ladies ran the castle. They supervised the household and discussed business and politics with important guests. Some women also fought to defend their castles against attack.

❓ WHICH RUSSIAN CZAR WAS TERRIBLE?

Ivan IV, who became Czar in 1533, when he was only three years old. He was clever but ruthless, and killed everyone who opposed him. He conquered many places, including Livonia, and passed laws turning all the peasants into serfs. Serfs (like slaves) were not free.

KNIGHTS JOUSTING

For fun, and to practice their skills, knights fought mock battles called tournaments or jousts.

THE GUILLOTINE
A prisoner lay his or her head on the wooden block at the base, and the blade fell to chop off the head.

❓ WHO FARMED LAND THEY DIDN'T OWN?

Poor peasant families. Under medieval law, all land belonged to the king, or to rich nobles. The peasants lived in little cottages in return for rent or for work on the land. Sometimes the peasants protested, or tried to run away.

❓ WHAT WAS THE ANCIEN REGIME?

This is French for "old order" and describes the government of France in the 1700s, when the king ruled without a parliament, supported by the Church and rich nobles. The Ancien Regime was overthrown by the French Revolution of 1789, when the poor rose up in protest against the king, the high taxes they had to pay, and their lack of a say in how things were run.

❓ WHICH FRENCH KING LOST HIS HEAD?

King Louis XVI. In 1793 he was executed by guillotine, along with thousands of nobles.

❓ WHO BUILT CASTLES AND CATHEDRALS?

Many people, including kings, queens, and rich nobles. The first castles were just rough wooden forts. Later, they were built of stone, and became impressive homes. Cathedrals were very big churches, in cities or towns. Master-craftsmen built them to reflect God's glory, and to create a beautiful place in which to worship, that would bring honor to their town.

❓ WHO WAS THE VIRGIN QUEEN?

Elizabeth I of England, who reigned from 1558 to 1603, at a time when many people believed that women were too weak to rule. Elizabeth proved them wrong. Under her leadership, England grew stronger. She never married and ruled alone.

❓ WHO PRAYED THE DAY AWAY?

Monks and nuns spent much of their lives at prayer. They promised never to marry and devoted their lives to God.

❓ WHO SWAPPED SALT FOR SANDALWOOD AND GOLD?

Merchants from the north coast of Africa. They traveled across the Sahara Desert to trade with people living in the West African kingdoms of Ghana, Mali, and Songhay, which were powerful from about AD 700 to 1600. Flakes of gold were found among gravel in West African rivers and streams; sweet smelling sandalwood came from tropical trees.

Who built his wife a beautiful tomb?

Mughal emperor Shah Jehan (ruled 1628–1658). He was so sad when his wife Mumtaz Mahal died that he built a lovely tomb for her, the Taj Mahal. It is made of pure white marble decorated with gold and semi-precious stones.

❓ WHO WAS THE GREAT SHE-ELEPHANT?

This was a title of respect given to the Queen Mother in southern African kingdoms, now part of present-day Botswana and neighboring lands. It honored her status as mother of the king, and showed her power.

❓ WHO LIVED IN A ROSE-COVERED PALACE?

The rulers of Vijayanagar, a kingdom in southern India. Their royal palace was covered in carvings of roses and lotus flowers, and surrounded by lakes and gardens. Vijayanagar was conquered by the Mughals in 1565.

❓ WHERE DID DHOWS SAIL TO TRADE?

Dhows were ships built for rich merchants living in trading ports like Kilwa, in East Africa. They sailed to the Red Sea and the Persian Gulf to buy pearls and perfumes, across the Indian Ocean to India to buy silks and jewels, and to Malaysia and Indonesia to buy spices.

❓ WHO WAS THE TIGER KING?

Tippu Sultan, king of the southern Indian state of Mysore from 1785 to 1799. Tippu means tiger—he fought as fiercely as a tiger to defend his land against British and Mughal soldiers.

TAJ MAHAL

One of the most beautiful buildings in the world, the Taj Mahal, near Agra in India, was completed in 1653.

WHICH KINGS BUILT TALL STONE TOWERS?

Shona kings of southeast Africa, who built the city of Great Zimbabwe. Zimbabwe means "stone houses." The city was also a massive fortress. From inside this fortress, the Shona kings ruled a rich empire from AD 1200 to 1600. The Shona were originally farmers, growing millet and raising cattle. Later they became skilled miners and metalworkers. They traded gold, copper, iron, ivory, and leather with Arab merchants living on the East African coast. In return they bought glass and fine porcelain.

HOW LONG DID THE MUGHALS RULE?

For more than three centuries, from 1526 to 1858. But from about 1750, Mughal emperors were weak and powerless. The last Mughal emperor was turned off his throne when the British government took control of India after Indian soldiers working for the British East India Company rebelled in 1857.

WHICH AFRICAN CITY HAD A FAMOUS UNIVERSITY?

Timbuktu, in present-day Mali, West Africa. The city was founded in the 11th century and became a great center of learning for Muslim scholars from many lands. Timbuktu also had many mosques and markets, a royal palace, and a library.

WHO FOUNDED A NEW RELIGION IN INDIA?

Guru Nanak, a religious teacher who lived in northwest India from 1469 to 1539. He taught that there is one God, and that people should respect one another equally, as brothers and sisters. His followers became known as Sikhs.

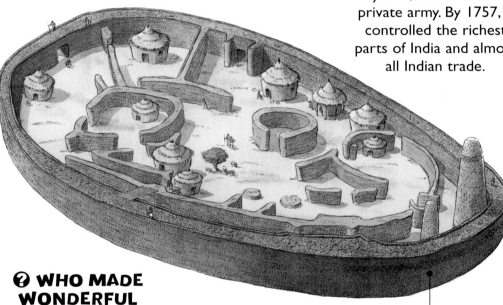

WHO MADE WONDERFUL STATUES OF BRASS AND BRONZE?

Artists and craftworkers living in the great rainforest kingdom of Benin (part of present-day Nigeria), which was powerful from about 1400 to 1900. The statues were used to decorate the royal palace, and were placed on family altars in honor of dead ancestors.

WHY DID BRITISH MERCHANTS TRAVEL TO INDIA?

To make their fortunes! They knew that Indian goods, especially cotton cloth, drugs, and dyes, fetched high prices in Europe. In 1600 they set up the East India Company, to organize trade. The Company grew very rich, and had its own private army. By 1757, it controlled the richest parts of India and almost all Indian trade.

THE FORTRESS-CITY OF GREAT ZIMBABWE

This vast fortress-city was built of carefully cut and shaped stones. The Shona kings lived there with their servants and warriors. Grain was stored in the tall towers. The houses were made of mud and roofed with grass thatch held up on wooden poles.

WHO CONQUERED A KINGDOM AGED ONLY 14?

Prince Babur, who was descended from the greatest Mongol warrior, Genghis Khan. He captured the city of Samarkand in 1497, then invaded Afghanistan, and conquered northern India in 1526. He founded a new empire in India, and a new dynasty of rulers, the Mughals—a north Indian way of writing "Mongols."

THE "VICTORIA"

Magellan set off from Europe with a fleet of five ships, but only the "Victoria" survived.

Who sailed around the world?

The first round-the-world trip was made by sailors in the ship "Victoria," owned by Ferdinand Magellan, a Portuguese explorer. In 1519 he sailed eastward from Europe, but was killed fighting in the Philippines. Most of his crew died too, from hunger or disease.

A few survivors, led by sea-captain Sebastian Elcano, managed to complete Magellan's planned voyage, and returned home to Europe, weak but triumphant, in 1522

❓ HOW DID THE MAORIS CROSS THE VAST PACIFIC OCEAN?

By sailing and paddling big outrigger canoes. They steered by studying the waves and the stars, and made maps out of twigs and shells to help themselves navigate.

❓ DID THE ABORIGINALS ALWAYS LIVE IN AUSTRALIA?

No, they probably arrived there from Southeast Asia about 60,000 years ago, at a time when the sea surrounding Australia was much shallower than today. They may have travelled by land or in small boats.

❓ HOW DID SAILORS HELP SCIENCE?

By observing the plants, fishes, and animals as they traveled, and by bringing specimens home with them. When Captain Cook explored the Pacific Ocean, he took artists and scientists with him to study and record what they saw.

❓ WHO ARRIVED IN AMERICA BY MISTAKE?

Italian explorer Christopher Columbus. In 1492, he sailed west across the Atlantic from Spain. He hoped to reach China or India, but arrived instead in America, which was unknown to Europeans.

A BRIEF HISTORY OF EXPLORATION ACROSS THE OCEANS OF THE WORLD

1304–1377 Ibn Battuta sails to India and China.
1405–1433 Cheng Ho's voyages to Africa and Indonesia.
1419 Portuguese explorers begin to sail along the west coast of Africa.
1492 Columbus sails by mistake to America.
1497 Vasco Da Gama sails around Africa to reach India.
1519–1522 Magellan's ship sails around the world.
1577–1580 Drake sails around the world.
1642 Tasman sails to Australia.
1768–1779 Captain Cook explores the Pacific.

❓ WHO LIVED IN THE AUSTRALIAN DESERT?

The Aboriginal people have lived in the desert for thousands of years. They learned how to find underground water, and to dig up nourishing roots hidden deep in the soil. They discovered which seeds, berries, grubs, and animals are poisonous, and which are good to eat. They perfected the use of wild herbs in natural remedies. They found out how to use fire to scorch the earth and encourage wild food plants to grow. In addition, they used throwing sticks called boomerangs for hunting kangaroos, and nets and traps for catching birds.

ABORIGINAL HUNTERS
Aboriginals used spears to kill kangaroos for food.

❓ WHO WERE THE FIRST PEOPLE TO DISCOVER NEW ZEALAND?

The Maoris. They began a mass migration from other Pacific Islands in about AD 1150, but remains dating back to AD 800 have been found.

❓ WHAT WERE DINGOES USED FOR?

Dingoes are descended from dogs introduced by aboriginal settlers thousands of years ago. They were used as guard dogs, and to keep Aboriginal people warm as they slept around campfires in the desert, which gets very cold at night.

❓ WHO EXPLORED THE EASTERN SEAS?

Muslim explorer Ibn Battuta, who was born in Tangiers, North Africa, sailed to India and China in the 14th century. He was followed by Cheng Ho, a Chinese admiral, who made seven long voyages between 1405 and 1433. Cheng explored the seas around India, Arabia, and the East Coast of Africa. He sailed south to Malaysia and Indonesia, and may even have sighted Australia.

❓ DID NATIVE AMERICANS LIVE IN BIG CITIES?

Yes, some of them. The people who lived in the Mississippi valley about AD 700 to 1300 built huge cities as centers of farming and trade. Their biggest city, Cahokia, was home to at least 20,000 people.

HOME ON THE PLAINS

A Native American woman and her child prepare to say goodbye to a hunter outside their tipi (tent) on the Great Plains. The hunter rides bareback (without a saddle). Moving camp, and setting it up again, was women's work. Working together, the women could clear a whole campsite in a morning.

Who lived in tents on the Great Plains?

Native American hunters, like the Sioux/Dakota, and the Cheyenne. After Europeans settled in America, bringing horses with them, Native Americans spent summer and autumn moving across the wide, rolling grasslands of the Great Plains, following herds of buffalo, which they killed for meat and skins. In winter time, they camped in sheltered valleys or woods. Before the Europeans brought the horses, Native Americans were mainly farmers. They had no animals to ride—the Native American horse died out about 13,000 BC.

❓ WHO WERE THE FIRST EUROPEANS TO SETTLE IN NORTH AMERICA?

Spanish colonists, who settled in present-day Florida and California from about 1540. English settlements began in Chesapeake Bay in 1607, and in Massachusetts in 1620.

WHAT STORIES DO TOTEM POLES TELL?

Native American peoples who lived in the forests of northwest North America carved tall totem poles to record their family's history, and to re-tell ancient legends about the powerful spirits that lived in all rocks, mountains, wild animals, and trees.

WHO WENT TO THE BOSTON TEA PARTY?

European settlers in America gave this famous demonstration. In 1773, they poured tons of tea imported from Britain into the waters of Boston harbor. They were protesting against paying taxes to help the British government fund the wars it was fighting in far-away Europe. They wanted to ban all British taxes, and campaigned for the freedom to rule their own land.

TOTEM POLE

Magical creatures are carved on this totem pole. It was made by skilled craftsmen in present-day Canada.

WHO OR WHAT WERE THE THREE SISTERS?

Beans, corn, and squash, three essential foodcrops that Native American farmers grew wherever they could.

WHY DID A CIVIL WAR BREAK OUT IN AMERICA?

The Civil War was caused mainly by a quarrel over slavery. The war lasted from 1861 to 1865 and was fought between the southern and northern states of the USA. The economy of the southern states relied on black slaves shipped from Africa to work in the cotton plantations of wealthy white owners. The northern states wanted slavery banned. There were also disagreements about law-making, politics, and trade. After four years, the northern states won, and most slaves were set free.

WHO BUILT STRANGE SHAPED MOUNDS?

The Hopewell Native American people, who lived on the banks of the Ohio River. They buried their dead under huge heaps of earth, and created massive earth-mound sculptures. The biggest, "Serpent Mound", dates from about AD 1070, and is about 1,330 feet (400 m) long.

WHEN DID THE USA BECOME INDEPENDENT?

On July 4, 1776, 13 English colonies (the land where most Europeans in America had chosen to settle) proclaimed a Declaration of Independence. They refused to be ruled by Britain any longer, and became a new nation, the United States of America. Britain sent troops to fight the USA and try and win the colonies back, but was defeated in 1783.

WHY DID THE PILGRIMS LEAVE HOME?

The Pilgrims were a group of English families with strong religious beliefs, who quarreled with Church leaders and the government. In 1620 they sailed in the "Mayflower" to America, to build a new community where they could practice their religion in peace.

A CONFEDERATE SOLDIER

A Confederate soldier from the southern states, which supported slavery.

A UNION SOLDIER

A Union soldier from the northern states, which opposed slavery.

What was the Industrial Revolution?

It was a big change in the way people worked and goods were produced. It began around 1775 in Britain and spread to Belgium, Germany, northern Italy, France, and, after 1850 the USA. Machines in huge factories replaced the craftworkers who used to make all kinds of goods slowly, one by one, at home. People had to learn new jobs operating machines that could mass-produce very large quantities of textiles, shoes, paper, metal, and wooden goods more quickly and cheaply than the craftworkers could.

❓ WHEN DID THE FIRST TRAINS RUN?

Horse-drawn railroad wagons had been used to haul coal, ore and stone from mines and quarries since the 1600s, but the first passenger railroad was opened by George Stephenson in the north of England in 1825. Its locomotives were powered by steam. People rode standing in open carriages.

"THE ROCKET"

"The Rocket" was the first inter-city steam locomotive.

LATE 19TH-CENTURY TOILET

By 1900 many ordinary homes had lavatories, but only the rich could afford a polished wooden seat and an elaborately painted pottery pan like this.

WHY WERE DRAINS AND TOILETS SO IMPORTANT?

Because without them, deadly diseases carried in sewage could spread very quickly through crowded industrial towns. Pottery-making was one of the first mass-production industries. Machines in 19th-century pottery factories produced millions of cups, plates—and toilets.

DID NEW INDUSTRIES MAKE PEOPLE RICH?

They made some inventors and factory owners very rich indeed. This angered many ordinary workers, who often earned barely enough to stay alive. Robert Owen founded the first trade union in 1833, to campaign for better pay and conditions.

WHO WORKED IN THE FIRST FACTORIES?

Thousands of poor men and women moved from the countryside to live in fast-growing factory towns. They hoped to find regular work and more pay. Wages in factories were better than those on farms, and some people enjoyed the excitement and bustle of living in a town. But working conditions in factories were often dirty and dangerous, and houses in factory towns were crowded, noisy, and full of disease.

DID CHILDREN LEAD BETTER LIVES THEN?

No, many worked 16 hours a day in factories and down mines. Large numbers were killed in accidents with machinery, or died from breathing coal dust, cotton fibers, or chemical fumes. But after 1833, governments began to pass laws to protect child workers, and conditions slowly improved.

HOW DID RAILROADS CHANGE PEOPLE'S LIVES?

They helped trade and industry grow, by carrying raw materials to factories, and finished goods from factories to shops. They carried fresh foods from farms to cities. They made it easier for people to travel, and encouraged a whole new holiday industry.

Who dropped the first atomic bomb?

On August 6, 1945, the USA bombed Hiroshima in Japan, killing 66,000 people and wounding another 69,000. By using this terrible new weapon on Japan, the USA, together with its allies, Britain, France and the Soviet Union, hoped to bring World War II (1939–1945) to an end. Japan was the strongest ally of Adolf Hitler, ruler of Nazi Germany. Hitler's invasions of European nations had led to the war breaking out in 1939. On August 9, the Americans dropped another atom bomb on the city of Nagasaki, and on August 10, Japan surrendered. The war ended on 14 August.

❷ WHO SHOT THE RUSSIAN CZAR?

In 1918, after the Russian Revolution (1917), Russian rebels called Bolsheviks killed the whole Russian royal family, including the czar, and set up a Communist government instead.

MUSHROOM CLOUD

Atomic explosions create huge mushroom-shaped clouds of boiling gas and give off deadly, invisible radiation.

MAO ZEDONG

In 1966 Mao started a Cultural Revolution among the younger generation in China. He wrote down his thoughts in his "Little Red Book."

❷ WHAT WAS THE LONG MARCH?

A gruelling march across China, covering 5,000 miles, made by around 100,000 communists escaping their their enemies. They were led by Mao Zedong, who became ruler of China in 1949. It began in October 1934 and lasted about a year.

❷ WHAT WAS THE COLD WAR?

A time of dangerous tension from the mid-1940s to the 1980s between the USA and the USSR, the two strongest nations in the world. They had very different political systems and distrusted and feared one another. The USA believed in democracy and capitalism; the USSR was Communist. The superpowers never fought face to face, but their enmity dew them into local conflicts in almost every corner of the globe.

❓ HOW HAS THE WORLD CHANGED SINCE 1900?

In many ways! European empires in Asia and Africa have collapsed, and new independent nations have taken their place. Women now play an important part in government. New scientific knowledge has saved millions of lives; cars and planes make travel faster than ever before; and phones, televisions, and computers send information rapidly all around the world. There are new dangers, too, such as over-population, mass terrorism, and pollution. Sadly, there is still a vast gap in living standards between rich and poor. And there are still many wars being fought.

❓ WHO FOUGHT AND DIED IN THE TRENCHES?

Millions of young men during World War I (1914–1918). Trenches were ditches dug deep into the ground. They were meant to shelter soldiers from enemy gunfire, but offered little protection from shells exploding overhead. The trenches filled up with mud, water, rats, and dead bodies, and many soldiers drowned in them, or died from disease.

❓ WHO MADE FIVE YEAR PLANS?

Joseph Stalin, the Russian Communist leader who ruled from 1924 to 1953. He reorganized the country in a series of Five Year Plans. He built thousands of new factories, took land away from ordinary people, and divided it into vast collective farms. Critics of his policies were often killed.

❓ WHO COMPETED IN THE SPACE RACE?

The USSR and the USA. Each tried to rival the other's achievements in space, because they hoped to prove that their nation was best. The USSR took the lead by launching the first satellite in 1957 and the first manned space flight in 1961, but America won the race by landing the first man on the Moon in 1969.

MAN ON THE MOON
American astronaut Neil Armstrong was the first person to walk on the Moon, on July 20, 1969.

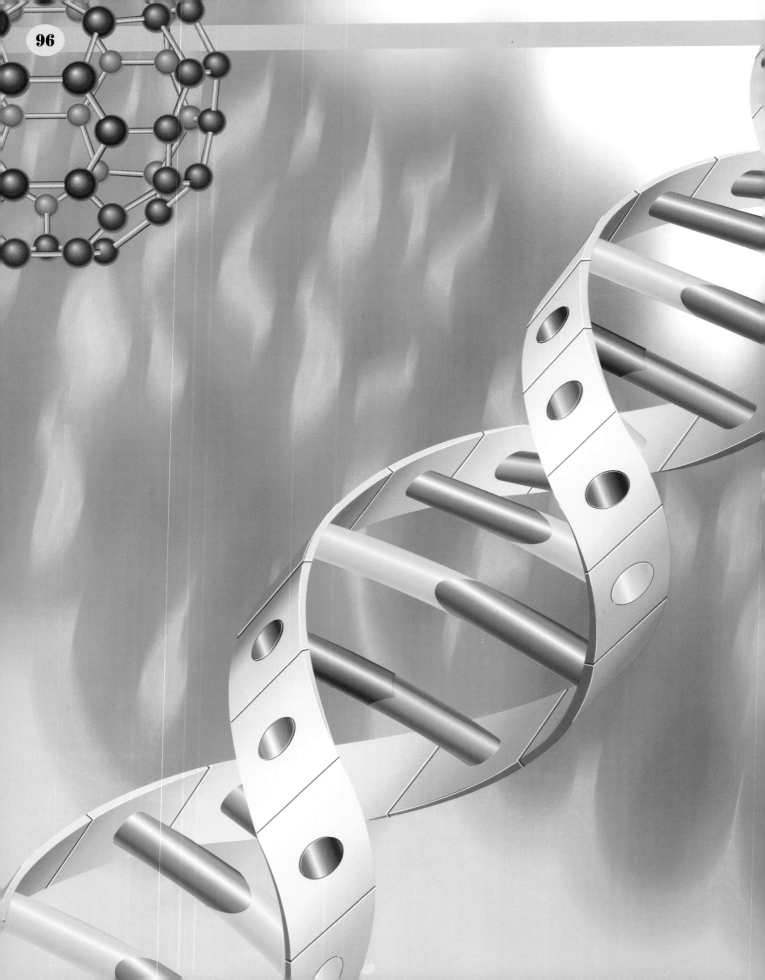

SCIENCE

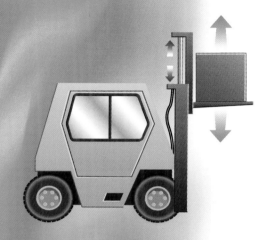

What happens in evaporation and condensation?

Evaporation happens when a liquid is warmed up and changes to a vapor. Particles at the liquid's surface vibrate so fast they escape altogether. Condensation happens when a vapor is cooled down and becomes liquid. Evaporation and condensation take place not only at boiling point, but also at much cooler temperatures.

❓ WHICH SUBSTANCE HAS THE LOWEST FREEZING POINT?

Mercury has the lowest freezing point of any metal, at -37.96°F (-38.87°C). Helium has the lowest freezing point of all substances, at -457.96°F (-272.2°C), which is less than 1° above absolute zero.

❓ WHEN DO THINGS FREEZE?

Things freeze from liquid to solid when they reach their freezing point. Most substances get smaller when they freeze as the particles pack closer together. But water gets bigger as it turns to ice, which is why frozen pipes burst in winter.

❓ WHAT IS A PLASMA?

A plasma is the fourth state of matter. It occurs only when a gas becomes so hot its atoms and molecules collide and electrons are ripped free. This happens inside the Sun, other stars, and lightning, and in gas neon tubes. Plasmas are good conductors of electricity.

❓ WHEN DO THINGS MELT?

Things melt from solid to liquid on reaching a temperature called the melting point. Each substance has its own melting point. Water's is 32°F (0°C); lead's is 621.5°F (327.5°C).

WATER AS SOLID, LIQUID, AND GAS
Solids do not always keep their shape. The ice in glaciers can flow very slowly.

❷ WHAT ARE SOLIDS?

Substances can be either solid, liquid, or gas—the three "states of matter." Substances move from one state to another when they are heated or cooled, boosting or reducing the energy of the particles they are made of. In solids, particles are locked together, so solids have a definite shape and volume. In liquids, particles move around a bit, so liquids can flow into any shape, but stay the same in volume. In gases, particles zoom about all over the place, so gases spread out to fill containers of any size or shape. When a liquid turns into a gas, this is called vapor.

❷ WHAT IS PRESSURE?

Pressure is the amount of force pressing on something. Air pressure is the force with which air presses. The force comes from the bombardment of the moving air particles.

❷ HOW DOES PRESSURE CHANGE?

If you squeeze a gas into half the space, the pressure doubles (as long as the temperature stays the same). This is Boyle's law. If you warm up a gas, the pressure rises in proportion (as long as you keep it the same volume). This is the Pressure law.

❷ WHEN DO THINGS BOIL?

Things boil from liquid to gas when they reach boiling point, which is the maximum temperature a liquid can reach. For water this is 212°F (100°C).

❷ WHAT SUBSTANCE HAS THE HIGHEST MELTING POINT?

The metal with the highest melting point is tungsten, which melts at 6,188°F (3,420°C). But the highest melting point of any substance belongs to carbon, which melts at 6,386°F (3,530°C).

CLOUDS
Clouds form when rising air gets so cold that the water vapor it contains condenses into water droplets.

What is an atom?

Atoms are what every substance is made of. Atoms are the smallest recognizable bit of any substance. They are so small that they are visible only under extremely high-powered microscopes—you could fit two billion atoms on the full stop at the end of this sentence. Yet atoms are largely composed of empty space—empty space dotted with even tinier clouds of energy called sub-atomic particles.

❷ HOW BIG ARE ATOMS?

Atoms are about a ten millionth of a millimetre across and weigh 100 trillionths of a trillionth of a gram. The smallest atom is hydrogen; the biggest is meitnerium. (Since they are so small, atoms are measured in terms of "moles,". A mole is a quantity of the substance containing the same number of atoms as 0.42 ounces (12 g) of a form of carbon called carbon 12.)

❷ WHAT IS THE NUCLEUS?

Most of an atom is empty space, but right at its center is a very tiny area that is densely packed with particles much bigger than electrons. This is the nucleus. It usually contains two kinds of nuclear particle—neutrons with no electrical charge, and protons with a positive electrical charge (opposite to the negative charge of electrons).

❷ WHAT ARE ELECTRONS?

Electrons are the very tiny electrically charged particles that whizz around inside an atom. They were discovered by the English physicist J.J. Thomson (1856–1940) in 1897 during some experiments with cathode ray tubes.

❷ WHO SPLIT THE ATOM?

Electrons can be split off from atoms easily, but in 1919, the New Zealand-born British physicist Ernest Rutherford (1871–1937) managed to split the nucleus of an atom by firing alpha particles at it. (Alpha particles are the nuclei of helium atoms.)

❷ WHAT HOLDS ATOMS TOGETHER?

Electrons are held to the nucleus by electrical attraction, because they have an opposite electrical charge to the protons in the nucleus. The particles of the nucleus are held together by a force called the strong nuclear force.

INSIDE A PROTON

Protons are made of even smaller particles (quarks joined by gluons).

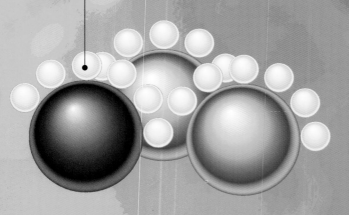

❷ WHAT ARE ELECTRON SHELLS?

Electrons behave as if they are stacked around the nucleus at different levels, like the layers of an onion. These levels are called shells, and there is room for only a particular number of electrons in each shell. The number of electrons in the outer shell determines how the atom will react with other atoms. An atom with a full outer shell, like the gas argon, is very stable. An atom with room for one or more extra electrons in its outer shell, like oxygen, is very reactive.

❓ HOW MANY KINDS OF PARTICLE ARE THERE?

Since the 1920s, scientists have discovered that there are at least 200 kinds of sub-atomic particle besides electrons, protons, and neutrons. Most of these are created in special conditions and exist only for a very short time.

❓ WHAT IS THE SMALLEST PARTICLE OF ALL?

No one is sure. Atoms are made of protons, neutrons, and electrons. In turn, these are made of even tinier particles—quarks and leptons. But one day, we might discover even smaller particles....

AN ATOM

At the center of an atom is the nucleus, made from protons and neutrons. Around the nucleus whirls a cloud of tiny negatively charged electrons.

❓ WHAT IS A MOLECULE?

Quite often, atoms cannot exist by themselves, and must always join up with others—either of the same kind, or with other kinds to form chemical compounds. A molecule is the smallest particle of a substance that can exist on its own.

❓ WHAT IS AN ION?

An ion is an atom that has either lost one or a few electrons, making it positively charged (cation) or gained a few, making it negatively charged (anion). Ions usually form when substances dissolve in a liquid.

❓ WHAT IS AN ELEMENT?

It is a substance that cannot be split up into other substances. Water is not an element because it can be split into the gases oxygen and hydrogen. Oxygen and hydrogen are elements because they cannot be split. Every element has its own atomic number. This is the number of protons in its nucleus, which is balanced by the same number of electrons.

Fluorine

❓ WHY IS CARBON SO SPECIAL?

Carbon is the most friendly element in the universe. With four electrons in the outer shell of its atom (and so four gaps), carbon atoms link very readily with other atoms.

❓ WHAT IS THE HEAVIEST ELEMENT?

The heaviest is hahnium. It has 105 protons and 157 neutrons in its nucleus. The atomic mass of hahnium is 262.

❓ WHAT ARE THE TRANSITION METALS?

Transition metals are the metals in the middle of the periodic table, such as chromium, gold, and copper. They are generally shiny and tough, but easily shaped. They conduct electricity well and have high melting and boiling points.

Silver

❓ WHAT ARE THE LANTHANIDES?

The lanthanides are a group of 15 elements in the middle of the periodic table that take their name from lanthanum. They are all shiny silvery metals and often occur naturally together. They all have two or three electrons in their outer electron shells. This makes them chemically similar—they are all very reactive.

❓ WHAT IS THE LIGHTEST ELEMENT?

The lightest element is hydrogen. It has just one proton in its nucleus and has an atomic mass of just one. The heaviest is osmium, which is 10 times denser than lead.

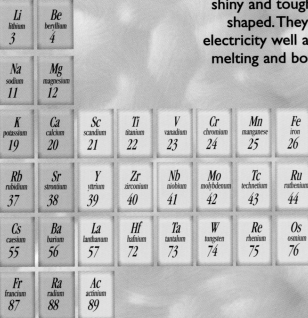

H hydrogen 1								
Li lithium 3	Be beryllium 4							
Na sodium 11	Mg magnesium 12							
K potassium 19	Ca calcium 20	Sc scandium 21	Ti titanium 22	V vanadium 23	Cr chromium 24	Mn manganese 25	Fe iron 26	Co cobalt 27
Rb rubidium 37	Sr strontium 38	Y yttrium 39	Zr zirconium 40	Nb niobium 41	Mo molybdenum 42	Tc technetium 43	Ru ruthenium 44	Rh rhodium 45
Cs caesium 55	Ba barium 56	La lanthanum 57	Hf hafnium 72	Ta tantalum 73	W tungsten 74	Re rhenium 75	Os osmium 76	Ir iridium 77
Fr francium 87	Ra radium 88	Ac actinium 89						

Ce cerium 58	Pr praseodymium 59	Nd neodymium 60	Pm promethium 61	Sm samarium 62
Th thorium 90	Pa protactinium 91	U uranium 92	Np neptunium 93	Pu plutonium 94

Copper

❓ WHAT IS ATOMIC MASS?

Atomic mass is the "weight" of one whole atom of a substance, which is of course very tiny! It includes all the particles in the atom—protons, neutrons, and electrons.

❓ WHY ARE SOME ELEMENTS REACTIVE?

Elements are reactive if they readily gain or lose electrons. Elements on the left of the periodic table, called metals, lose electrons very easily. The farther left they are, the more reactive they are. So Group I metals (called the alkali metals) including sodium, potassium, and francium are very reactive.

What is the periodic table?

All the elements can be ordered according to their properties, forming a chart called the periodic table. Columns are called groups, rows are called periods. Elements in the same group have the same number of electrons in the outer shell of their atoms and similar properties.

								He helium 2
			B boron 5	C carbon 6	N nitrogen 7	O oxygen 8	F fluorine 9	Ne neon 10
			Al aluminium 13	Si silicon 14	P phosphorus 15	S sulphur 16	Cl chlorine 17	Ar argon 18
Ni nickel 28	Cu copper 29	Zn zinc 30	Ga gallium 31	Ge germanium 32	As arsenic 33	Se selenium 34	Br bromine 35	Kr krypton 36
Pd palladium 46	Ag silver 47	Cd cadmium 48	In indium 49	Sn tin 50	Sb antimony 51	Te tellurium 52	I iodine 53	Xe xenon 54
Pt platinum 78	Au gold 79	Hg mercury 80	Ti thalium 81	Pb lead 82	Bi bismuth 83	Po polonium 84	At astatine 85	Rn radon 86

Eu europium 63	Gd gadolinium 64	Tb terbium 65	Dy dysprosium 66	Ho holmium 67	Er erbium 68	Tm thulium 69	Yb ytterbium 70	Lu lutetium 71
Am americium 95	Cm curium 96	Bk berkelium 97	Cf californium 98	Es einsteinium 99	Fm fermium 100	Md mendelevium 101	No nobelium 102	Lr lawrencium 103

HIGHLY RADIOACTIVE

The actinides are a group of 15 elements at the bottom of the periodic table that take their name from actinium. They include radium and plutonium, and are all very radioactive.

WHO DISCOVERED RADIUM?

The Polish–French physicist Marie Curie (1867–1934), born Marya Sklodowska, was the first woman to win not one, but two, Nobel prizes. The first, in 1903, was for her part in the discovery of radioactivity, and the second, in 1911, for her discovery of the elements polonium and radium.

Sulfur

HOW MANY ELEMENTS ARE THERE?

New elements are sometimes discovered, but the total number identified so far is 112.

WHAT ARE NOBLE GASES?

Group 0 is the farthest right-hand column of the periodic table. This group is called the noble gases, because they do not readily react with other elements. But kyrpton, radon and xenon do combine with fluorine and oxygen to form compounds. They are sometimes called inert gases.

Uranium

WHAT IS A METAL?

Most people can recognize a metal. It is hard, dense, and shiny, and goes "ping" when you strike it with something else made of metal. It also conducts both electricity and heat well. Chemists define a metal as an electropositive element, which basically means that metals easily lose negatively charged electrons. It is these lost, "free" electrons that make metals such excellent conductors of electricity.

Gold

❓ WHAT ARE COMPOUNDS?

They are substances made from two or more elements joined together. Every molecule in a compound is the same combination of atoms. Sodium chloride, for instance, is one atom of sodium joined to one of chlorine. Compounds have different properties to the elements that make them up. Sodium, for instance, spits when put in water; chlorine is a thick green gas. Yet sodium chloride is ordinary table salt!

❓ WHAT IS ELECTROLYSIS?

Electrolysis is a chemical reaction caused when an electric current is passed through a substance, the electrolyte. The effect is to make positive ions (or cations) move to the negative terminals (the cathode) and negative ions (or anions) move to the positive terminal (the anode).

❓ WHAT IS A CHEMICAL FORMULA?

A chemical formula is a shorthand way of describing an atom, an ion, or a molecule. Initial letters (sometimes plus an extra letter) usually identify the atom or ion; a little number indicates how many atoms are involved. The formula for water is H_2O, because each molecule consists of two hydrogen atoms and one oxygen atom.

❓ HOW DO THINGS DISSOLVE?

When solids dissolve in liquid, it may look as if the solid disappears. Its atoms, ions, or molecules are, in fact, still intact—but are separated and evenly dispersed throughout the liquid.

❓ WHAT IS A MIXTURE?

Mixtures are substances that contain several chemical elements or compounds mixed in together, but not chemically joined. The chemicals intermingle but do not react with each other, and with the right technique can often be separated.

❓ WHAT IS THE SEA MADE OF?

The sea is water with oxygen, carbon dioxide, nitrogen, and various salts dissolved in it. The most abundant salt is common salt (sodium chloride). Others include Epsom salt (magnesium sulphate), magnesium chloride, potassium chloride, potassium bromide, and potassium iodide.

❓ HOW DO BATTERIES WORK?

Batteries create electric currents from the reaction between two chemicals, one forming a positive electrode and the other a negative. The reaction creates an excess of electrons on the negative electrode, producing a current. Chemicals used include zinc chloride, strong alkaline chemicals, and lithium.

A CAR BATTERY

In a lead-acid car battery, alternating plates of lead and lead oxide form negative and positive terminals, linked by a bath of dilute sulfuric acid, the electrolyte.

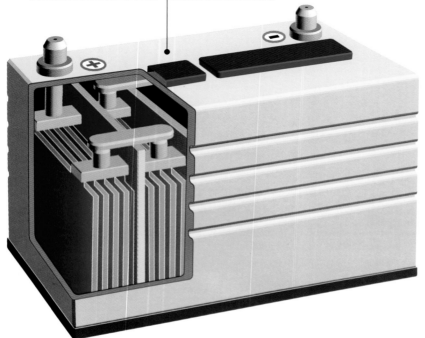

How do chemicals react?

When substances react chemically, their atoms, ions, and molecules interact to form new combinations, separating elements from compounds or joining them together to form different compounds. Nearly all chemical reactions involve a change in energy, usually heat, as the bonds between particles are broken and formed.

❷ WHAT IS THE AIR MADE OF?

Pure air is 78.9% nitrogen, 20.95% oxygen. There are traces of argon (0.93%), carbon dioxide (0.03%), helium (0.0005%), neon (0.018%), krypton (0.001%), xenon (0.0001%), and radon.

FIRE

Fire is a chemical reaction in which one substance gets so hot that it combines with oxygen in the air.

How do nuclear power stations work?

Inside the reactor there are fuel rods made from pellets of uranium dioxide, separated by spacers. When the station goes "on-line," a nuclear fission chain reaction is set up in the fuel rods. This is slowed down by control rods, which absorb the neutrons so that heat is produced steadily to drive the steam turbines that generate electricity.

❓ HOW CAN RADIOACTIVITY BE USED TO INDICATE AGE?

Radioactivity proceeds at a very steady rate. So by measuring how much of a substance has decayed radioactively, you can tell how old it is. With once-living things, the best radioactive isotope to measure is carbon-14. This form of dating is called carbon dating.

❓ WHAT IS AN ATOMIC BOMB?

An atomic bomb or A-bomb is one of the two main kinds of nuclear weapon. It relies on the explosive nuclear fission of uranium-235 or plutonium-239. Hydrogen bombs, also called H-bombs or thermonuclear weapons, rely on the fusion of hydrogen atoms to create explosions a thousand times more powerful.

❓ WHY IS NUCLEAR POWER AWESOME?

The energy that binds together an atomic nucleus is enormous, even though the nucleus itself is so small. In fact, as Einstein showed in 1905, the particles of the nucleus can also be regarded as pure energy. This enables nuclear power stations to generate huge amounts of power with just a few tons of nuclear fuel.

❓ WHO INVENTED THE ATOMIC BOMB?

The first atomic bombs were developed in the USA toward the end of World War II by a team of scientists under the leadership of Robert Oppenheimer (1904–1967).

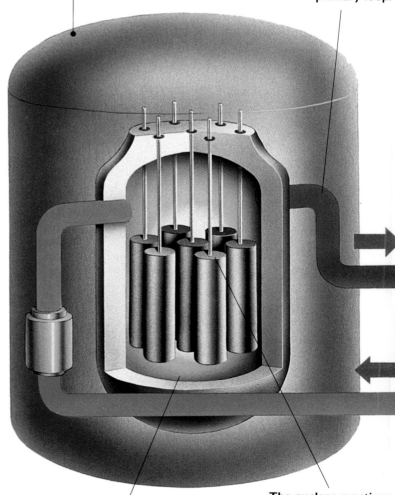

A NUCLEAR POWER STATION

A containment building houses the reactor vessel, keeping in heat, radioactivity, and other energy.

Warmth from the nuclear reaction superheats water under very high pressure in the primary loop.

In the reactor vessel, nuclear fission releases tremendous amounts of heat energy.

The nuclear reactions take place in fuel rods in the reactor core.

❷ WHAT EXACTLY IS RADIOACTIVITY?

The atoms of an element may come in several different forms or isotopes. Each form has a different number of neutrons in the nucleus, indicated in the name, as in carbon-12 and carbon-14. The nuclei of some of these isotopes—the ones scientists call radioisotopes—are unstable, and they decay (break up), releasing radiation, consisting of streams of particles called alpha, beta, and gamma rays. This is what radioactivity is.

NUCLEAR FISSION

A nucleus splits, and each part makes another nucleus split, and so on, in a fission chain reaction.

❷ WHAT IS HALF-LIFE?

No-one can predict when an atomic nucleus will decay. But scientists can predict how long it will take for half the atoms in a given quantity of radioactive element to decay. This is its half-life. Strontium-90 has a half-life of 9 minutes. Uranium-238 has a half-life of 4.5 billion years.

❷ WHAT IS NUCLEAR FUSION?

Nuclear energy is released by fusing or joining together small atoms like those of deuterium (a form of hydrogen). Nuclear fusion is the reaction that keeps stars glowing and provides energy for thermonuclear warheads. Scientists hope to find a way of harnessing nuclear fusion for power generation.

❷ WHAT IS NUCLEAR FISSION?

Nuclear fission releases nuclear energy by splitting big atomic nuclei, usually those of uranium. Neutrons are fired at the nuclei. As the neutrons smash into the nuclei, they split off more neutrons, which bombard other nuclei, setting off a chain reaction.

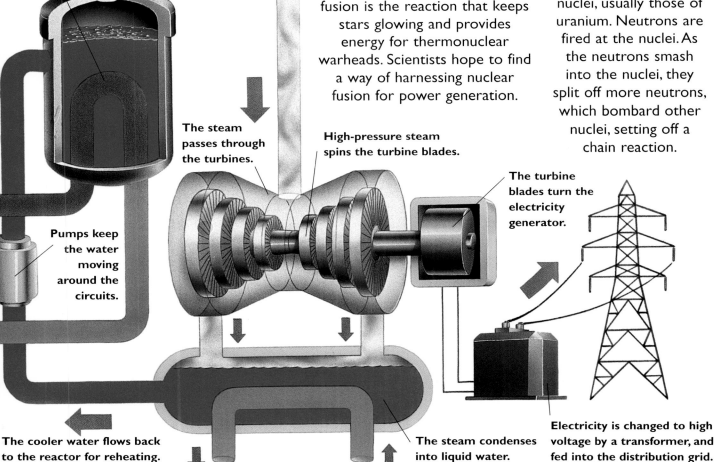

The superheated water in the primary loop boils water in the secondary loop into high-pressure steam.

The steam passes through the turbines.

Pumps keep the water moving around the circuits.

High-pressure steam spins the turbine blades.

The turbine blades turn the electricity generator.

The cooler water flows back to the reactor for reheating.

The steam condenses into liquid water.

Electricity is changed to high voltage by a transformer, and fed into the distribution grid.

What is hydroelectric power?

Hydroelectric power (HEP) is electricity generated by turbines turned by falling water. Typically, hydroelectric power stations are sited inside dams built to create a big fall or "head" of water.

❷ WHO MADE THE FIRST WATERWHEELS?

Nobody knows for sure, but wheels turned by water to generate power were described by ancient Greek writers over 2,000 years ago.

❷ WHAT IS HEAVY WATER?

Heavy water is deuterium oxide, water that is a little heavier than ordinary water because it contains the hydrogen isotope deuterium rather than ordinary hydrogen. Heavy water is used in the nuclear industry to slow down nuclear reactions.

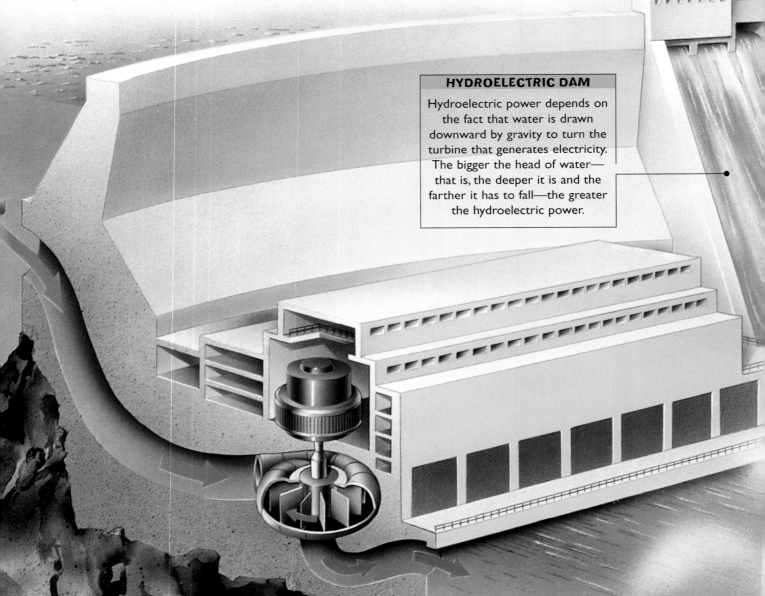

HYDROELECTRIC DAM

Hydroelectric power depends on the fact that water is drawn downward by gravity to turn the turbine that generates electricity. The bigger the head of water—that is, the deeper it is and the farther it has to fall—the greater the hydroelectric power.

❓ WHAT'S SO SPECIAL ABOUT WATER?

Water is essential to all living things. It is chemically neutral, yet dissolves many substances, which is why it is so important for life. It is denser as a liquid than a solid and so expands when it freezes. Water is found naturally as solid ice, liquid water, and gaseous water vapor. This is unusual and happens because of the strong bonds between its two hydrogen atoms and one oxygen atom. When cooled, most substances with similar-sized atoms to water do not freeze until -22°F (-30°C). Water freezes at a much higher temperature, 32°F (0°C).

❓ WHY DO ICEBERGS FLOAT IN THE SEA?

When most things get colder they contract, and when most liquids freeze they get very much smaller. Water is unique in that it contracts only down to a certain temperature, 39.2°F (4°C). If it gets colder still, it begins to expand, because the special bonds between the hydrogen atoms in the water begin to break down. When it freezes, water expands so much that ice is actually lighter (less dense) than water, so ice floats. But it is only a little lighter, so icebergs float with almost nine-tenths below the water line, which is why they are so dangerous to ships.

❓ WHY DOES SWEATING KEEP YOU COOL?

Because sweat is nearly all water, and water needs warmth to turn to vapor, which we call "drying." Watery sweat dries from the skin by taking warmth from the body. This makes the body cooler.

❓ WHY DO PLANTS NEED WATER?

Plants need water for building cells, and also for transporting nutrients from the roots to the leaves where they are needed.

❓ WHAT IS HYDRAULIC POWER?

Fluids like water are incompressible—that is, they cannot be squashed. So if you push fluid through a pipe, it will push out the other end. Hydraulic power uses fluid-filled pipes working like this to drive things very smoothly. Hydraulic means water, but most hydraulic systems use oil to avoid rust problems.

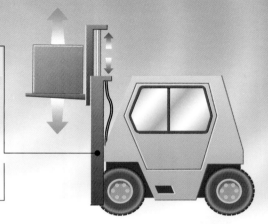

HYDRAULIC LIFT TRUCK

Pumping fluid into the forklift truck's hydraulic pipes raises the load. Slowly releasing the fluid lets the load back down.

❓ HOW MUCH WATER IS THERE IN THE BODY?

Water is found in nearly every cell of the body, which is why human bodies are almost 75% water. Women's bodies have slightly less water than men's, and children's bodies slightly less than women's.

❓ WHY DO THINGS FLOAT?

When an object is immersed in water, the weight of the object pushes it down. But the water around it pushes it back up with a force equal to the weight of water displaced (pushed out of the way). The object sinks until its weight is equalled by the upthrust, then floats.

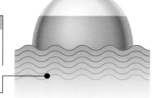

A BUOY AT SEA

Buoys at sea are used to signal all kinds of information to shipping, including potential dangers.

❷ HOW IS NATURAL OIL MADE?

Oil is formed from tiny plants and animals that lived in warm seas millions of years ago. As they died, they were slowly buried beneath the seabed. As the seabed sediments hardened into rock, the remains of the organisms were turned to oil and squeezed into cavities in the rock.

❷ WHAT IS CELLULOSE?

Cellulose is a natural fiber found in the walls of all plant cells. It is a polymer, made of long chains of sugar molecules. These long chains make it tough and stringy, which is why we can't digest it when we eat plants. It passes through our bodies largely intact.

❷ WHAT IS ORGANIC CHEMISTRY?

Organic chemistry is the chemistry of carbon and its compounds. Carbon's unique atomic structure means it links atoms together in long chains, rings, or other shapes to form thousands of different compounds. These include complex molecules such as DNA, which are the basis of life.

DNA MOLECULE

The "ropes" of the DNA molecule are alternating groups of chemicals called sugars and phosphates.

The "rungs" of DNA are pairs of chemicals called bases, linked together by chemical bonds.

What is DNA?

DNA is deoxyribonucleic acid. This is the amazing long, double-spiral molecule that is found inside every living cell. It is made up of long chains of sugars and phosphates linked by pairs of chemical "bases"—adenine, cytosine, guanine, and thymine. The order in which these bases recur provides in code form the instructions for all the cell's activities, and for the lifeplan of the entire organism.

❷ WHAT IS A POLYMER?

Polymers are substances made from long chains of thousands of small carbon-based molecules, called monomers, strung together. Some polymers occur naturally, such as wool and cotton, but plastics such as nylon and polythene are human-made polymers.

❓ WHAT ARE AROMATICS?

Chemicals that have a benzene ring are called aromatics, because benzene has a distinctive aroma. Benzene is a clear liquid organic chemical found in coal tar. It can be harmful, but has many uses, for example as a cleaning fluid and in manufacturing dyes. It has distinctive hexagonal molecules made of six carbon atoms and six hydrogen atoms, and called a benzene ring.

❓ WHAT IS THE CARBON CYCLE?

Carbon circulates like this: animals breathe out carbon as carbon dioxide. Plants take in carbon dioxide from the air and convert it into carbohydrates. When animals eat plants, they take in carbon again.

❓ WHAT ARE CARBOHYDRATES?

Carbohydrates are chemicals made only of carbon, hydrogen, and oxygen atoms, including sugars, starches, and cellulose. Most animals rely on carbohydrate sugars such as glucose and sucrose for energy.

❓ WHAT ARE OILS?

Oils are thick liquids that won't mix with water. Mineral oils used for motor fuel are hydrocarbons—that is, complex organic chemicals made from hydrogen and carbon.

❓ WHAT IS A CARBON CHAIN?

Carbon atoms often link together like the links of a chain to form very long, thin molecules, as in the molecule of propane, which consists of three carbon atoms in a row, with hydrogen atoms attached.

❓ HOW IS OIL REFINED?

Oil drilled from the ground, called crude oil, is separated into different substances, mainly by distillation. This means the crude oil is heated until it evaporates. Substances are then drawn off and condensed from the vapor at different temperatures. The molecules of heavier oils may then be "cracked" by heating under pressure.

❓ WHO DISCOVERED THE SHAPE OF DNA?

The discovery in 1953 that every molecule of DNA is shaped like a twisted rope ladder or "double helix" was one of the great scientific breakthroughs of the 20th century. Maurice Wilkins and Rosalind Franklin did the groundwork for the discovery. Francis Crick and James Watson, two young researchers at Cambridge University, UK, had the inspiration and won the Nobel Prize.

❓ HOW IS PLASTIC MADE?

Most plastics are made from ethene, one of the products of cracked oil. When heated under pressure, the ethene molecules join in chains 30,000 or more long. These molecules get tangled like spaghetti. If the strands are held tightly together, the plastic is stiff. If the strands can slip easily over each other, the plastic is bendy, like polythene.

❓ WHAT ARE BUCKYBALLS?

Before 1990, carbon was known in two main forms or allotropes: diamond and graphite. In 1990, a third allotrope was created. Its molecule looks like a football or the domed stadium roofs created by American architect Buckminster Fuller, so this allotrope is called, after him, a buckyball.

CARBON BUCKYBALL
This is one molecule of buckminster fullerene made from dozens of carbon atoms linked together in a ball.

❷ WHAT IS A KNOCK-ON EFFECT?

When two objects collide, their combined momentum remains the same if nothing else interferes. So if one object loses momentum, this momentum must be passed on to the other object, making it move. This is essentially a knock-on effect.

❷ WHO WAS EINSTEIN?

Albert Einstein (1897–1955) was the scientific genius who transformed science with his two big theories—Special Relativity (1905) and General Relativity (1915). The theory of Special Relativity was developed while he was working in the Swiss Patent Office in Bern.

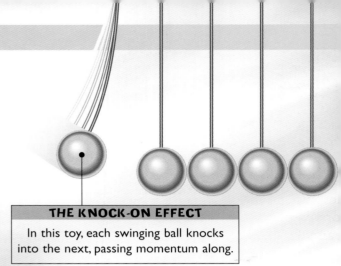

THE KNOCK-ON EFFECT

In this toy, each swinging ball knocks into the next, passing momentum along.

❷ WHAT IS A TURNING FORCE?

When something fixed in one place is pushed or pulled elsewhere, it turns around a fulcrum. When you push a door shut, the push is the turning force, and the hinge is the fulcrum.

How do things get moving?

Things only move if forced to move. So when something starts moving, there must be a force involved, whether it is visible, like someone pushing, or invisible, like gravity, which makes things fall. Once moving, things will carry on moving at the same speed and in the same direction until another force is applied, typically friction.

❷ WHAT'S THE DIFFERENCE BETWEEN VELOCITY AND SPEED?

Speed is how fast something is going. Velocity is how fast something is going and in which direction. Speed is called a scalar quantity; velocity a vector.

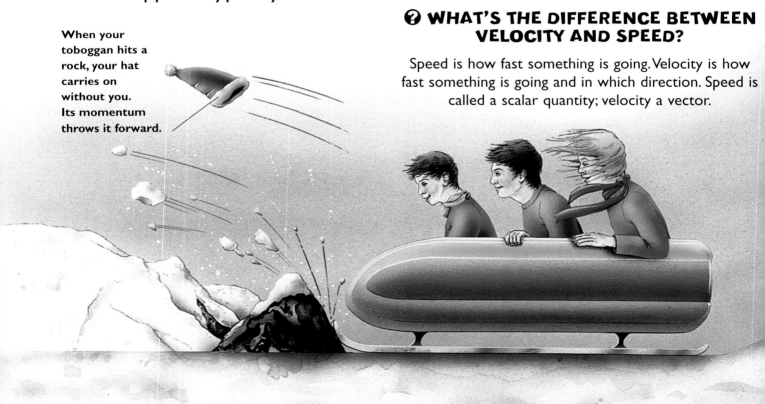

When your toboggan hits a rock, your hat carries on without you. Its momentum throws it forward.

❷ WHY DO THINGS GO ROUND?

If only one force is involved, things will always move in a straight line. This is called linear motion. Things go round when there is more than one force involved. A ball loops through the air because gravity is pulling it down while its momentum is pushing it on, less and less strongly. A wheel goes round on its axle because there is one force trying to make it carry on in a straight line and another keeping it the same distance from the axle.

❷ WHAT IS SPECIAL RELATIVITY?

The theory of Special Relativity shows how both space and time can be measured only relatively, that is, in comparison to something else. This means that time can speed up or slow down, depending on how fast you are moving.

❷ WHAT'S THE FASTEST THING IN THE UNIVERSE?

Light, which travels at 186,000 miles (300,000 km) per second. This is the one speed in the universe that is constant—it is always the same, no matter how fast you are going when you measure it.

❷ WHAT IS UNIFORM MOTION?

Uniform motion is when an object carries on traveling at exactly the same speed in exactly the same direction.

A TOBOGGAN RIDE
Once gravity has overcome your toboggan's inertia and got you swishing downhill, its momentum will keep it going until something stops it.

❷ WHAT WAS NEWTON'S BREAKTHROUGH?

Sir Isaac Newton's breakthrough in 1665 was to realize that all movement in the universe is governed by three simple rules, which we now called Newton's Laws of Motion. The First is about inertia and momentum. For his three Laws of Motion, read on.

❷ WHAT'S THE DIFFERENCE BETWEEN INERTIA AND MOMENTUM?

Inertia is the tendency of things to stay still unless they are forced to move. Momentum is the tendency for things to keep going once they are moving, unless forced to stop or slow. This is the First Law of Motion.

❷ WHAT IS ACCELERATION?

Acceleration is how fast something gains speed. The larger the force and the lighter the object, the greater the acceleration. This is Newton's Second law of Motion.

❷ WHAT HAPPENS WITH EVERY ACTION?

This is Newton's Third Law of Motion—for every action, there is an equal and opposite reaction. Which means that whenever something moves, there is a balance of forces pushing in opposite directions. When you push your legs against water to swim, for instance, the water pushes back on your legs equally hard.

Why do satellites go round the Earth?

Satellites are whizzing through space at exactly the right height for their speed. The Earth's gravity tries to pull them down to Earth, but they are traveling so fast that they go on zooming round the Earth just as fast as the Earth pulls them in.

ORBITING THE EARTH

The Moon is also a satellite. It orbits the Earth because they are held together by mutual gravitational pull.

❷ WHAT'S THE DIFFERENCE BETWEEN MASS AND WEIGHT?

Mass is the amount of matter in an object. It is the same wherever you measure it, even on the Moon. Weight is a measure of the force of gravity on an object. It varies according to where you measure it.

❷ WHAT DID A GREAT SCIENTIST LEARN FROM AN APPLE?

The mathematician and physicist Sir Isaac Newton is said to have developed his ideas about gravity while sitting one day under an apple tree. As he watched an apple fall to the ground, it occurred to him in a flash that the apple was not merely falling, but was being pulled toward the ground by an invisible force. This is the force he called gravity.

The satellite is traveling forward so fast that it never gets close to the Earth.

Gravity is tugging the satellite downward all the time.

❷ WHAT IS POWER?

Power is the rate at which work is done. A high-powered engine is an engine that can move a great deal of weight very quickly. Power is also the rate at which energy is transferred. A large amount of electric power might be needed to heat a large quantity of water.

❓ WHAT IS GRAVITY?

Gravity is the invisible force of attraction between every bit of matter in the universe. Its strength depends on the mass of the objects involved and their distance apart.

❓ WHAT DID GALILEO DO ON THE TOWER OF PISA?

Galileo Galilei (1564–1642) is said to have dropped metal balls of different weights from the Leaning Tower of Pisa to show that they all fall at the same speed.

A typical space rocket has fuel tanks filled with liquid propellant fuel and liquid oxygen for the motors to burn.

❓ HOW FAST DOES A STONE FALL?

At first the stone falls faster and faster at a rate of 32 feet (9.8 m) per second at every second. But as the stone's speed accelerates, air resistance increases until it becomes so great that the stone cannot fall any faster. It now continues to fall at the same velocity, called the terminal velocity.

❓ WHY CAN YOU JUMP HIGHER ON THE MOON?

The Moon is much smaller than the Earth, so its gravity is much weaker. Astronauts weigh six times less on the Moon than they do on Earth, and can jump much higher!

❓ HOW DOES GRAVITY HOLD YOU DOWN?

The mutual gravitational attraction between the mass of your body and the mass of the Earth pulls them together. If you jump off a wall, the Earth pulls you toward the ground. You also pull the Earth toward you, but because you are tiny and the Earth is huge, you move a lot and the Earth barely moves at all.

❓ WHAT IS FRICTION?

Friction is the force between two things rubbing together, which may be brake pads on a bicycle wheel or air molecules against an aeroplane. Friction tends to slow things down, making them hot as their momentum is converted into heat.

❓ WHAT IS A FORCE?

A force makes something move, by pushing or pulling it. Gravity is an invisible force. Other forces, such as a kick, we can see. To overcome Earth's gravity and fly into space, a rocket must reach a speed of roughly 25,000 mph (40,000 km/h)—this is known as escape velocity. The farther the rocket goes, the smaller Earth's gravitational pull becomes. At 1,500 miles (2,500 km) away, it is only half as strong. Forces work in pairs. For every force pushing in one direction, there is an equal and opposite force pushing in the opposite direction.

BLAST OFF!

Hot gas rushes out from a rocket's motors at enormous speed. The momentum of the gas rushing out in one direction gives the rocket equal momentum in the opposite direction, thrusting it upward.

❓ HOW IS FORCE MEASURED?

Force is measured in newtons. A newton is the force needed to accelerate 2.2 pounds (1 kg) by 3.2 feet (1 m) per second every second.

❓ DOES GRAVITY VARY?

An object's gravitational pull varies with its mass and its distance. In fact, gravity diminishes precisely in proportion to its distance away, squared. You can work out the force of gravity between two objects by multiplying their masses and dividing by the square of the distance between them. This sum works all over the universe with pinpoint accuracy.

HOW FOSSIL FUELS WERE FORMED

Millions of years ago, plants absorbed the Sun's energy and converted it into new fibers as they grew. The stored energy in the plant fibers was concentrated into coal as the fibers were buried and squeezed beneath layers of sediment over millions of years.

Where does our energy come from?

Nearly all of our energy comes to us ultimately from the Sun. Some we get directly via solar power cells. Most comes indirectly via fossil fuels (coal and oil), which got their energy from the fossilized plants (and other organisms) of which they are made. The plants got their energy directly from the Sun by a process called photosynthesis.

❓ HOW ARE ENERGY AND MASS LINKED?

Energy is a form of mass; mass is a form of energy. In nuclear reactions, tiny amounts of mass are changed into huge quantities of energy.

The deepest coal (anthracite) is squashed to almost pure black carbon, and provides a very concentrated form of energy.

Fuel buried less deep is less squashed. This less concentrated fuel is called brown coal or lignite.

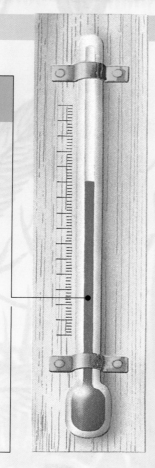

SPIRIT THERMOMETER FOR MEASURING NORMAL AIR TEMPERATURES

720 million°F (400 million°C) is the highest temperature ever measured. It happened in a nuclear fusion experiment in the USA.

The highest air temperature ever recorded is 136°F (58°C) in Libya, North Africa.

Earth's lowest air temperature ever measured was -190°F (-88°C). It was recorded in Antarctica.

The lowest temperature ever measured was -459.67°F (-273.15°C) in a Finnish laboratory.

❓ HOW IS TEMPERATURE MEASURED?

Temperature is usually measured with a thermometer. Some thermometers have a metal strip that bends according to how hot it is. But most contain a liquid, such as mercury, in a tube. As it gets warmer, the liquid expands, and its level rises in the tube. The level of the liquid indicates the temperature.

❓ HOW IS ENERGY CONSERVED?

Energy can be neither created nor destroyed. When energy is converted from one form to another, there is always exactly the same amount of energy afterward as there was before. In this way energy is conserved, even when converted into a different form.

❓ WHAT'S THE DIFFERENCE BETWEEN HEAT AND TEMPERATURE?

Heat is molecules moving. It is a form of energy, the combined energy of all the moving molecules. Temperature, on the other hand, is simply a measure of how fast all the molecules are moving.

❓ HOW DO YOU CONVERT FAHRENHEIT TO CELSIUS?

You can convert from Fahrenheit to Celsius by subtracting 32, then dividing by nine, and multiplying by five. You can convert from Celsius to Fahrenheit by dividing by five, multiplying by nine, and adding 32.

❓ WHAT IS CONDUCTION?

Conduction is one of the three ways in which heat moves. It involves heat spreading from hot areas to cold areas as moving particles knock into one another. The other ways are convection, in which warm air or water rises, and radiation, which is rays of invisible infrared light.

❓ WHAT IS ABSOLUTE ZERO?

Absolute zero is the coldest possible temperature, the temperature at which atoms stop moving altogether. This happens at -459.67°F (-273.15°C), or 0 on the Kelvin scale.

❓ WHAT IS ENERGY EFFICIENCY?

Some machines waste a great deal of energy, while others waste very little. The energy efficiency of a machine is measured by the proportion of energy it wastes. Waste energy is usually lost as heat.

❓ WHAT IS ENERGY?

Energy takes many forms. Heat energy boils water, keeps us warm, and drives engines. Chemical energy fuels cars and airplanes. Electrical energy drives many small machines and keeps lights glowing. Almost every form of energy can be converted into other forms. But whatever form it is in, energy is essentially the capacity for making something happen or, as scientists put it, "doing work."

❓ HOW DO THINGS ABSORB LIGHT?

When light rays hit a surface, some bounce off, but others are absorbed by atoms in the surface, warming it up very slightly. Each kind of atom absorbs particular wavelengths (colors) of light. The color of the surface depends on which wavelengths of light are absorbed and which reflected. You see a leaf as green because the leaf has soaked up all colors but green, and you see only the reflected green light.

How do mirrors work?

Most mirrors are made of ordinary glass, but the back is silvered—coated with a shiny metal that perfectly reflects all the light that hits it—at exactly the same angle. The image in a mirror is back-to-front, or reversed. Left is on the right, and right is on the left—a mirror image! A photograph gives a true right-way-round image.

REFLECTION
You can see an object such as a plant in a pot by the light reflected from it.

❓ WHAT HAPPENS AT AN INTERFERENCE FRINGE?

Interference is what happens when two light waves meet each other. If the waves are in step with each other, they reinforce each other. This is positive interference, and you see bright light. If they are out of step, they may cancel each other out. This is negative interference, and you see shadow. Interference fringes are bands of light and shade created by alternating positive and negative interference.

❓ WHAT IS AN INCIDENT RAY?

When scientists talk about reflections, they distinguish between the light falling on the reflector (which may be a mirror) and the light reflected. Incident rays are the rays hitting the reflector.

❓ WHAT ARE PHOTONS?

Photons are almost infinitesimally small particles of light. They have no mass and there are billions of them in a single beam of light.

DOES LIGHT TRAVEL IN WAVES?

In the last century, most scientists believed light did travel in tiny waves rather than bullet-like particles. Now they agree it can be both, and it is probably best to think of light as vibrating packets of energy.

WHY IS THE SKY BLUE?

Sunlight is white, which means it contains all the colors of the rainbow. The sky is blue because air molecules scatter—reflect in all directions—more blue from sunlight toward our eyes than they do other colors.

HOW IS LIGHT BENT?

Light rays are bent when they are refracted. This happens when they strike a transparent material like glass or water, at an angle. The different materials slow the light waves down so that they slew round, like car wheels driving on to sand.

HOW DO YOUR EYES SEE THINGS?

Light sources such as the Sun, stars, and electric light shine light rays straight into your eyes. Everything else you see only by reflected light, that is, by light rays that bounce off things. So you can see things only if there is a light source throwing light onto them. Otherwise, they look black, and you can't see them at all.

WHY IS THE SUN RED?

The Sun is only red at sunrise and sunset, when the Sun is low in the sky and sunlight reaches us only after passing a long way through the dense lower layers of the atmosphere. Particles in the air absorb shorter, bluer wavelengths of light or reflect them away from us, leaving just the red.

REFRACTION
A straight rod dipped in a glass of water seems to bend in the middle, because the glass and water refract (bend) the light.

IMAGE
The reflection of the plant forms an image that appears to be behind the mirror, as if you were looking at it through a window.

HOW DO FIBER-OPTIC CABLES BEND LIGHT?

Actually they don't bend light, but reflect it round corners. Inside a cable are lots of bundles of glass fibers. Light rays zig-zag along the inside of each fiber, reflecting first one side, then the other. In this way, light can be transmitted through the cable no matter what route it takes.

❷ WHAT IS THE ELECTROMAGNETIC SPECTRUM?

Light is just a small part of the wide range of radiation emitted by atoms—the only part we can see. This range of radiation is called the electromagnetic spectrum and ranges from long waves, such as radio waves and microwaves, to short waves, such as X-rays and gamma rays.

❷ WHAT IS INFRARED?

Infrared is light with wavelengths too long for the human eye to register. But you can often feel infrared light as warmth.

RAINBOWS

Rainbows are formed by the reflection of the Sun off billions of drops of moisture in the air.

What are the colors of the rainbow?

The colors of the rainbow are all the colors contained in white light. When white light hits raindrops in the air, it is split up into a rainbow of colors, because each color of light is refracted by the rainbow to a different extent. The colors of the rainbow appear in this order: red, orange, yellow, green, blue, indigo, violet.

❓ HOW DO TV SIGNALS TRAVEL?

TV signals travel in one of three ways. Terrestrial broadcasts are beamed out from transmitters as radio waves to be picked up by TV aerials. Satellite broadcasts are sent up to satellites as microwaves, then picked up by satellite dishes. Cable broadcasts travel as electrical or light signals along underground cables, straight to the TV set.

❓ WHY CAN'T YOU SEE ULTRAVIOLET?

Ultraviolet light is light with wavelengths too short for the human eye to register.

❓ HOW DO CT SCANS WORK?

CT (computed tomography) scans run X-ray beams right around the body, and pick up how much is absorbed with special sensors. A computer analyzes the data to create a complete "slice" through the body.

ELECTROMAGNETIC SPECTRUM

All the different colors of light have different wavelengths. The longest waves we can see are red (far left). The shortest waves of light we can see are violet (above).

❓ HOW DOES A PRISM SPLIT COLORS?

Prisms split white light into separate colors by refracting (bending) it. The longer the wavelength of the light, the more it is refracted. So long wavelength colors emerge from the prism at a different point from short wavelength colors.

❓ WHO MADE THE FIRST RADIO BROADCAST?

Italian inventor Guglielmo Marconi first sent radio signals over 1 mile (1.6 km) in 1895. In 1898, he sent a message in Morse code across the English Channel. In 1901, he sent a radio message across the Atlantic Ocean.

RAINDROP

Light refracted through a raindrop

❓ HOW DO X-RAYS SEE THROUGH YOU?

X-rays are stopped only by the bones and especially dense bits of the body. They pass through the soft bits to hit a photographic plate on the far side of the body, where they leave a silhouette of the skeleton.

What makes lightning flash?

Lightning flashes produce 100 million volts of static electricity. Lightning is created when raindrops and ice crystals inside a thundercloud become electrically charged as they are flung together, losing or gaining electrons from each other. Negatively charged particles build up at the base of the cloud. When this charge has built up enough, it discharges as lightning, either flashing within the cloud or forking between the cloud and the ground.

DISCHARGING

Lightning flashes to the ground to discharge, because it always carries a slight positive electrical charge.

❷ HOW DO ELECTRIC CURRENTS FLOW?

The charge in an electric current is electrons that have broken free from their atoms. None of them moves very far, but the current is passed on as they bang into each other like rows of marbles.

❷ WHAT IS A SILICON CHIP?

A silicon chip is an electronic circuit implanted in a small crystal of semi-conducting silicon, in such a way that it can be manufactured in huge numbers. This was the predecessor to the microprocessors that make computers work.

❷ WHAT IS AN ELECTRIC CURRENT?

A current is a continuous stream of electrical charge. It happens only when there is a complete, unbroken "circuit" for the current to flow through, typically a loop of copper wire.

SILICON CHIP

Complex electrical circuits can be printed on to a tiny silicon chip.

LIGHT BULB
The pressure of the electric current through the bulb's thin wire filament makes it glow.

❓ WHY DOES YOUR HAIR GO FRIZZY?

When you comb dry hair, tiny electrons are knocked off the atoms in the comb as it rubs past. Your hair is coated with these tiny negative electrical charges and so is attracted to anything that has its normal quota of electrons, or more. An electric charge made like this is called "static," because it does not move. Try rubbing a balloon on your jumper to create a static charge, then you can stick it on the wall.

❓ WHAT IS AN ALTERNATING CURRENT?

A direct current (DC) flows in one direction only. Most hand-held flashlights use DC. Electricity in the house is alternating current (AC), which means it continually swaps direction as the generator's coil spins around past its electrodes.

❓ WHO INVENTED TRANSISTORS?

Transistors were invented by three scientists working at the Bell Laboratories in the USA in 1948: William Shockley, Walter Brattain, and John Bardeen.

❓ WHAT ARE THE BEST CONDUCTORS?

The best conductors are metals such as copper and silver. Water is also a good conductor. Superconductors are materials like aluminium, which is cooled until it transmits electricity almost without resistance.

WHAT IS A VOLT?

Electrical current flows as long as there is a difference in charge between two points in the circuit. This difference is called a potential and is measured in terms of volts. The bigger the difference, the bigger the voltage.

FLASHES OF LIGHT
Lightning flashes from a thundercloud when a massive electrical charge builds up in the base of the cloud.

❓ WHAT IS A SEMI-CONDUCTOR?

Semi-conductors are materials such as silicon or germanium, which are partly resistant to electric current and partly conducting. They can be set up so that the conductivity is switched on or off, creating a tiny electrical switch. They are used to make diodes, transistors, and chips, and so are essential to electronics.

❓ WHAT IS RESISTANCE?

Not all substances conduct electric currents equally well. Resistance is a substance's ability to block a flow of electric current.

❓ HOW DOES ELECTRIC LIGHT WORK?

An electric bulb has a very thin filament of tungsten wire inside a glass bulb filled with argon or nitrogen gas. When current flows through such a thin wire, the resistance is so great that the wire heats up and glows brightly. If it wasn't surrounded by non-reactive nitrogen or argon gas, it would quickly burn through.

What is a magnetic pole?

Magnetism is the invisible force that draws together some metals, such as iron and steel, or pushes them apart. This force is especially strong at each end of the magnet. These two powerful ends are called poles. One is called the north (or north-seeking) pole, because if the magnet is suspended freely this pole swings round until it points north. The other is called the south pole. If the opposite poles of two magnets meet, they will be drawn together. If the same poles meet, the magnets will push each other apart.

EARTH'S MAGNETIC FIELD

The Earth's magnetic field is called the magnetosphere and extends far out into space.

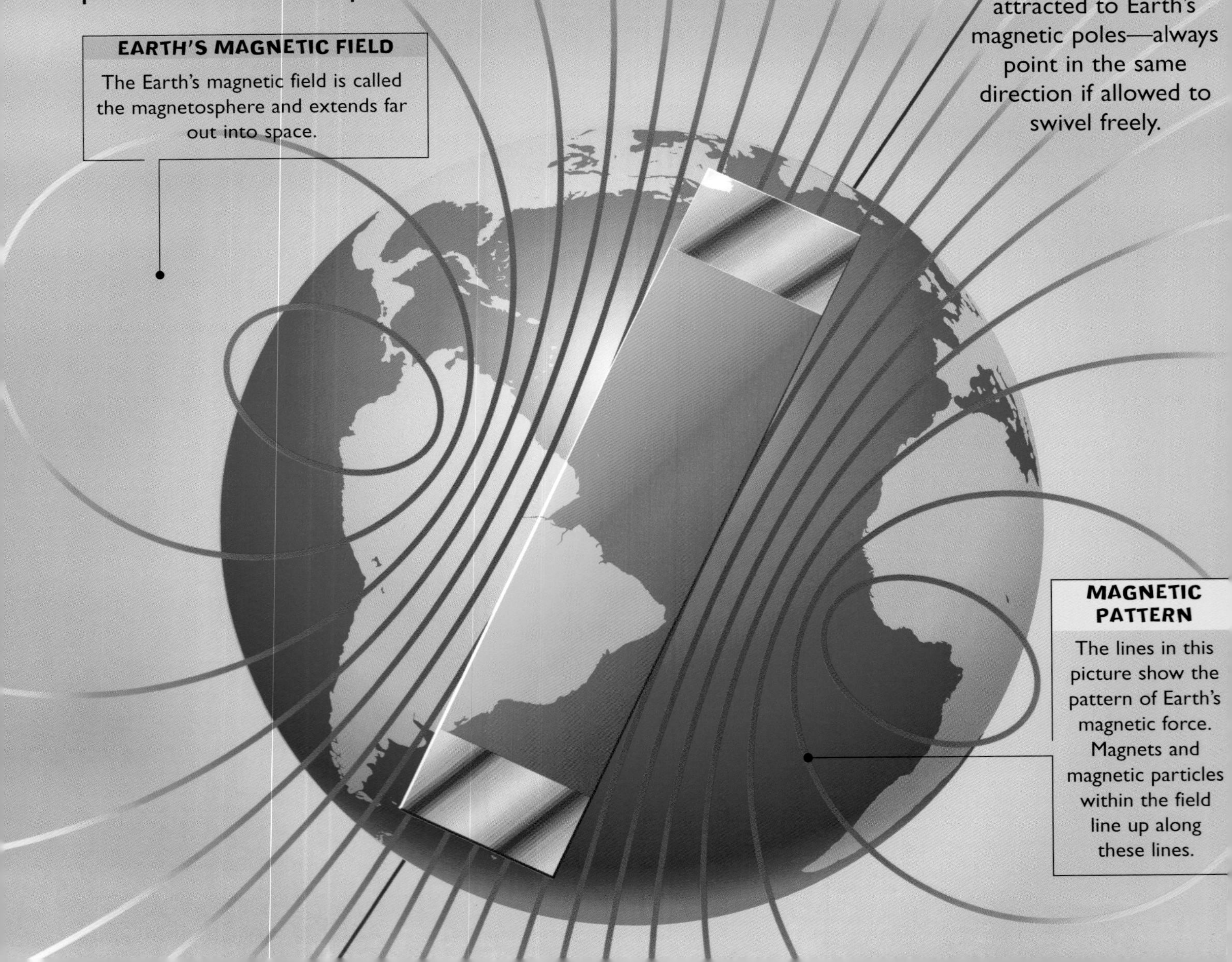

❓ WHY IS THE EARTH LIKE A MAGNET?

As the Earth spins, the swirling of its iron core turns the core into a giant magnet. It is a little like the way a bicycle dynamo generates an electric current. Like smaller magnets, the Earth's magnet has two poles, a north and a south. It is because the Earth itself is a magnet that small magnets—attracted to Earth's magnetic poles—always point in the same direction if allowed to swivel freely.

MAGNETIC PATTERN

The lines in this picture show the pattern of Earth's magnetic force. Magnets and magnetic particles within the field line up along these lines.

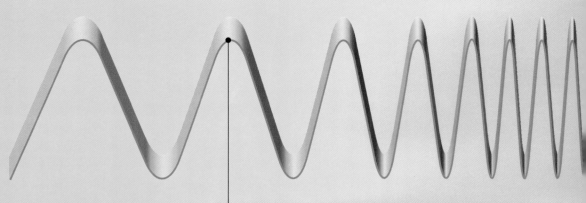

❓ HOW DOES SOUND TRAVEL?

Every sound is created by vibration, be it an elastic band twanging or a loudspeaker cone shaking to and fro. Sound reaches your ears as a vibration, normally of the air. When a sound source vibrates to and fro, it pushes the air around it to and fro. The sound travels through the air as it is pushed to and fro in a knock-on effect, that is by being alternately stretched and squeezed. This moving stretch and squeeze of air is called a sound wave. You can't hear any sounds in a vacuum.

SOUND WAVES

Long, low-frequency sound waves give low-pitched sounds. Short, high-frequency sound waves give high-pitched sounds.

❓ WHAT IS SOUND FREQUENCY?

Some sounds, like a car's squealing brakes, are very high-pitched. Others, like a booming bass drum, are very low-pitched. What makes them different is the frequency of the sound waves. If the sound waves follow very rapidly one after another, they are high-frequency and make a high sound. If there are long gaps between each wave, they are low-frequency and make a low sound. A low-frequency sound is about 20 Hz or waves per second. A high-frequency sound is 20,000 Hz or waves per second.

❓ WHAT IS RESONANCE?

An object always tends to vibrate freely at the same rate. This is its natural frequency. You can make it vibrate faster or slower by jogging it at particular intervals. But if you can jog it at just the same rate as its natural frequency, it vibrates in sympathy and the vibrations become stronger. This is resonance.

❓ WHAT IS A LODESTONE?

Thousands of years before people learned how to make steel magnets, they found that lumps of certain types of rock attracted or repelled each other, or bits of iron. These rocks are called lodestones. They contain iron oxide, which makes them naturally magnetic.

STEEL HORSESHOE MAGNET

When the paper clips come within the magnet's magnetic field, they become magnetized too, and so attract other paper clips.

❓ WHAT IS AN ECHO?

An echo is when you shout in a confined space, such as a tunnel, and you hear the noise ringing back out at you a moment or two later. The echo is simply the sound of your voice bouncing back from the walls. Echoes only bounce back clearly off smooth, hard surfaces, and in confined spaces. But the wall must be at least 55 feet (17 m) away, because you will hear an echo only if it bounces back at least 0.1 second after you shouted.

❓ WHAT IS A MAGNETIC FIELD?

The magnetic field is the area around the magnet in which its effects are felt. It gets gradually weaker farther away from the magnet. The Earth's magnetic field extends some 50,000 miles (80,000 km) into space.

ANIMALS

Why do beavers build dams?

DORMOUSE

The desert dormouse weighs less than 1 oz (28 g), but it puts on extra fat before it rest for long periods.

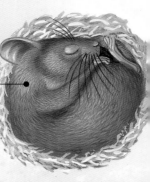

Beavers build their homes, or lodges, in streams or rivers. But first they need to build a dam to make an area of still water, or the current would wash the lodge away. With their huge front teeth, the beavers cut down trees to build the dam. They plaster the sides with mud and fill gaps with stones and sticks. The lodge is built of sticks behind the dam and has an underwater entrance. The beavers sleep, store food, and care for their young in the lodge. They have to keep repairing both the dam and the lodge with more sticks and mud. Beavers live in North America and in parts of Europe and Asia.

❓ DO DORMICE REALLY SLEEP A LOT?

Most dormice do sleep through the winter. This is called hibernation. It may start in October and last until April, or longer in cold climates. The dormouse sleeps in in a cozy nest on the ground or in trees.

A BEAVER'S LODGE

The living chamber in the beaver's lodge is built above the water level.

❓ HOW BIG IS A BEAVER?

A fully grown beaver can measure over 40 inches (101 cm) long, including its long, flat tail. It can weigh as much as 85 pounds (38.5 kg) and is the heaviest rodent in North America and Eurasia.

❓ WHICH IS THE BIGGEST RODENT?

The largest rodent is the capybara of South America. It measures up to 4 feet (1.25 m) long and weighs up to 145 pounds (66 kg). Capybaras live in marshy places and feed on grasses.

❓ HOW MANY KINDS OF RODENT ARE THERE?

There are more than 2,000 different species of rodent, including squirrels, hamsters, and beavers, as well as rats and mice. Rodents live all over the world in every kind of habitat, from the icy Arctic to scorching deserts and humid rainforests.

PORCUPINE
If attacked, the porcupine runs backward at its enemy, driving in its sharp spines.

❓ WHERE DO PORCUPINES LIVE?

There are two groups of porcupines. New World porcupines live in North and South America, mostly in trees. Old World porcupines live in Africa and parts of Asia. They are mostly ground-dwelling animals. All porcupines are covered in long, sharp spines, which look fearsome and help protect them from their enemies.

❓ WHICH IS THE SMALLEST RODENT?

One of the smallest rodents is the pygmy mouse of North America. It is only about 4 inches (10 cm) long, including its tail, and weighs just 0.25 ounce (7 g). The harvest mouse of Europe and Asia is only slightly bigger.

❓ WHAT DO BEAVERS EAT?

Beavers eat plant food. In spring and summer they feed on fresh green leaves and grasses. In the fall they gather woody stems to eat. Some of these are stored under water near the lodge to keep fresh for the winter months.

❓ CAN FLYING SQUIRRELS REALLY FLY?

No, but they can glide some distance from tree to tree. When the flying squirrel leaps into the air, it stretches out the skin flaps at the sides of its body. These act like a parachute, enabling it to glide gently down from one branch to another.

❓ WHEN IS A DOG REALLY A RAT?

A prairie dog is actually not a dog at all. It is a type of rodent, and lives in North America. Prairie dogs live in family groups of one adult male and several females and their young. The family, or coterie, makes a burrow of connecting chambers and tunnels. Groups of coteries live near each other in huge areas of burrows called towns. Prairie dogs feed mostly on grasses and other plants. While the family is feeding, one prairie dog keeps watch.

❓ IS A GUINEA PIG A RODENT?

Yes. Wild guinea pigs, also known as cavies, live in South America, where they feed on leaves and grasses. Most cavies are about 9 inches (22 cm) long, but one type, the long-legged, harelike mara, is up to 30 inches (75 cm) long.

❓ WHY DO RODENTS GET LONG IN THE TOOTH?

The two sharp teeth, called incisors, at the front of the rodent's jaw are the ones it uses for gnawing. A rodent's incisors get worn down as it gnaws tough food, but they keep on growing throughout its life.

SHARP TEETH
A beaver can gnaw through a small tree trunk in just a few minutes.

❓ DO BEARS SLEEP THROUGH THE WINTER?

Brown bears, Polar bears and American and Asian black bears that live in the far north do sleep for much of the winter. Food supplies are poor and the bears hide themselves away in warm dens and live off their own fat reserves. Before their long sleep and fast, the bears eat as much food as they can to build up their body fat. They may not eat or drink again for six months. A bear's body temperature drops only slightly during the winter sleep, and it wakes easily if disturbed. Female bears may give birth to a litter of cubs during this time.

❓ WHAT DO GIANT PANDAS EAT?

The giant panda's main food is bamboo. An adult eats up to 40 pounds (18 kg) of bamboo leaves and stems a day. Pandas also eat small amounts of other plants and some small animals.

BROWN BEAR

A full-grown male brown bear stands up to 7.5 feet (2.3 m) tall and weighs up to 1,760 pounds (800 kg). Bears reach up into trees to pick juicy fruit or berries.

❓ HOW BIG IS A BABY BEAR?

Although adult bears are huge, they have tiny babies. A polar bear weighing more than several people gives birth to cubs of only about 2.2 pounds (1 kg), far smaller than most human babies. Baby pandas are tinier still. The mother weighs up to 180 pounds (80 kg), but her newborn cubs can weigh as little as 3 ounces (85 g).

❓ HOW DO WOLF CUBS LEARN HOW TO HUNT?

Wolf cubs learn how to hunt by watching their parents and playing with other pack members. As the cubs run around and pounce on one another, they are also learning how to attack and ambush prey.

How many kinds of bear are there?

There are eight species of bear. They range in siz from the sun bear, which weighs as little as 6 pounds (27 kg), to huge polar bears and brow bears. The brown bear is the most widespread bea It lives in northern North America (where it is als called the grizzly) and parts of Europe and Asia Brown bears have a varied diet. They eat grasse roots, and berries, but they also catch insects fish, and other larger animals, as well a scavenging the carcasses of dead creature such as deer and seals

GIANT PANDA

The panda's front paws have a special extra "toe" to help it grip bamboo stems.

❓ IS THE GIANT PANDA A BEAR?

For years experts argued about whether this animal should be grouped with bears or raccoons or classed in a family of its own. Genetic evidence now suggests that the panda is a member of the bear family.

❓ WHERE DO GIANT PANDAS LIVE?

Giant pandas live in bamboo forest reserves in west and central China, where they are protected.

❓ HOW MANY KINDS OF WILD DOG ARE THERE?

There are about 35 species in the dog family, including foxes, wolves, coyotes, and hunting dogs. Antarctica is the only continent where there are no wild dogs. All are good runners and hunt other animals to eat.

❓ WHICH IS THE BIGGEST BEAR?

The polar bear of the Arctic is one of the largest. Fully grown males are up to 8.5 feet (2.6 m) long. Polar bears have thick white fur to keep them warm in their icy homes. They hunt seals and occasionally also young walruses and birds.

❓ WHAT DO FOXES EAT?

Foxes, such as the red fox, are hunting animals. They kill and eat small creatures, including rats, mice, and rabbits. But foxes are very adaptable and will eat more or less anything that comes their way, such as birds and birds' eggs, insects, and even fruit and berries. More and more foxes in cities are feasting on our discarded food from garbage cans and compost heaps.

❓ WHAT IS A DINGO?

Dingoes are the wild dogs of Australia. They are probably descended from dogs domesticated more than 3,500 years ago by Aborigines. Dingoes hunt sheep and rabbits. A 3,107-mile-long (5,000 km) fence has been built across southeastern Australia to keep dingoes out of sheep-grazing lands.

❓ HOW BIG IS A WOLF PACK?

In areas where there are plenty of large animals to catch, a pack may contain up to 30 wolves. Hunting in a pack means that the wolves can kill prey much larger than themselves, such as moose. A wolf pack has a home range, or territory, which it defends against other wolves.

❓ CAN POLAR BEARS SWIM?

Polar bears can swim well and spend long periods in the freezing Arctic water. They are well equipped to survive the cold. A polar bear has a dense layer of underfur as well as a stiff, shiny outer coat. Under the skin is a thick layer of fat to give further protection.

❓ ARE THERE BEARS IN THE JUNGLE?

Yes, there are two kinds of bear that live in jungle, or rainforest. Spectacled bears live in the cloudforests of South America, and the sun bear lives in rainforests in parts of Southeast Asia.

RED FOX

A red fox is up to 42 inches (105 cm) long. Its bushy tail adds 16 inches (40 cm).

❓ WHY DO TIGERS HAVE STRIPES?

A tiger's stripes help it hide among grasses and leaves so it can surprise its prey. Tigers cannot run fast for long distances, so they depend on being able to get close to their prey before making the final pounce. The stripes help to break up their outline, making them harder for prey to see.

❓ WHICH CAT RUNS THE FASTEST?

The cheetah is the fastest running cat and one of the speediest of all animals over short distances. It has been timed running at 58 mph (93 km/h) over a distance of 1000 feet (300 m). Olympic sprinters can reach only about 18 mph (30 km/h).

❓ WHAT IS A SNOW LEOPARD?

The snow leopard is a big cat that lives in the mountains in central Asia. Its beautiful pale coat with dark markings has made it the target of fur poachers. Killing snow leopards for their fur is now illegal, but poaching still goes on.

STRIPES

The pattern of stripes on a tiger's fur is unique. No two tigers have quite the same pattern.

Which big cat is the biggest?

Tigers are the biggest of the big cats. They measure up to 10 feet (3 m) long including the tail, and weigh 550 pounds (250 kg) or more. Tigers are now very rare. They live in parts of Asia, from snowy Siberia in the north to the tropical rainforests of Sumatra, Indonesia. There is only one species of tiger, but those in the north tend to be larger and have thicker, lighter colored fur than their relations farther south. Tigers live alone, coming together only to mate. The female rears her cubs without the help of the male. At first the cubs stay close to the den, but when they are about six months old they go with their mother on hunts and start to make kills at 18 months.

❓ WHY ARE LIONS UNLIKE OTHER CATS?

Unless they are rearing their young, most cats, including tigers and cheetahs, live alone. But lions live and hunt in a group called a pride. A lion pride includes several generations of lionesses and their cubs and one or two lions who defend the pride's territory. Working together, lions can bring down animals much larger than themselves, such as zebras.

❓ WHAT DO LIONS DO ALL DAY?

Like domestic cats, lions sleep for a surprisingly large part of the day. As many as 20 hours a day are spent resting and grooming. The rest of the time is taken up with looking for prey, hunting, and feeding. Lionesses do most of the hunting. They share the catch with the rest of the pride.

❓ WHAT DOES A MONGOOSE EAT?

The mongoose is a fast-moving little hunter. It kills small creatures such as rats, mice, and frogs, and also eats insects and birds' eggs. It will even tackle a large snake.

❓ IS A CIVET A KIND OF CAT?

No, civets belong to a separate family, which includes mongooses, meerkats, and genets. Most civets live in tropical forests in Southeast Asia or Africa. They have long, slender bodies, short legs, and long tails. The African civet is about 36 inches (91 cm) long with a 24-inch-long (61 cm) tail. It hunts small mammals, birds, reptiles, and insects.

❓ HOW MANY KINDS OF CAT ARE THERE?

There are about 36 species of wild cat, ranging from the tiger to the African wild cat, which is closely related to the domesticated cat. Cats live in most parts of the world in every sort of habitat, from tropical rainforest and desert to the icy lands of Siberia. There are no wild cats in Antarctica, Australia, or New Zealand.

❓ WHAT IS A PANTHER?

A panther is simply a leopard with a black coat instead of spots. It is not a separate species of cat. Leopards live in Africa and Asia.

MEERKATS ON GUARD

Meerkats thrive in the hostile Kalahari desert by working as a team. A group of adults watches out for predators while others are foraging or napping.

❓ WHERE DO JAGUARS LIVE?

Jaguars live in the forests of Central and South America. They are the largest South American cats, measuring up to 6 feet (1.8 m) long, with tails up to 36 inches (90 cm) long. Despite its size, the jaguar is a good climber and often clambers up a tree to watch for prey. It hunts forest animals such as peccaries and capybaras, as well as birds, turtles, and fish.

❓ WHAT IS A MEERKAT?

A meerkat is closely related to the mongoose. Meerkats live in Africa in large groups of up to 30 or more animals. They share the task of guarding the young and finding food. Sentry meerkats often stand up on their hind legs to watch out for danger.

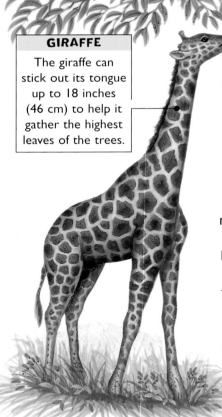

❓ HOW TALL IS A GIRAFFE?

A male giraffe stands up to 18 feet (5.5 m) tall to the tips of its horns. It has an extraordinarily long neck, and its front legs are longer than its back legs, so the body slopes down toward the tail. The long neck allows it to feed on leaves that other animals cannot reach.

❓ HOW MANY BONES ARE THERE IN A GIRAFFE'S NECK?

A giraffe has only seven bones in its neck, just like other mammals, including humans. But the giraffe's neck bones are much longer than those of other animals, and have more flexible joints between them.

❓ CAN HIPPOS SWIM?

The hippo spends most of its day in or near water and comes out onto land at night to feed on plants. It is a powerful simmer and can walk or run along the bottom of the river at surprisingly fast speeds.

❓ WHAT IS AN OKAPI?

An okapi is a relative of the giraffe. It lives in the African rainforest and was unknown until 1900. The male has small horns on its head and a long tongue like a giraffe's, but it does not have a long neck.

❓ HOW LONG ARE AN ELEPHANT'S TUSKS?

An elephant's tusks grow throughout its life, so the oldest elephants have the longest tusks. One pair in the British Museum weighs 293 pounds (133 kg), and one of them measures 11. 5 feet (3.5m).

What do elephants do with their trunks?

The elephant's trunk is very useful. Without it, an elephant could not reach the ground to feed because its neck is too short. The trunk is also used for taking food from high in the trees and for breaking off branches. The elephant can smell with its trunk pick up tiny objects, and gently caress its young. It drinks by sucking up water into its trunk and squirting it into its mouth. It also sprays water or dust over itself to clean its skin.

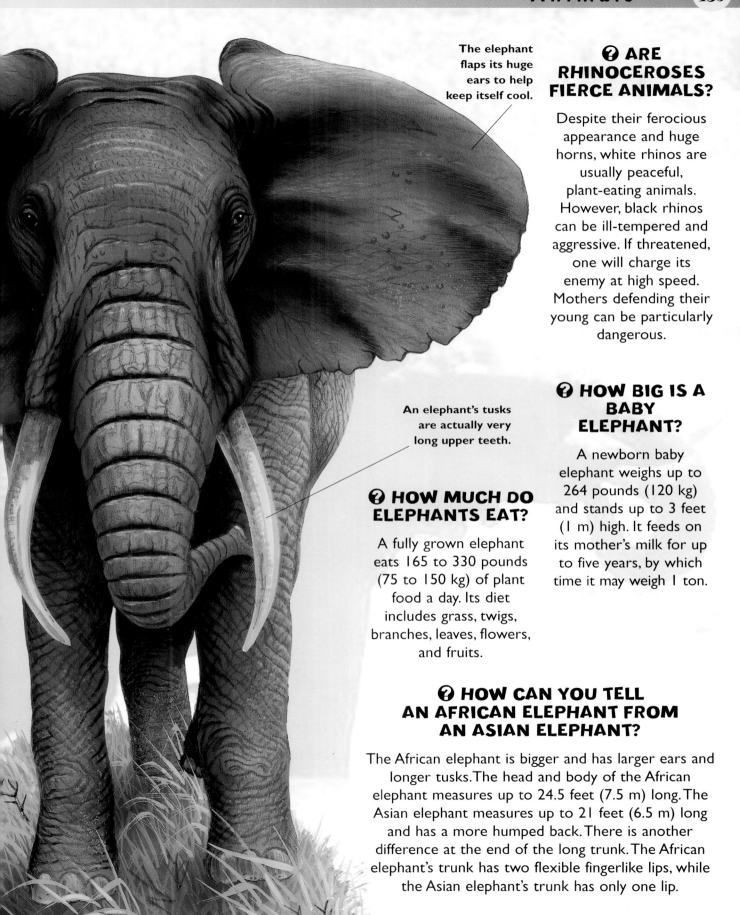

The elephant flaps its huge ears to help keep itself cool.

An elephant's tusks are actually very long upper teeth.

❓ ARE RHINOCEROSES FIERCE ANIMALS?

Despite their ferocious appearance and huge horns, white rhinos are usually peaceful, plant-eating animals. However, black rhinos can be ill-tempered and aggressive. If threatened, one will charge its enemy at high speed. Mothers defending their young can be particularly dangerous.

❓ HOW BIG IS A BABY ELEPHANT?

A newborn baby elephant weighs up to 264 pounds (120 kg) and stands up to 3 feet (1 m) high. It feeds on its mother's milk for up to five years, by which time it may weigh 1 ton.

❓ HOW MUCH DO ELEPHANTS EAT?

A fully grown elephant eats 165 to 330 pounds (75 to 150 kg) of plant food a day. Its diet includes grass, twigs, branches, leaves, flowers, and fruits.

❓ HOW CAN YOU TELL AN AFRICAN ELEPHANT FROM AN ASIAN ELEPHANT?

The African elephant is bigger and has larger ears and longer tusks. The head and body of the African elephant measures up to 24.5 feet (7.5 m) long. The Asian elephant measures up to 21 feet (6.5 m) long and has a more humped back. There is another difference at the end of the long trunk. The African elephant's trunk has two flexible fingerlike lips, while the Asian elephant's trunk has only one lip.

❓ HOW MUCH DOES A KOALA EAT EVERY DAY?

A koala eats between seven and eighteen ounces (200–500 g) of eucalyptus leaves a day. The leaves do not provide much energy, but koalas are slow-moving and sleep up to 20 hours a day.

❓ DO ALL MARSUPIALS LIVE IN AUSTRALIA?

Most of the 260 or so species of marsupial live in Australia and New Guinea, but there are about 80 species of marsupial opossum in South America. One of these also lives in North America.

KOALA BEAR

The koala has strong claws to help it hold on to branches as it climbs in search of food.

❓ WHAT IS A TASMANIAN DEVIL?

The Tasmanian devil is the largest of the carnivores, or flesh-eating marsupials. It is about 36 inches (90 cm) long, including its tail, and has sharp teeth and strong jaws. The devil feeds mostly on carrion—the flesh of animals that are already dead—but it does also kill prey such as sheep and birds.

Is a koala really a kind of bear?

No, it's a marsupial like a kangaroo and not related to bears at all. Koalas live in Australia in eucalyptus forests. They feed almost entirely on eucalyptus leaves, preferring those of only a few species. A baby koala spends its first six or seven months in the pouch and then rides on its mother's back until it is able to fend for itself. A baby measures around 0.75 inches (2 cm) and weighs around 0.2 ounces (6 g) at birth, but when fully grown the average koala measures about 30 inches (78 cm) long and weighs up to 24 pounds (11 kg)

❓ DO ALL MARSUPIALS HAVE A POUCH?

Most female marsupials have a pouch, but not all. Some very small marsupials such as the shrew opossums of South America do not have a pouch. Others, such as the American opossums, simply have flaps of skin around the nipples and not a full pouch. The tiny young cling on to the nipples.

❓ WHICH IS THE SMALLEST MARSUPIAL?

The smallest marsupials are the mouselike ningauis, which live in Australia. These little creatures are only about 2 inches (5 cm) long and can weigh as little as 0.1 ounces (2.8 g). They feed on insects.

❓ WHAT ARE BANDICOOTS?

Bandicoots are a group of small marsupials that live in Australia and New Guinea. Most have short legs, rounded bodies, and long, pointed noses. They have strong claws, which they use to dig for insects and plant food.

❓ WHY DOES A KANGAROO HAVE A POUCH?

At birth, kangaroos are very tiny and underdeveloped. They measure only about 0.75 inch (2 cm) long when born. The female kangaroo has a pouch so that its young can complete their development in safety. The tiny newborn crawls up to the pouch by itself and starts to suckle on one of the nipples inside the pouch. A young kangaroo, or joey, stays in the pouch until it weighs about 20 pounds (9 kg). Pouched animals like kangaroos are called marsupials.

❓ HOW MANY KINDS OF KANGAROO AND WALLABY ARE THERE?

There are more than 50 different species of kangaroo and wallaby. All live in Australia or New Guinea. The red kangaroo, which weighs about 200 pounds (90 kg), is the largest, and the tiny musky rat kangaroo, weighing only 1.2 pounds (0.5 kg), is the smallest.

❓ IS A PLATYPUS A MARSUPIAL?

No, the platypus is not a marsupial, but it is an unusual animal and it does live in Australia. Unlike most mammals, which give birth to live young, the platypus lays eggs. The mother leaves her two to four eggs to incubate in a burrow for up to ten days. When they hatch, the young suck milk from the mother from special mammary hairs.

❓ WHAT IS A WOMBAT?

A wombat is a small bearlike marsupial with a heavy body and short, strong legs. It digs burrows to shelter in and feeds mostly on grass. Its pouch opens to the rear so that it does not fill up with soil when the wombat is burrowing.

❓ HOW FAST DO KANGAROOS MOVE?

A kangaroo bounds along on its strong back legs at up to 31 mph (50 km/h). It can cover about 44 feet (13.5 m) in one giant bound.

❓ DO ANY MARSUPIALS SWIM?

The water opossum of South America is an excellent swimmer and has webbed back feet. Strong muscles keep its pouch closed when the opossum is in water.

❓ WHAT DO KANGAROOS EAT?

Kangaroos eat grass and the leaves of low-growing plants, just like deer and antelopes do in the northern hemisphere.

RED KANGAROO
In the eastern part of its range, the female red deer is bluish gray rather than red.

CHIMPANZEE

Chimpanzees climb well and find much of their food in trees.

❓ WHERE DO ORANGUTANS LIVE?

Orangutans live in the rainforests of Sumatra and Borneo in Southeast Asia. This ape has long, reddish fur and spends most of its life in the trees. Fruit is its main food, but the orangutan also eats leaves, insects, and even eggs and small animals. The orangutan is active during the day. At night it sleeps on the ground or in a nest of branches in the trees.

❓ WHERE DO CHIMPANZEES LIVE?

Chimpanzees live in forest and grasslands in Equatorial Africa. There is another less familiar chimpanzee species called the pygmy chimpanzee, or bonobo, which lives in rainforests in the Congo region of Africa. It has longer limbs than the common chimpanzee, and spends more of its time in trees.

❓ WHY DOES A MONKEY HAVE A LONG TAIL?

To help it balance and control its movements as it leaps from branch to branch in the rainforest. The tails of South American monkeys are even more useful than those of their African and Asian relatives, because they are prehensile. A prehensile tail has special muscles that the monkey can use to twine around branches and help it climb—almost like having a fifth limb. The naked skin on the underside of the tail is ridged to improve grip.

❓ WHAT DO GORILLAS EAT?

Gorillas eat plant food such as leaves, buds, stems, and fruit. Because their diet is juicy, gorillas rarely need to drink.

❓ WHAT IS AN APE?

Apes are the most advanced animals in the primate group, which also includes animals such as lemurs, bushbabies, and monkeys. There are three families of apes. One includes all the different kinds of gibbons. The second contains the gorilla, chimpanzee, and orangutan, and the third has one species only—humans.

❓ DO CHIMPANZEES LIVE IN FAMILY GROUPS?

Yes, in very large families that may include between 20 and 100 animals, led by a dominant male. Each group has its own home range.

❓ HOW MANY KINDS OF MONKEY ARE THERE?

About 133 species in three main groups. One group lives in Africa and Asia. The other two groups live in Central and South America.

❓ DO CHIMPANZEES HUNT PREY?

Yes, they do. Although fruit is the main food of chimpanzees, they also eat insects and hunt young animals, including monkeys. The hunt alone or in groups. Working together as a group, some of the chimps will chase a couple of animals away from the herd and drive them toward the other chimps, who make the kill. The rest of the troop then joins in to share the meat.

Which is the biggest ape?

The gorilla. A fully grown male stands up to 5.5 feet (1.7 m) tall and weighs as much as 400 pounds (180 kg). Gorillas live in the forests of West and Central Africa. A family group contains one or two adult males, several females, and a number of young of different ages. The male, known as a silverback because of the white hair on his back, leads the group.

❓ WHICH MONKEY MAKES THE LOUDEST NOISE?

Howler monkeys shout louder than other monkeys and are among the noisiest of all animals. Their voices carry for more than 0.6 miles (1 km).

❓ DO ANY MONKEYS LIVE IN COLD PLACES?

Most monkeys are found in warm areas near to the equator, but some macaque monkeys live in cooler places. The rhesus macaque lives in the Himalayas and parts of China and India, and the Japanese macaque survives freezing winters in Japan with the help of its thick fur coat.

❓ DO CHIMPANZEES USE TOOLS?

Yes. The chimpanzee can get food by poking a stick into an ants' nest. It pulls out the stick and licks off the ants. It also uses stones to crack nuts, and it makes sponges from chewed leaves to mop up water or wipe its body.

❓ WHICH IS THE SMALLEST MONKEY?

The smallest monkey is the pygmy marmoset of the South American rainforests. It is about 6 inches (14 cm) long plus tail, and weighs only about 3–5 ounces (85–141 g).

❓ HOW DEEP DO SEALS DIVE?

The Weddell seal of Antarctic waters is one of the deepest-diving seals. It can dive to depths of more than 1,968 feet (600 m) in search of food. When it dives, blood flow is cut off to all but essential organs such as the heart.

❓ ARE ANY SEALS VERY RARE?

Yes, monk seals, which live in the Caribbean, Mediterranean, and Hawaiian seas, are extremely rare. The Caribbean monk seal is probably already extinct. Monk seals live closer to human activity than most other seals, so they have suffered greater habitat disturbance.

❓ HOW BIG ARE SEA LIONS?

The biggest sea lion is the huge steller sea lion. It is about 90 inches (230 cm) long and weighs as much as 2,200 pounds (1,000 kg). Females are much smaller and weigh only about 595 pounds (270 kg). The smallest is probably the Galapagos fur seal, which weighs about 140 pounds (64 kg).

❓ HOW BIG IS A WALRUS?

The largest male walruses are more than 10 feet (3 m) long and weigh up to 3,700 pounds (1,700 kg). Females are smaller, averaging 9 feet (2.7 m) long and weighing about 1,800 pounds (800 kg). The walrus's skin is up to 1.5 inches (4 cm) thick and is covered with coarse hairs. The thick skin helps protect the walrus from the tusks of other walruses.

❓ WHICH IS THE BIGGEST SEAL?

The male elephant seal is the biggest of all the seals. It is 16 feet (5 m) long and weighs 5,300 pounds (2,400 kg)—nearly as much as an elephant.

❓ ARE BABY SEALS AND SEA LIONS BORN IN WATER?

No, they are born on land. Seals and sea lions spend most of their lives in water, but come out onto land to give birth. They remain on land for a number of weeks, feeding their young on their rich milk.

How can you tell a seal from a sea lion?

With practice! Seals and sea lions both have streamlined bodies adapted to marine living, and flippers instead of limbs. But there are several differences between them. Sea lions have small ear flaps, whereas seals have only ear openings. Sea lions can bring their back flippers under the body to help them move on land. Seals cannot do this—they simply drag themselves along. Sea lions swim by moving their front flippers. Seals swim by using their hind limbs in side to side strokes.

HARP SEAL

In the late winter harp seals migrate to breeding grounds near Newfoundland and in the Greenland and White seas.

❓ DO SEALS LIVE IN FRESH WATER?

Yes, there is a species of freshwater seal in Lake Baikal in Russia. Baikal is the deepest freshwater lake in the world and holds more water than any other. Thousands of seals live there, feeding on freshwater fish and resting on the remote islands in the middle of the lake.

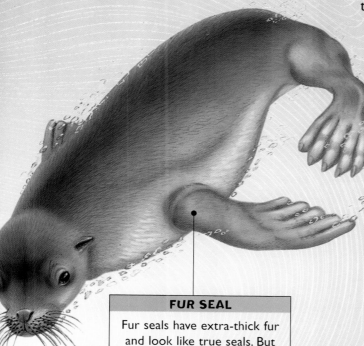

FUR SEAL

Fur seals have extra-thick fur and look like true seals. But their small ear flaps show they are really types of sea lion.

❓ DO SEALS AND SEA LIONS BREATHE AIR?

Seals and sea lions are mammals, so they have to come to the surface regularly to breathe air. But they can stay underwater much longer than we can. Dives lasting 20 minutes or more are common, and the Weddell seal has been timed making a dive lasting more than an hour.

❓ HOW DO SEALS KEEP WARM IN COLD SEAS?

A layer of fatty blubber under the skin helps to keep seals and sea lions warm. The blubber may be up to 4 inches (10 cm) thick. These animals also have a covering of fur.

❓ HOW LONG ARE A WALRUS'S TUSKS?

The tusks of an adult male walrus can be up to 22 inches (55 cm) long. Tusks are used as hooks for climbing on to ice and as weapons for fighting.

❓ WHICH IS THE SMALLEST SEAL?

The Baikal seal is the smallest seal in the world. It is about 4 feet (1.2 m) long and weighs between 139 and 154 pounds (63 and 70 kg) . The Baikal seal is only found in Russia's Lake Baikal. It is the only seal to live solely in fresh water.

❓ WHAT DO SEALS AND SEA LIONS EAT?

Fish is their main diet, but some also eat shellfish and catch larger prey. Some seals have a more varied diet. The crabeater seal feeds mostly on krill—small shrimplike crustaceans. The bearded seal eats seabed creatures such as clams, and the leopard seal preys on the young of other seals as well as birds and fish.

❓ HOW MANY KINDS OF SEAL AND SEA LION ARE THERE?

There are about 14 species of sea lion, 18 species of seal and one species of walrus. Most sea lions live along North Pacific coasts and on the southern coasts of Africa, Australia, and South America. Most seals live in waters to the far north and south of the world, and the walrus lives in Arctic seas.

❓ HOW FAST CAN SEALS AND SEA LIONS SWIM?

Sea lions can reach swimming speeds of 25 mph (40 km/h). On land the crabeater seal can move at up to 16 mph (25 km/h) as it toboggans over ice.

CALIFORNIAN SEA LION

The sea lion can rotate its hind flippers forward to use all four limbs on land.

Which is the biggest whale?

The blue whale is the largest whale, and also the largest mammal that has ever lived. It measures more than 100 feet (30 m) long and weighs at least 90 tons. The biggest blue whales may weigh more than twice this amount. Although it is so huge, the blue whale is not a fierce hunter. It eats tiny shrimplike creatures called krill. It may gobble up as many as four million of these in a day.

❓ WHY DO SOME WHALES MIGRATE?

Whales such as humpbacks migrate—travel seasonally—to find the best conditions for feeding and breeding. They spend much of the year feeding in the waters of the Arctic and Antarctic, where krill are plentiful. When it is time to give birth, the humpbacks travel to warmer waters near the equator.

❓ HOW DOES A BLUE WHALE FEED?

A blue whale filters small shrimplike creatures called krill from the water. Hanging from the whale's upper jaw are lots of plates of a fringed bristly material called baleen. The whale opens its mouth and water full of krill flows in. The whale forces the water through the baleen with its tongue. The water flows out at the sides of the mouth, leaving the krill behind on the baleen for the whale to swallow.

❓ WHICH WHALE DIVES DEEPEST?

The sperm whale routinely dives to at least 0.6 miles (1 km) beneath the surface of the sea and may go down to even greater depths when chasing giant squid to eat.

❓ DO HUMPBACK WHALES REALLY SING?

Yes. They make a series of sounds, including high whistles and low rumbles, that may continue for more than 20 minutes. No one knows why the humpback whale sings, but it may be to court a mate or to keep in touch with others in the group.

❓ IS A DOLPHIN A KIND OF WHALE?

A dolphin is a small whale. Most of the 32 or so species of dolphin live in the sea, but there are five species that live in rivers. The biggest dolphin is the killer whale, or orca, which grows up to 32 feet (9.8 m) long. Dolphins have a streamlined shape and a beaked snout containing lots of sharp teeth. They are fast swimmers and catch sea creatures such as fish and squid to eat. A form of ultrasound helps dolphins find their prey. A dolphin gives off a series of high-frequency clicking sounds that bounce off anything in their path. The echoes tell the dolphin about the size and direction of the prey.

❓ HOW BIG IS A BABY BLUE WHALE?

A baby blue whale is about 26 feet (8 m) long at birth and is the biggest baby in the animal kingdom. It weighs about 3 tons.

❓ DO WHALES EVER COME TO LAND?

No, whales spend their whole lives in the sea. But they do breathe air and have to come to the surface regularly to take breaths.

❓ WHAT IS A PORPOISE?

A porpoise is a small whale with a rounded head, not a beaked snout like a dolphin. There are about six species of porpoise. They live in coastal waters in the Atlantic, Pacific and Indian Oceans, and feed on fish and squid.

❓ HOW FAST DO WHALES SWIM?

Blue whales normally swim at about 5 mph (8 km/h), but can move at speeds of up to 18 mph (30 km/h) when disturbed. Small whales such as dolphins may swim at more than 30 mph (50 km/h).

❓ DO WHALES GIVE BIRTH IN THE WATER?

Yes, they do. The baby whale comes out of the mother's body tail first so that it does not drown during birth. As soon as the head emerges, the mother and the other females attending the birth help the baby whale swim to the surface to take its first breath.

❓ WHAT IS A NARWHAL?

A narwhal is a whale with a single long tusk at the front of its head. The tusk is actually a tooth, which grows out from the upper jaw. It can be as much as 10 feet (3 m) long. Only the males have tusks. They may use them in battles with other males.

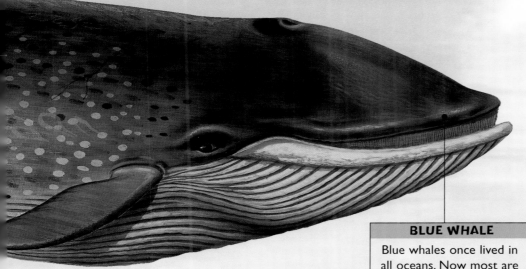

BLUE WHALE

Blue whales once lived in all oceans. Now most are found in Antarctic waters.

How big is a great white shark?

Great white sharks are mostly about 23 feet (7 m) long, but some can grow to 40 feet (12 m). They live in warm seas all over the world. Great white sharks are fierce hunters and attack large fish and other creatures such as sea lions and porpoises. Their main weapons are their large, jagged-edged teeth, which they use to kill prey and to tear it apart. Behind these teeth are rows of new ones, ready to replace teeth at the front that get damaged or broken.

GREAT WHITE SHARK

A shark is able to swim at speeds of up to 25 mph (40 km/h) for short periods.

❓ ARE ELECTRIC EELS REALLY ELECTRIC?

Yes, they are. The electric eel's body contains special muscles that can release electrical charges into the water. These are powerful enough to stun its prey.

❓ WHICH IS THE FIERCEST FRESHWATER FISH?

The piranha, which lives in rivers in tropical South America, is the fiercest of all freshwater fish. Each fish is only about 10–24 inches (25–60 cm) long, but a shoal of hundreds attacking together can kill and eat a large mammal very quickly. The piranha's weapons are its very sharp, triangular-shaped teeth, which it uses to chop flesh from its victim. But not all piranhas are dangerous killers. Some species feed only on plants.

❓ ARE ALL SHARKS KILLERS?

No, two of the largest sharks, the whale shark and the basking shark, eat only tiny shrimplike creatures. They filter these from the water through sievelike structures in the mouth.

❓ ARE FLATFISHES BORN FLAT?

No, young flatfishes have normal bodies with an eye on each side. As they grow, the body flattens and one eye moves, so that both are on the upper surface. The fish lies on the seabed with its eyed side uppermost so it can see.

PUFFER FISH
This fish puffs up its body when disturbed or threatened.

❓ DOES A STINGRAY STING?

A stingray gets its name from the sharp spine near the base of its tail. The stingray lives in warm shallow waters, where its spine can cause a nasty wound if stepped on.

❓ WHY DOES A FLYING FISH "FLY"?

A flying fish usually lifts itself above the water to escape from danger. It has extra large fins, which act as "wings." After building up speed under the water, the fish lifts its fins and glides above the surface for a short distance.

❓ ARE THERE ANY POISONOUS FISH?

Yes, there are—and the puffer fish is one of the most poisonous of all. It has a powerful poison in some of its internal organs, such as the liver, which can kill a human. Despite this, puffer fish is a delicacy in Japan, where chefs are specially trained to remove the poisonous parts and prepare the fish. A puffer fish also has another way of defending itself. It can puff up its body with water and air until it is at least twice its normal size. This makes it very hard for any predator to swallow. Some puffer fish are covered with spines that stick up when the body is inflated.

❓ HOW FAST DO FISH SWIM?

The sailfish is one of the fastest fish. It can move at speeds of more than 70 mph (110 km/h). Marlins and tunas are also fast swimmers. All these fish have sleek, streamlined bodies.

❓ HOW MANY KINDS OF SHARK ARE THERE?

There are over 300 different species of shark. They range in size from dwarf dogfish measuring only 20 cm long to the giant whale shark, which can grow to 15 m.

❓ HOW MANY TYPES OF FROG AND TOAD ARE THERE?

There may be as many as 4,000 species of frog and toad. They live on all continents except Antarctica. Most live in areas with plenty of rainfall, but some manage to live in drier lands by sheltering in burrows.

FLYING FROG

Flaps of skin help the frog glide through the air.

❓ WHAT DO FROGS EAT?

Adult frogs catch insects and spiders and other small creatures such as crayfish—and even other frogs—to eat. Tadpoles usually feed on small water plants.

❓ WHY DO FROGS CROAK?

Male frogs make their croaking calls to attract females. The frog has a special sac of skin under its chin, which it inflates to help make the call louder.

❓ HOW CAN TREEFROGS CLIMB TREES?

Treefrogs are excellent climbers. On each of their long toes is a round, sticky pad, which allows them to cling to the undersides of leaves and to run up the smoothest surfaces. Treefrogs spend most of their lives in trees, catching insects to eat, and only come down to the ground to lay their eggs in or near water.

Can the flying frog really fly?

No, but it can glide up to 50 feet (15 m) through the air between trees. When the frog jumps into the air, it stretches out its legs and toes so that its webbed feet act like parachutes. Small flaps of skin on the legs also help the frog to glide. The flying frog lives in rainforests in Southeast Asia and spends most of its life in trees. Being able to "fly" in this way means that it does not have to go down to the ground and climb back up again to move from tree to tree.

❓ WHAT IS AN AMPHIBIAN?

An amphibian is a creature that lives in water and on land. Amphibians evolved from fish and were the first vertebrates (creatures with backbones) to live on land. There are more than species of amphibian, including frogs, toads, newts, and salamanders.

❓ DO ALL FROGS LAY THEIR EGGS IN WATER?

No, some frogs have very unusual breeding habits. The male marsupial frog (and sometimes the female) carries his mate's eggs in a pouch on his back or hip. The male Darwin's frog keeps his mate's eggs in its vocal pouch until they have developed into tiny frogs.

❓ HOW DID THE SPADEFOOT TOAD GET ITS NAME?

The spadefoot toad got its name from the hard spadelike projections on each back foot, which it uses for digging its burrow. The toad backs into the ground, pushing soil away with its "spades." It usually spends the day deep in its burrow and comes out at night to find food.

❓ WHAT IS A SALAMANDER?

A salamander looks like a lizard, with its long body and tail, but is an amphibian like frogs and toads. There are over 350 different kinds. The biggest is the giant salamander, which can grow as big as 5 feet (1.5 m) long.

❓ WHAT IS A TADPOLE?

A tadpole is the young, or larva, of an amphibian such as a frog or newt. The amphibian egg is usually laid in water and hatches out into a small, swimming creature called a tadpole, with a long tail. The tadpole feeds on water plants and gradually develops into its adult form.

POISON-ARROW FROG
The poison-arrow frog is one of the most poisonous of all animals.

❓ WHICH IS THE SMALLEST FROG?

The smallest frog, and the smallest of all amphibians, is the Cuban frog, which measures around 0.4 inches (9.8 mm) long. The tiny gold frog, which lives in Brazilian rainforests, is probably about the same size. .

❓ ARE FROGS AND TOADS POISONOUS?

Some are—the cane toad can squirt poison at an enemy from glands near its eyes, and the fire-bellied toad has poison in its skin. But most deadly of all are the poison-arrow frogs that live in South American rainforests. Their skin contains one of the most powerful poisons known—a tiny drop can kill a person. Local people tip their hunting arrows with this deadly substance by simply rubbing the arrow over the skin of a frog. Poison-arrow frogs live in trees and are usually very brightly colored. Their bold markings warn predators that they are poisonous and should be left alone. But there is a frog-eating snake in the rainforest that seems to be able to eat the frogs without coming to any harm.

❓ HOW BIG IS A GIANT TOAD?

The giant, or cane toad, which is native to parts of the southern United States and South America, is up to 9.5 inches (24 cm long). It eats beetles, and was introduced into Australia by farmers, in an effort to control the beetles that eat crops such as sugarcane. Unfortunately, it didn't control the beetles and is now a pest itself.

❓ DO TURTLES EVER COME TO LAND?

Female sea turtles do come to land to lay their eggs. The female turtle drags herself up on to a sandy beach and digs a deep pit. She lays lots of eggs and covers them with sand. She then returns to the sea. When the young hatch, they must dig their own way out and struggle down the beach to the sea. Green turtles also come to land to bask in the sun.

❓ WHICH IS THE BIGGEST TURTLE?

The leatherback is the largest of all the turtles. It grows up to 8 feet (2.4 m) long.

❓ WHAT DO SEA TURTLES EAT?

Most sea turtles eat a range of underwater creatures, such as clams, shrimps, and snails, but some concentrate on certain foods. The hawksbill is one of the few creatures that feed mostly on sponges. The leatherback's main food is jellyfish, while the green turtle eats sea grass.

GREEN TURTLE

The green turtle's broad shell is up to 3.2 feet (1 m) long. Turtles "fly" through the water with the help of their paddle-shaped flippers.

How can you tell a crocodile from an alligator?

You can recognize a crocodile because its teeth stick out when its mouth is shut! In many ways, crocodiles and alligators are very similar. They both have long bodies covered with thick scales. And they both have long jaws with lots of sharp teeth. But when they shut their mouths, there is one difference between them that is easily spotted. In alligators, the fourth pair of teeth on the lower jaw disappears into pits in the upper jaws, but in crocodiles, these teeth slide outside the mouth into notches in the upper jaw, and are visible.

CROCODILE

The crocodile's body is well armored with lots of hard scales and rows of bony plates.

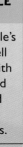

❓ HOW BIG IS A GIANT TORTOISE?

Giant tortoises grow to over 4.25 feet (1.3 m) long and weigh more than 300 pounds (140 kg). They live on the Galapagos Islands in the Pacific and on the island of Aldabra in the Indian Ocean. Seychelles giant tortoises were thought to be extinct in the wild—to have died out completely—but a few individuals have recently been discovered. Efforts are being made by conservationists to breed more tortoises in captivity and release them into the wild.

❓ WHICH IS THE BIGGEST CROCODILE?

The Nile crocodile grows up to 19.5 feet (6 m) long, but the Indopacific crocodile is even larger. This mighty crocodile, which lives in parts of Southeast Asia, may be even larger.

❓ WHAT DO CROCODILES EAT?

Baby crocodiles start by catching insects and spiders to eat. As they grow, fish and birds form a larger part of their diet. Fully grown crocodiles prey on anything that comes their way, even large animals such as giraffes. The crocodile lies in the water near where animals come to drink, then suddenly lurches forward to seize the prey.

❓ HOW MANY TYPES OF CROCODILE ARE THERE?

There are around 14 species of crocodile, one species of gavial, two species of alligator, and several species of caiman. The gavial is very like the crocodile and the alligator, but has a long, very slender snout.

❓ DO CROCODILES LAY EGGS?

Most crocodiles do lay eggs and they look after them very carefully. The female crocodile digs a pit into which she lays 30 or more eggs. She covers them over with soil or sand. While the eggs incubate for about three months, the female crocodile stays nearby guarding the nest. When the young hatch, the mother gently lifts them out of the pit with her mouth.

CHAMELEON
A chameleon can remain quite still for long periods, waiting for insect prey.

❓ WHERE DO CHAMELEONS LIVE?

There are about 85 different sorts of chameleon and most of these live in Africa and Madagascar. There are a few Asian species and one kind of chameleon lives in parts of southern Europe.

❓ WHICH IS THE LARGEST LIZARD?

The Komodo dragon. It lives on some Southeast Asian islands, grows up to 10 feet (3 m) long, and hunts animals such as wild pigs and small deer.

❓ HOW MANY KINDS OF LIZARD ARE THERE?

There are probably over 3,000 species of lizard. These belong to different groups, such as the geckos, iguanas, skinks, and chameleons. Lizards live on all the continents except Antarctica, mostly in warm parts of the world.

❓ WHY DOES A RATTLESNAKE RATTLE?

Rattlesnakes make their rattling noise to warn their enemies to stay well away. The rattle is made by a number of hard rings of skin at the end of the tail that make a noise when shaken. Each ring was once the tip of the tail. A new one is added every time the snake grows and sheds its skin.

Why does a chameleon change color?

Changing color helps the chameleon get near to its prey without being seen and allows it to hide from its own enemies. The color change is controlled by the chameleon's nervous system. Nerves cause areas of color in the skin to be spread out or to become concentrated in tiny dots. Chameleons are said to go darker in color when they are cold and lighter when they are hot.

❓ HOW MANY KINDS OF SNAKE ARE THERE?

There are about 2,500 species of snake. They live on all continents except Antarctica, but there are no snakes in Ireland, Iceland, or New Zealand. All snakes are carnivorous, which means that they feed on other animals.

❓ WHICH IS THE MOST DANGEROUS SNAKE?

The saw-scaled carpet viper is probably the world's most dangerous snake. It is extremely aggressive and its poison can kill humans. Saw-scaled carpet vipers live in Africa and Asia.

❓ HOW FAST DO SNAKES MOVE?

The fastest-moving snake on land is thought to be the black mamba, which lives in Africa. It can slither along at up to 7 mph (11 km/h).

❓ ARE THERE ANY POISONOUS LIZARDS?

There are only two poisonous lizards in the world, the gila monster and the Mexican beaded lizard. Both of these live in south-western North America. The poison is made in glands in the lower jaw. When the lizard seizes a prey and starts to chew, poison flows into the wound and the victim soon stops struggling.

RETICULATED PYTHON

The python can coil its strong body around its prey and crush it to death. Its jaws open so wide that it can swallow prey larger than itself.

❓ ARE THERE ANY SNAKES IN THE SEA?

Yes, there are about 50 to 60 different species of snake that spend their whole lives in the sea. Most are completely helpless on land. They eat fish and other sea creatures, such as shrimp, and all are extremely poisonous. One species, the beaked sea snake, is potentially lethal.

❓ WHY DO SNAKES SHED THEIR SKIN?

Snakes shed their skin, or moult, to allow for growth and because their skin gets worn and damaged. Some snakes, even as adults, shed there skin every 20 days.

❓ ARE ALL SNAKES POISONOUS?

Only about a third of all snakes are poisonous and fewer still have poison strong enough to harm humans. Non-poisonous snakes either crush their prey to death or simply swallow it whole.

❓ WHICH IS THE BIGGEST SNAKE?

The world's longest snake is the reticulated python, which lives in parts of Southeast Asia. It grows to an amazing 33 feet (10 m) long. The anaconda, which lives in South American rainforests, is heavier than the python but not quite as long. Pythons and anacondas are not poisonous snakes. They kill by crushing prey to death. A python wraps the victim in the powerful coils of its body until it is suffocated.

Which is the biggest penguin?

The emperor penguin lives in Antarctica and is the biggest penguin in the world. It stands about 45 inches (115 cm) tall. Like all penguins, it cannot fly, but is an expert swimmer and diver, using its wings as paddles. It spends most of its life in the water, where it catches fish and squid to eat. Emperor penguins do come to land to breed, however. The female lays one egg, which the male keeps warm on his feet. The female goes back to the sea, but the male stays and incubates the egg for about 60 days. He cannot leave it, even to feed. The female returns when the egg hatches, and she cares for the chick while the hungry male goes to find food.

? WHAT IS A TROPICBIRD?

A tropicbird is a seabird with two very long, central tail feathers. There are three species, all of which fly over tropical oceans.

? HOW FAST DO PENGUINS SWIM?

Some penguins can swim at 8 mph (13 km/h), but they may move even faster for short periods. They can dive under water for two minutes or more. Some penguins are believed to be able to stay under water for more than 20 minutes.

? WHICH IS THE SMALLEST PENGUIN?

The little, or fairy, penguin is the smallest penguin. It is only about 16 inches (40 cm) long. It lives in waters off the coasts of New Zealand and Tasmania, Australia.

EMPEROR PENGUINS
The emperor penguin has waterproof feathers and a thick layer of fat to keep out the cold of Antarctica.

❓ DO ALL PENGUINS LIVE IN ANTARCTICA?

Most of the 18 species of penguin live in or near Antarctica, but some are found in warmer areas. There are several species around New Zealand, several around South American, one in the tropical Galapagos Islands, and one on South Africa's coasts. There are no penguins in the northern hemisphere.

❓ HOW MANY KINDS OF GULL ARE THERE?

There are about 45 species of gull. They live in all parts of the world, but there are more species north of the equator. Gulls range in size from the little gull, at only 11 inches (28 cm) long, to the great black-backed gull, at 26 inches (65 cm) long. Many gulls find food inland as well as at sea, and some even scavenge in towns and cities.

❓ HOW DOES A GANNET CATCH ITS FOOD?

The gannet catches fish and squid by making spectacular dives into the sea. This graceful seabird flies over the water looking for prey. When it sees something, it plunges from as high as 100 feet (30 m) above the ocean, dives into the water with its wings swept back, and seizes the catch in its daggerlike beak.

❓ WHICH BIRD MAKES THE LONGEST MIGRATION?

The Arctic tern makes the longest migration journey of any bird. Each year it makes a round trip of more than 22,000 miles (35,400 km). The bird nests in the Arctic during the northern summer and then travels south to escape the northern winter, spending the southern summer near Antarctica, where food is plentiful.

❓ CAN ALL SEABIRDS SWIM?

Not all seabirds can swim. Frigatebirds cannot swim and avoid going into the water. They seize food from the surface or rob other birds of their catches. Storm petrels, too, rarely land on the water, preferring to swoop close to the surface.

❓ WHICH BIRD HAS THE LONGEST WINGS?

The wandering albatross has the longest wings of any bird. When fully spread, they measure up to 11 feet (3.3 m) from tip to tip. This majestic seabird spends much of its life soaring over the ocean, and may travel many miles a day. It lays its eggs and cares for its young on islands near Antarctica.

WANDERING ALBATROSS
The wandering albatross has a strong hooked beak used for catching its slippery prey.

❓ IS A PUFFIN A KIND OF PENGUIN?

No, puffins belong to a different family of birds, called auks. They live in the northern hemisphere, particularly around the Arctic. Auks are good swimmers and divers, like penguins, but can also fly.

❓ CAN ALL CORMORANTS FLY?

There are about 30 different kinds of cormorant and all but one can fly. The flightless cormorant lives in the Galapagos Islands off the coast of South America. It has tiny wings and cannot fly, but is an expert swimmer. It catches all of its food in the water.

❓ WHY DOES A PELICAN HAVE A POUCH?

The pelican has a pouch to help it catch fish to eat. When the bird plunges its open beak into the water, the pouch fills up with water and fish. As it brings its head up again, the water drains from the pouch, leaving any fish behind to be swallowed.

Do vultures hunt and kill prey?

Vultures do not usually kill their prey. They are scavengers, feeding on animals that are already dead or have been killed by hunters such as lions. They have strong claws and beaks, and the bald head allows them to plunge into carcasses without dirtying their feathers. The bearded vulture, or lammergeier, picks up bones and drops them from a great height onto rocks to smash them open, so it can feed on the marrow inside.

❓ WHICH IS THE FASTEST FLYING BIRD?

As it dives to catch other birds in the air, the peregrine falcon may move at more than 200 mph (320 km/h)—faster than any other bird. The falcon circles above its victim before making its fast dive and killing the prey on impact.

❓ DO EAGLES REALLY CATCH SNAKES?

Yes, serpent eagles feed mostly on snakes and lizards. The rough surface of the serpent eagle's toes helps it hold on to slippery snakes.

GRIFFON VULTURES SURROUND A CARCASS

The griffon vulture has a weak bill, so the flesh it pulls at must be soft or rotten.

❓ HOW MANY KINDS OF OWL ARE THERE?

There are about 145 species of owl in two families. The barn owl family contains about 10 species and the true owl family about 135 species. Owls live in most parts of the world, except a few islands. They usually hunt at night, catching small mammals, birds, frogs, lizards, insects, and even fish.

❓ HOW CAN OWLS HUNT AT NIGHT?

Owls have excellent sight, even in low light, and extremely sharp hearing. Even in complete darkness they can pinpoint where a sound is coming from and swoop. Owls also have special soft-edged wing feathers that make very little noise as they beat their wings. This allows them to approach prey making scarcely a sound.

❓ DO EAGLES BUILD NESTS?

Yes, and the nest made by the bald eagle is the biggest made by any bird. Some bald eagle nests are up to 18 feet (5.5 m) deep. They are used again and again, with the eagles adding more nesting material each year.

❓ WHICH IS THE BIGGEST BIRD OF PREY?

The Andean condor is the biggest bird of prey. It measures up to 43 inches (110 cm) long and weighs up to 25 pounds (12 kg). Its wingspan is over 10 feet (3 m) across.

❓ WHAT DOES AN OSPREY EAT?

The osprey feeds mostly on fish. When it sees something near the surface, it dives down toward the water and seizes the fish in its feet. The soles of its feet are covered with small spines to help it hold on to the slippery fish.

❓ WHICH IS THE BIGGEST EAGLE?

The biggest eagle in the world is the great harpy eagle, from the rainforests of South America. It is up to 3.3 feet (1 m) long and has huge feet and sharp talons, which it uses to kill its prey. Unlike other eagles, the harpy does not soar high in the air looking for food. It hunts creatures such as monkeys and sloths in the trees, chasing its victims from branch to branch at high speed. Almost as big is the rare Philippine monkey-eating eagle, from the rainforests of the Philippines in Southeast Asia.

❓ HOW DO EAGLES KILL THEIR PREY?

An eagle kills with the four long, curved claws on each of its feet. It drops down on to its prey, seizes it in its long talons, and crushes it to death. The eagle then tears the flesh apart with its strong, hooked beak.

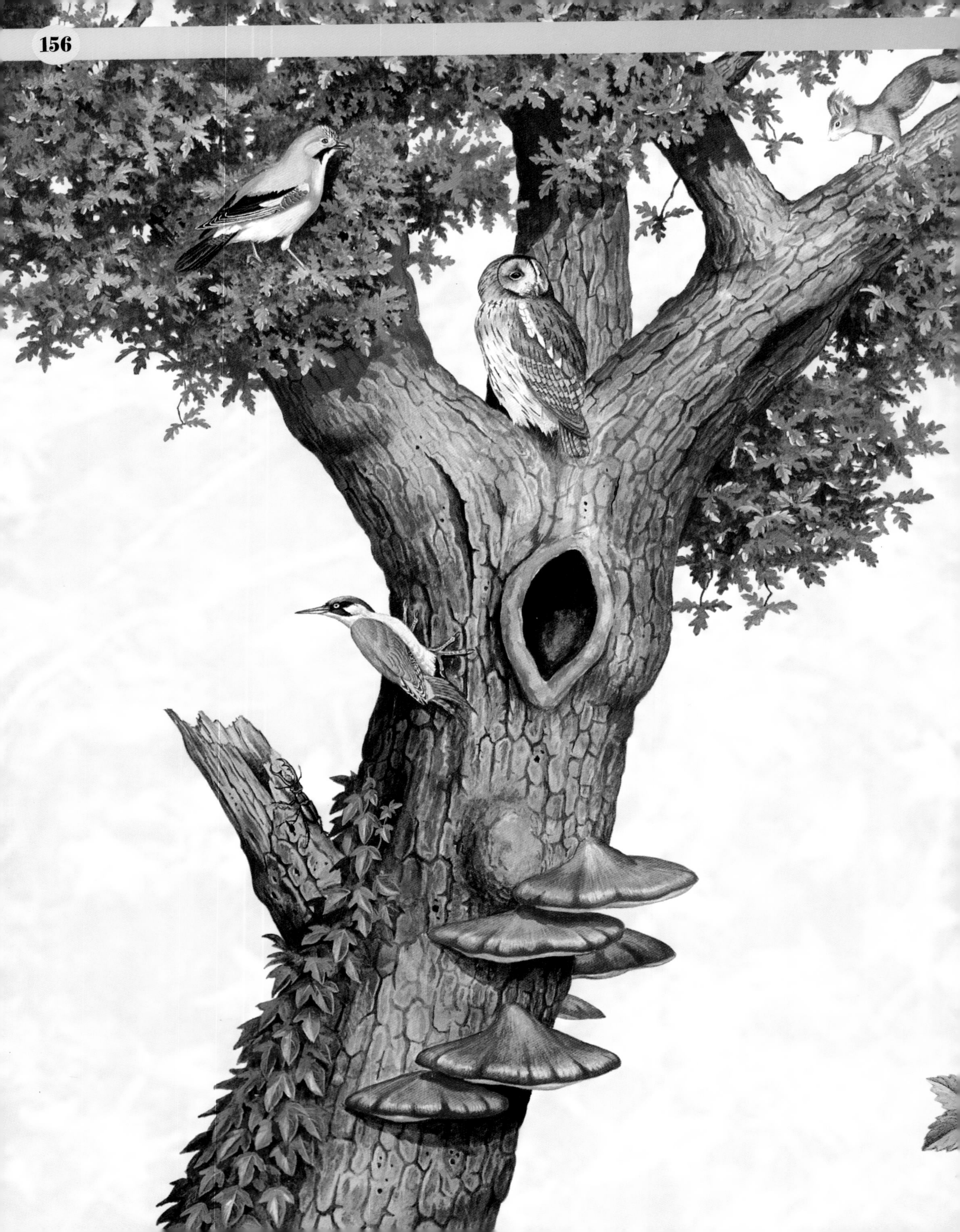

PLANTS

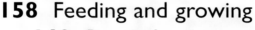

❓ WHY ARE MOST PLANTS GREEN?

Most plants are green because they contain the green pigment chlorophyll in their stems and leaves. Sometimes the green pigment is masked by other colors, such as red. This means that not all plants that contain chlorophyll look green.

❓ HOW DO GREEN PLANTS FEED?

Green plants make their own food in a process called photosynthesis. Chlorophyll helps to trap energy from the Sun. Plants use this energy to convert water and carbon dioxide into sugars and starch.

THE DEVELOPMENT OF A POPPY FLOWER

The poppy flower is ready to burst from its bud.

How does a flower form so quickly?

When a flower opens out from a bud, it may appear like magic in just a day or even a few hours. This is possible because the flower is already formed in miniature inside the bud, just waiting to open out. If you cut open a flower bud, you can see that all the flower's parts are there inside the bud. The bud opens as its cells take in water and grow. Many flowers form their buds in the fall, winter, or early spring, ready to open quickly in the warmer, sunnier weather of spring or early summer.

The bud turns up toward the Sun and the petals open further.

The bud begins to open in the warm sunshine.

❓ WHY DO SHOOTS GROW UPWARD?

Most shoots grow upward, toward the sunlight. The growing tip of the shoot can detect the direction of the light, and chemicals are released that make it grow more on the lower or darker side, thus turning the shoot upward.

❓ WHAT MAKES A SEED GROW?

To grow, a seed needs moisture, warmth, and air. Some seeds can only germinate (begin to grow) if they have first been in the low temperatures of winter. The seeds of some plants can lie dormant (inactive) for years before germinating.

❓ WHAT DO PLANTS NEED TO GROW?

Plants need water, mineral salts, and foods such as carbohydrates. Green plants make their own foods, while other plants may take in food from decaying plants or animals, or direct from other living plants.

❷ HOW DO PLANTS TAKE IN WATER?

Plants use their extensive root systems to take in water from the ground. Each root branches into a network of rootlets, which in turn bear root hairs. Water passes into the root across the cell walls of millions of tiny root hairs.

❷ WHY DO ROOTS GROW DOWNWARD?

Roots generally grow downward because they can detect the pull of gravity. The root responds to gravity by releasing chemicals that cause more growth on the upper side, thus turning the root downward.

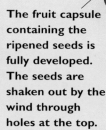

The fruit capsule containing the ripened seeds is fully developed. The seeds are shaken out by the wind through holes at the top.

The petals have fallen off, leaving the seed capsule.

❷ HOW DOES A VENUS FLY-TRAP CATCH ITS PREY?

The fly-trap is a carnivorous (meat-eating) plant that catches insects and other small animals. The trap is a flattened, hinged pad at the end of each leaf, fringed with bristles. When an insect lands on the pad and touches one of the sensitive hairs growing there, the trap is sprung and closes over the insect.

IN FULL FLOWER
The poppy is now fully open with its petals unfurled.

❷ HOW DOES A PARASITIC PLANT FEED?

Parasitic plants do not need to make their own food, and many are not green. Instead, they grow into the tissues of another plant, called the host, and tap into its food and water transportation system, taking all the nourishment they need from its sap.

❷ HOW FAST DOES SAP FLOW THROUGH A TREE?

In warm conditions, with a plentiful supply of water to the roots, and on a breezy day, sap may flow through a tree as fast as 40 inches (100 cm) every hour.

❷ HOW MUCH SUGAR DOES PHOTOSYNTHESIS MAKE IN A YEAR?

Plants turn the sugar they make by photosynthesis into other chemical compounds that they need for growth and development. They also use sugar to make energy. Some scientists have estimated that the total mass of green plants alive in the entire world make more than 167 billion tons of sugar every year by photosynthesis.

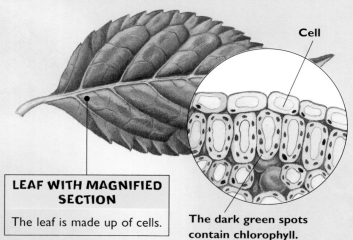

Cell

LEAF WITH MAGNIFIED SECTION
The leaf is made up of cells.

The dark green spots contain chlorophyll.

How are flowers pollinated?

Pollination is an important part of reproduction in plants. The pollen, containing the male sex cells, fertilizes the ovules, which are the female sex cells. This can happen in several ways. The flowers of many trees release masses of tiny pollen grains into the air, and the breeze takes some to their destination. Water plants often produce pollen that floats downstream. Many flowers have evolved their structure, colors, and scent to attract bees, wasps, and butterflies to pollinate them. The animal lands on the flower to feed from its nectar, gets showered with pollen, then moves to the next flower, transporting the pollen. Some tropical flowers are pollinated by birds, bats, and even small mammals.

❷ CAN PLANTS REPRODUCE WITHOUT SEEDS?

Some plants, such as mosses, liverworts, and ferns, do not produce seeds. Instead, they spread by dispersing spores. But even among seeding plants, reproduction without seeds is possible. Many plants can reproduce vegetatively by sending out runners or splitting off from bulbs, or swollen stems.

A FLOWER IN CROSS-SECTION

At the end of the flower's stalk are the flowers, where the reproductive parts are found.

Stigma

Stamen

❷ WHICH FLOWERS LAST FOR ONLY ONE DAY?

The flowers of morning glory open each morning and shrivel and die toward evening. Day lilies also produce flowers that last one day.

Flower stalk

Style

Ovary

Ovule

❓ WHAT HAPPENS IN A FLOWER AFTER POLLINATION?

After pollination, the pollen that has landed on the stigma of another flower of the same species will begin to germinate, if conditions are right. It sends a tube down into the style and eventually into the ovary of the flower, which it enters to fertilize an ovule.

❓ WHERE DO SEEDS DEVELOP?

Each ovule is destined to become a seed, and develops inside the ovary of the flower. An ovule consists of the zygote, or fertilized egg, surrounded by the endosperm, the seed's food store.

❓ WHICH PLANTS HAVE THE SMALLEST SEEDS?

Orchids produce huge numbers of microscopic seeds that drift invisibly through the air. As many as two million seeds may be produced from a single orchid seedpod.

❓ WHY ARE MANY SEEDS POISONOUS?

Many mammals and birds eat seeds. Some plants have seeds that are poisonous to mammals and birds, which prevents them being eaten. Poisonous seeds are often brightly colored, so the seed-eaters quickly learn to avoid them.

❓ HOW MUCH POLLEN DO FLOWERS MAKE?

Flowers can produce enormous quantities of pollen. Some American ragweeds can produce one billion pollen grains, and each grain can travel more than 100 miles (160 kilometre) from its source – which is bad news for sufferers of hay-fever!

❓ WHICH FLOWERS ARE POLLINATED BY MAMMALS?

The flowers of the African baobab tree are pollinated by bushbabies and bats.

❓ HOW ARE SEEDS DISPERSED?

Many seeds are dispersed by animals. Birds eat berries and pass out the tougher seeds unharmed in their droppings. Some fruit capsules have hooks that catch in animal fur and are transported that way. Both small and large seeds can be carried by the wind. The sycamore has "helicopter" wings to carry them, and dandelion seeds have feathery plumes.

A STRAWBERRY PLANT

Strawberries reproduce vegetatively by sending out runners. The plantlet develops at the end of the runner and eventually grows into a separate plant.

❓ HOW MANY SEEDS CAN A PLANT PRODUCE?

In the tropical forests of Central and South America, a single trumpet tree produces 9,000 seeds which are about 1.9 mm long. Many of these end up in the soil and germinate when there is a gap in the canopy.

❓ WHY DO FLOWERS OPEN IN SPRING AND SUMMER?

In temperate regions, this is the best time of year to attract insect pollinators. Ideally, the flowers open as early as possible in the season so that they can use the warm summer to grow and develop their seeds.

❓ WHAT HAPPENS TO ALL THE LEAVES THAT FALL?

Huge quantities of leaves fall each season from forest trees, but they do not build up on the woodland floor from year to year. The dead leaves are attacked, for example by fungi and bacteria, and break down, gradually becoming part of the soil. The leaves are also eaten by many animals, including worms, insects, slugs, snails, millipedes, and woodlice.

What lives in a tree?

Trees provide homes for countless animals, and also for other plants. The tree's leaves are eaten by the caterpillars of moths and butterflies and other insects, and many species of beetle lay their eggs in the tree's bark. Birds select a fork in a branch to build a nest, or use a natural hole in the trunk, and wild bees may also choose to nest inside a hollow tree. Many mammals are also tree dwellers, including squirrels, monkeys, sloths, bats, and koalas. In moist climates, other plants—especially mosses and ferns, and in the tropics orchids and bromeliads—can grow directly on the tree, in hollows where leaf litter gathers; they are known as epiphytes.

WILDLIFE IN AN OAK TREE

An oak tree is home to many birds, such as jays, owls, and woodpeckers. Woodpeckers clamber up the branches to feed, and may also dig a nesting hole in the trunk. Tawny owls often roost close to the main trunk, and jays feed on the tree's acorns.

? HOW DO FORESTS HELP IMPROVE THE AIR?

They do this by releasing huge quantities of water vapor and oxygen into the atmosphere. Plants also absorb carbon dioxide, and help prevent this gas from building up to damaging levels.

? HOW DO PLANTS HELP US RECLAIM LAND?

Several types of grass, including marram, can be planted on coastal dunes. Their roots anchor the sand and help to stop it blowing away. Plants can even begin to reclaim land contaminated by industrial poisons. Some species have evolved forms that can tolerate toxic substances. They gradually improve the fertility and build up the soil so that other plants can grow there too.

? HOW DO PLANTS RECYCLE WATER?

Plants help to return water to the air through the process of transpiration. This is when water evaporates from the stems and leaves of plants. Water enters the plant through its roots. A column of water moves up through the plant, from the roots right through the trunk or stem, into the leaves.

? WHAT IS THE NITROGEN CYCLE?

Bacteria in the soil use nitrogen from the air and turn it into a form that plants can use. Plants then use the nitrogen in their cells to make many complex compounds. When animals eat plants, the nitrogen returns to the soil in their droppings. It also returns when plant and animal bodies decay and rot.

? HOW ARE PLANTS USED TO CLEAN UP SEWAGE?

Sewage works use tiny algae and other microscopic organisms in their filter beds. These algae and other organisms feed on the pollutants in the water and help to make it clean.

FUNGI

Many fungi, such as these bracket fungi, may grow from the oak tree's trunk.

? HOW CAN PLANTS BE USED TO HELP STOP EROSION?

Erosion is when soil is loosened and removed by the action of natural forces such as wind and water. This can often be reduced or prevented by using plants. The roots of the plants trap the loose soil and stop it being blown away.

? HOW DO PLANTS MAKE THE SOIL MORE FERTILE?

When plants die, they decompose, releasing the chemicals in their tissues into the surrounding soil. The mixture of rotting leaves and other plant material in the soil is called humus, and this makes the soil more fertile.

? HOW DO PLANTS COLONIZE BARE GROUND?

Some plants can quickly colonize bare soil by germinating rapidly from lightweight, wind-blown seeds. Some colonizing plants spread by putting out runners, which split off, becoming new plants.

❓ HOW BIG IS THE LARGEST CACTUS?

The largest of all cacti is the giant cactus or saguaro, of the southwestern USA and Mexico. A 125 year old saguaro can measure up to 16 feet (15 m) tall and weigh as much as 6 tons.

❓ WHICH IS THE COLDEST DESERT?

Antarctica is sometimes called a cold desert, and is in fact extremely dry, because all its water is locked up as ice. The deserts of Central Asia—in Mongolia and western China—are chilled in winter by cold air from the Arctic. Even in summer, when the days are hot, the temperature can drop at night to below freezing.

What is a desert?

Deserts make up about a third of the land surface of the world. They are found wherever there is not enough water available to support much plant growth. Examples of deserts are the Sahara, Namib, and Kalahari deserts in Africa; the Atacama in Chile; and the Sonora in North America. Central Asia and Australia also have large deserts. Antarctica is also sometimes called a desert—although it is frozen, it is also very dry.

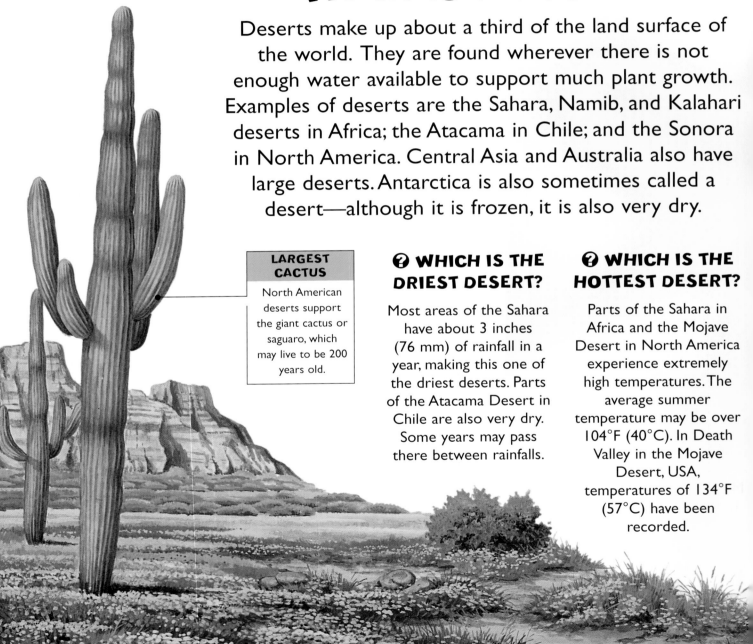

LARGEST CACTUS

North American deserts support the giant cactus or saguaro, which may live to be 200 years old.

❓ WHICH IS THE DRIEST DESERT?

Most areas of the Sahara have about 3 inches (76 mm) of rainfall in a year, making this one of the driest deserts. Parts of the Atacama Desert in Chile are also very dry. Some years may pass there between rainfalls.

❓ WHICH IS THE HOTTEST DESERT?

Parts of the Sahara in Africa and the Mojave Desert in North America experience extremely high temperatures. The average summer temperature may be over 104°F (40°C). In Death Valley in the Mojave Desert, USA, temperatures of 134°F (57°C) have been recorded.

A CACTUS IN FLOWER
Cacti are protected by sharp spines. Many kinds also produce large, colorful flowers.

❓ WHAT LIVES IN A LARGE CACTUS?

Cacti are home to a variety of wildlife. Their flowers are visited by butterflies and moths, and also by hummingbirds. Holes in cactus stems provide nest sites for desert rodents, and also for birds like the tiny elf owl.

❓ WHAT IS AN OASIS?

An oasis is a place in the desert where water is in plentiful supply, such as at a pool permanently fed by a spring. Many plants can grow at an oasis, even in the heat of the desert. Date palms are commonly planted at oases, both for shade and to provide fruit.

❓ HOW DO DESERT FLOWERS SURVIVE DROUGHTS?

Many desert flowers live for only a short time, but survive as seeds in the desert soil. When the next rains fall, they trigger the seeds to germinate.

❓ HOW DEEP DO THE ROOTS OF DESERT PLANTS GO?

Some desert plants have very long roots that can tap into deep underground water sources. Mesquite roots often grow as deep as 70 feet (20 m) in search of water.

❓ HOW DO "RESURRECTION" PLANTS SURVIVE THE DROUGHT?

When conditions get very dry, the leaves of these plants shrivel up and turn brown. This cuts down the loss of water. When it rains, they turn green again.

❓ WHAT IS THE STRANGEST DESERT PLANT?

Welwitschia is probably the strangest desert plant of all. It lives for centuries, growing very slowly and producing just two twisted leathery leaves. It lives in the coastal deserts of southwest Africa, and gets its water mainly from sea fog.

AMERICAN DESERT SCENE
Some deserts become a sheet of flowers after a rainfall.

❓ WHAT ARE LIVING STONES?

Living stones are special desert plants from southern Africa. They have swollen leaves and grow low down among the sand and gravel of the desert surface, looking very much like small pebbles or rocks. It is only when they flower that they reveal their true nature.

❓ HOW DOES A CACTUS SURVIVE IN THE DESERT?

Cacti have generally leafless, swollen stems that store water. Since they lack leaves, they do not lose much water through transpiration. Most cacti are spiny, which probably protects them from being eaten by hungry (and thirsty) desert animals.

❓ WHAT IS A JOSHUA TREE?

The Joshua tree grows in the Mojave Desert, California. It grows only about 4 inches (10 cm) a year, and its leaves can last for 20 years. The fibers inside the leaves can be used to make paper.

❓ WHY ARE SOME DESERTS EXPANDING?

The Sahara is growing larger each year partly because the climate is getting gradually warmer, but mainly because the plant life on the edges of the desert has been destroyed by grazing animals.

❓ WHERE IS THE PAMPAS?

The pampas stretches across Argentina, Uruguay, and southeastern Brazil, on the lowlands around the River Plate. The pampas is the largest area of temperate grassland in the southern hemisphere.

❓ WHERE ARE THE STEPPES?

The steppes—the grasslands of Asia—cover a huge swathe of country from eastern Europe, through southern Russia, right across Asia to Mongolia in the east.

❓ WHAT ANIMALS LIVE IN THE GRASSLANDS OF ASIA?

Wild horses once grazed on the Asian steppe, along with antelopes and deer, but they are rare today. Many rodents live in the steppe, such as hamsters, voles, mice, and sousliks (a kind of ground squirrel).

❓ HOW DO THE PLANTS SURVIVE FIRE?

Some grassland plants survive fires by persisting as thickened roots, and sprouting again after the fire has passed. Others may die, but germinate again later, from seeds left behind in the soil.

What makes grassland?

In temperate regions with warm or hot summers and cold winters, natural grassland develops in areas that don't have enough rainfall for trees and woods to grow. Many types of grasses dominate in these habitats. Mixed in with the grasses are other, mostly low-growing, plants, many of which have bright, colorful flowers to attract insects in the spring and summer. Grasslands have rich, fertile soils that have built up gradually as generations of grasses have grown up and died down, returning their goodness to the soil.

❓ WHERE ARE GRASSLANDS FOUND?

There are grasslands in Central Asia, North America, Argentina, and southern Africa. The Asian grasslands are called the steppes, and the North American grasslands are the prairies. In Argentina they are called pampas, and in southern Africa the veld. Smaller areas of natural grassland are found in parts of New Zealand and Australia. The steppes cover the largest area, stretching from Hungary to Mongolia.

A SCENE ON THE PAMPAS OF SOUTH AMERICA

Many parts of the pampas are dominated by tussock grasses. Very few trees break the monotony of the landscape.

❷ WHAT ANIMALS LIVE IN THE GRASSLANDS OF SOUTH AMERICA?

The animals of the pampas include the unusual mara (long-legged and harelike) and the plains viscacha (related to the chinchilla), as well as wild guinea pigs, giant anteaters, the maned wolf, and the rhea—a large, flightless bird.

❷ HOW DO GRASSLAND FIRES START IN NATURE?

Fires can start quite naturally, for example when lightning strikes dead or dying grass. If a wind is blowing, the sparks can quickly turn into a fire that begins to spread. Grassland fires are most likely in the summer months.

❷ WHY DON'T TREES TAKE OVER THE GRASSLAND?

Trees cannot survive easily in natural grassland areas, mainly because the rainfall is too low to support their growth. But in areas where the rainfall is higher, trees will gradually invade, unless they are chopped down or eaten by grazing animals.

❷ WHAT ANIMALS LIVE IN THE GRASSLANDS OF NORTH AMERICA?

The original animals of the prairie were buffalo and deer, and smaller species such as ground squirrels and prairie dogs. The wild buffalo once numbered some 40 million, but it was almost wiped out by settlers.

❷ WHAT ARE GRASSLANDS USED FOR?

Grasslands have long been used for grazing herds of domestic animals, especially bison. But because the soils are so fertile, much of the original prairie land has now been plowed up and planted with crops such as wheat and corn.

❷ WHICH GARDEN FLOWERS COME FROM NATURAL GRASSLANDS?

From the grasslands of Europe and Asia come flowers such as adonis, anemones, delphiniums, and scabious. Flowers from the prairie grasslands of North America include the coneflower, sunflower, and blazing star.

❷ WHERE ARE THE PRAIRIES?

The prairies extend from central southern Canada, through the mid-west of the USA, right down into northern Mexico, to the east of the Rocky Mountains. The area is known as the Great Plains, reflecting the open, treeless expanse of natural grassland.

LAND GOOD FOR CATTLE
Cattle ranching is a common form of farming in many parts of the pampas.

How does the plant life change as you go up a mountain?

Conditions generally get harsher the higher you go up a mountain, and the plant life reflects this. There may be temperate woodland in the lowlands, but as you climb, this changes, typically to coniferous woodland, then to mountain scrub, then to grassland, then again, with increasing height, to a tundralike vegetation, and to rocky screes and snow patches.

❓ HOW DO SOME MOUNTAIN PLANTS REPRODUCE WITHOUT FLOWERS?

Many mountain plants have dispensed with flowers because of the lack of insects to pollinate them, and reproduce vegetatively instead. For example, some grasses grow miniature plants where the flowers should be. These drop off and grow into new plants.

❓ WHY DO DIFFERENT PLANTS GROW ON DIFFERENT SIDES OF A MOUNTAIN?

Different sides of a mountain have different climates. On the south side (or north side in the southern hemisphere), there is more sunshine and conditions are warmer, while on the other side the snow and ice stay on the ground much longer.

ALPINE FLOWERS

Above the tree line in the mountains, many plants such as edelweiss and mountain avens grow well in the poor, rocky soils.

❷ WHAT LIMITS PLANT GROWTH IN THE MOUNTAINS?

The climate changes as the land rises from valley to mountain. It gets colder with increased height, and also windier. There is also usually much less level ground in the mountains, and the soils are thinner. Other factors that influence plant growth are the amount of sunshine, and the pattern of snow and ice accumulation. In very exposed sites, the wind chills the ground and prevents snow from gathering, creating conditions that defeat even the hardiest of plants.

GENTIAN
Many alpine plants, like this gentian, have showy flowers.

❷ HOW DO MOUNTAIN PLANTS ATTRACT POLLINATORS?

Many mountain plants have large, colorful flowers to attract the few insects that live there. Some, such as mountain avens, track the Sun to warm their flowers, which attracts insects to sunbathe there.

❷ HOW CAN PLANTS SURVIVE THE SNOW AND ICE?

Few plants can survive being completely frozen, but many can thrive under the snow. Snow acts like a blanket to keep the freezing ice and wind at bay, and saves the plants from being killed. Alpine grasses stay alive and green under the snow, ready to grow again as soon as it melts.

❷ WHY IS IT COLDER IN THE MOUNTAINS?

The Sun heats the ground and this heat is trapped close to the ground by the Earth's atmosphere. As you go up a mountain, and rise above the zone in which the heat is held, the atmosphere becomes thinner and the air gets colder. It falls about 1° in temperature for every 500 feet (150 m) you ascend in height.

❷ HOW DO MOUNTAIN HERBIVORES FIND THEIR FOOD?

Many mountain mammals burrow under the snow and continue to feed on mountain plants even at high altitudes. Others, such as marmots, store fat in their bodies and hibernate during the winter.

❷ WHY ARE ALPINE FLOWERS SO POPULAR IN GARDENS?

Many mountain plants, such as gentians and saxifrages, are known as alpines because they come from the alpine tundra. They are popular for their bright flowers, and also because they tend to grow well even in poor conditions, such as on a rock garden.

❷ HOW DO PLANTS SURVIVE THE COLD?

Plants have evolved many different ways of surviving mountain conditions. Many grow close to the ground in cushionlike shapes, which keeps them out of the wind. Some have thick, waxy, or hairy leaves to help insulate them.

❷ WHAT IS THE TREE LINE?

Trees cannot grow all the way up a mountain, and the highest level for them is known as the tree line. This varies according to the local climate of the region, but is about 5,900 feet (1,800 m) in the Alps. Trees at this level grow slowly and are often stunted.

ROCK GARDEN
These alpine flowers are growing in a natural rock garden.

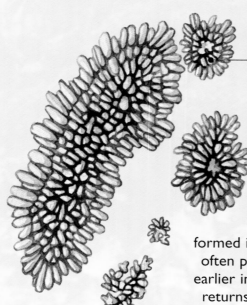

LICHEN

Many lichens are able to survive the cold and wind of the tundra.

❓ WHY ARE MANY ARCTIC SHRUBS EVERGREEN?

Many Arctic shrubs keep some or all of their leaves throughout the winter. Leaves formed in late summer stay on the plant, often protected by dead leaves formed earlier in the year. As soon as the spring returns, the green leaves are ready to photosynthesize, losing no time to make their food over the short summer months.

❓ ARE THERE LOTS OF PLANTS IN THE ARCTIC?

The northern parts of many land masses—Canada, Greenland, Europe, and Siberia, for example—extend into the Arctic region, and provide many open habitats for plants, especially in the summer. About 900 species are native to the Arctic tundra.

❓ HOW DO SOME POLAR PLANTS MELT THE SNOW?

Several Arctic and mountain plants that survive under the snow have dark colored leaves and stems. When the Sun begins to shine, they absorb the heat and melt the snow around them.

What is the tundra like?

The most striking feature of the tundra is its total lack of trees. Woody plants cannot survive here unless they are very small—there is simply not enough warmth in the summer for their growth. The dominant plants are grasses and sedges, mosses and lichens, with shrubs such as heathers, and dwarf willows and birches. There are also many flowers such as saxifrages, avens, and Arctic poppies.

❓ WHY DO MANY ARCTIC PLANTS HAVE SWOLLEN ROOTS?

Many Arctic plants have swollen roots or underground stems. They contain food reserves in readiness for a quick spurt of growth in the following summer.

❓ WHY ARE MANY TUNDRA FLOWERS WHITE OR YELLOW?

Most tundra flowers are pollinated by insects. However, there are relatively few bees this far north, and the main pollinators are flies. Flies cannot distinguish colors like bees can, so the flowers do not need to be so colorful.

❓ WHERE IS THE TUNDRA?

The tundra lies north of the coniferous forest belt, in a band roughly following the Arctic Circle. It covers about 10 million square miles (25 million sq km), from Alaska, through Canada, Greenland, Iceland, northern Norway, Finland and Sweden into Siberia. Only a small area of the Antarctic has similar conditions, on the northern tip nearest South America.

❓ WHAT PLANTS DO CARIBOU EAT?

Caribou survive the Arctic winter by foraging for food. They dig beneath the snow with their hooves and antlers, seeking out tender lichens, mosses, sedges, and grasses.

❓ WHY ARE THERE SO FEW PLANTS IN THE ANTARCTIC?

Most of Antarctica is covered with snow and ice all year. Only the Antarctic Peninsula has habitats where plants can survive, because it is warmed by the sea. Only two kinds of flowering plant—a hairgrass and a cushion plant—are native to Antarctica.

❓ WHAT IS PERMAFROST?

Even where the surface soil in the Arctic thaws in the summer, deeper down it is permanently frozen. This icy layer is known as permafrost. Because the ice prevents rain water seeping deeper down, the surface can be wet.

❓ WHAT IS THE MOST NORTHERLY FLOWER?

A species of poppy has been found growing farther north than any other flower, at 83°N, or on a level with the north of Greenland.

ARCTIC SCENE
The plants of the Arctic include pretty flowers such as the Arctic poppy, low-growing cushion plants, and tiny trees such as dwarf birch and willow.

What is the temperate forest like in summer?

In summer the temperate deciduous forests are humming with life—birds and insects call from the trees, mice and voles rustle in the undergrowth, and plant growth is at its height. The leaf canopy is fully developed, cutting out much of the sunlight from the forest floor. Nevertheless, most forests have well developed shrub and herb layers as well, with plants such as roses, honeysuckle, dogwoods, and hazel, and flowers including anemones, sorrel, and bluebells.

❓ WHAT IS THE TEMPERATE FOREST LIKE IN WINTER?

In winter, the tall trees forming the woodland canopy have lost all their leaves, most insects are quiet— they have either died or gone into hibernation—and there is not so much bird song. Many of the loudest songbirds are summer visitors and have migrated south. Most of the flowers have died back. Evergreen species such as holly, ivy, and yew stand out at this time of year, and provide valuable cover for birds and other animals.

❓ WHICH FOREST TREE CAN BE TRACKED DOWN BY ITS SOUND?

The leaves of the aspen tree move from side to side in the wind and rustle against each other, even in the lightest breeze. A practiced ear can easily track down an aspen.

❓ HOW OLD CAN FOREST TREES GET?

Many forest trees reach a great age, notably oaks, which live between 200 and 400 years. Most elms live to about 150 years.

❓ HOW ARE TEMPERATE FORESTS HARVESTED FOR WOOD?

Many temperate forests are not natural, but have been managed for centuries to provide timber. Traditional management involves a rotation of timber extraction, with only a proportion of the tree being removed at one time. This allows the forest to regenerate. Sometimes poles are cut from trees, and the trees can then re-sprout from the base, to provide another crop of poles later. This is called coppicing.

❓ WHAT ELSE DO WE GET FROM TEMPERATE FORESTS?

Lots of things! Charcoal is made by slowly burning certain kinds of wood. In the past, people depended upon woodland animals such as wild boar and deer for food and skins. Many edible fungi, including chanterelle, penny-bun, and truffles grow in temperate woods. Woodland brambles and wild strawberries have edible fruits, and cherries and currants were originally woodland plants.

A YEAR IN A TEMPERATE FOREST

The trees in temperate woodlands lose their leaves in an annual cycle. Early flowers can benefit from the extra light filtering through in spring.

❓ WHY DO TREES LOSE THEIR LEAVES IN THE FALL?

Trees and other plants that lose their leaves all at once each year are known as deciduous. Most lose their leaves in the fall, and remain bare through the winter. This way they shut down their main life processes—transpiration and photosynthesis—remaining largely dormant until the spring.

❓ WHAT LIVES ON THE FOREST FLOOR?

Invertebrates thrive in the dead leaves, twigs, fungi, and roots of the woodland floor. Beetles, woodlice, worms, slugs, snails, springtails, ants, mites, and millipedes, to name but a few, help break down the organic material, as well as providing food for mice and voles.

❓ WHY DO MOST WOODLAND FLOWERS APPEAR IN SPRING?

developing early, they can benefit from the sunlight efore it is shut out by the trees. Insects, which help o pollinate flowers, may also find it easier to spot them before the rest of the vegetation grows.

❓ WHICH CONIFER IS DECIDUOUS?

Larch is a coniferous tree—it bears cones. But unlike most conifers, larch loses its leaves all at once, in the fall, so it is also deciduous. In fact, there are also broadleaved trees that are evergreen, such as the oaks of the Mediterranean regions.

❓ WHAT ARE LIANES?

Lianes, or lianas, are plants that clamber over and dangle down from rainforest trees. They grow very long and use the trees as supports. Animals such as monkeys and squirrels use lianes to help them move about in the branches.

❓ HOW MUCH RAIN FALLS IN THE RAINFOREST?

The tropical rainforests are warm and wet. In many, the rainfall is more than 80 inches (2,000 mm) per year. It may rain at any time, but there are often storms in the afternoon.

❓ WHY ARE TROPICAL RAINFOREST SO RICH IN SPECIES?

No one knows fo certain, but it may because they have been undisturbed f so long, and also perhaps because th have such a stable warm climate.

How rich are the rainforests?

They are the richest habitats on earth, containing 50 per cent of the world's plants. Just 2.5 acres (1 ha) of tropical rainforest can contain 600 species of trees. The forests also contain untold riches in the shape of timber, fruits and herbs that can be used as food and medicine. The rainforests are important not just for their rich wildlife, but also because they help to preserve climate and soil stability. Without them, climate change would almost certainly accelerate—the forests help preserve the atmosphere, releasing huge quantities of water vapor and oxygen, and absorbing carbon dioxide.

❓ WHAT IS AN AIR-PLANT?

An air-plant grows without anchoring itself to the ground. Air plants are common in some tropical forests. They ge the moisture they need direct from the damp air.

❓ WHERE ARE THE RAINFORESTS?

The world's largest rainforest is in Brazil, covering the Amazon River basin, and also along the foothills of the Andes Mountains. The world's main areas of tropical rainforest are in South and Central America, West and Central Africa, Southeast Asia, and northern Queensland, Australia.

❓ WHAT DO WE GET FROM RAINFORESTS?

We get many things from rainforests, including timber, Brazil nuts, fruit, rubber, rattan (a kind of palm from which furniture is made), cosmetics, and medicines.

❓ WHICH PLANTS CAN TRAP THEIR OWN RAIN WATER?

It rains very often in the tropical rainforest, and many plants trap the water before it reaches the ground. Bromeliads have special leaves that form a waterproof cup for this purpose.

SUPPORTING OTHER PLANTS

Epiphytes such as ferns and bromeliads find a root-hold in crevices on trunks and branches of the trees.

❓ WHAT STOPS THE TALL TREES FROM BLOWING OVER?

Many of the taller forest trees have special supporting flanges, called stilts or buttresses, near the base of their trunks. These make the tree less liable to be pushed over in a storm.

❓ WHY ARE RAINFORESTS BEING CUT DOWN?

Many rainforests are destroyed so the land can be used for crops, or for grazing. Tropical forest soils are fertile, and many crops, such as cocoa and sugar cane, can be grown after the trees have been felled. However, the fertility of the soil is short-lived.

❓ HOW FAST ARE THE RAINFORESTS BEING DESTROYED?

Rainforests are being destroyed at a speed of 70 acres (28 ha) a minute. Every year an area the size of the state of Wisconsin is lost or badly damaged. When the forest is cleared, the tropical rainstorms work directly on the soil, erosion sets in, and in a short time all the fertile topsoil is washed away, making the ground useless for crops.

❓ HOW TALL ARE THE BIGGEST RAINFOREST TREES?

The main canopy of the rainforest develops at around 95 feet (30 m), with occasional taller trees (known as emergents) rising above these to an incredible 165 feet (50 m) or more.

How do water plants stay afloat?

Some water plants stay afloat because their tissues contain chambers of air, making their stems and leaves buoyant. Others, such as water lilies, have flat, rounded leaves that sit boatlike on the water's surface. They may also have waxy leaves, which repel the water and help keep the leaves afloat, or the leaves may have up-curved rims. Some combine wax with hairs so that the leaves are unwettable. Duckweeds are so small and light that the surface tension of the water is enough to keep them afloat, and the water hyacinth has inflated leaf-bases that act as floats.

❷ HOW DO WATER PLANTS DISPERSE THEIR FRUITS?

The running water of streams and rivers carries floating fruits along, and there is usually some water movement even in ponds and lakes. Many floating fruits have tough coats that stop them from germinating too soon, so that they can travel a good distance.

❷ HOW ARE WETLANDS DAMAGED?

When soil is drained, or too much water is pumped from the land nearby, wetlands suffer as the water table is lowered. They are easily damaged by pollution as well. Sewage and chemicals released from factories find their way into streams, where they can upset the balance of nature and poison the wildlife

❷ HOW DO WATER PLANTS GET THEIR FLOWERS POLLINATED?

Even though their growth is mainly below the surface, most water plants hold their flowers above the water, for pollination by the wind or by insects. Some, like the water starwort, have water-resistant floating pollen that drifts to the female flowers.

❷ WHY DO MOST WATER PLANTS GROW ONLY IN SHALLOW WATER?

Most plants need to root themselves in the soil, even if they live mainly submerged in the water. In deep water there is not enough sunlight for plants to grow successfully.

❓ HOW DO RIVER PLANTS COPE WITH THE CURRENT?

In the current of fast rivers, tiny algae encrust stones on the riverbed. In slower currents by the bank, river plants anchor themselves firmly with roots. They tend to grow narrow ribbon- or straplike leaves that offer little resistance to the water flow. Water milfoil has finely divided, feathery leaves, for the same reason.

❓ HOW DOES BLADDERWORT FEED?

Bladderwort is a carnivorous plant found in boggy pools. The underwater stems develop small bladders, each with a trigger. When a small animal, such as a water flea, bumps into the trigger, the bladder springs open, sucking in the animal with the water.

❓ WHY IS THE WATER HYACINTH SOMETIMES A PROBLEM?

Water hyacinth is a floating plant with beautiful mauve flowers. However, it is also a fast-growing weed, and can spread rapidly to choke waterways, alter the ecology, and impede boat traffic.

❓ WHY DO SOME LAKES HAVE VERY FEW PLANTS?

Lakes vary in the chemical composition of their water. Some lakes, such as those draining from lime-rich soils, are very fertile and can support a lot of plants. Others, especially those with high acidity in the water (as in granite areas), are poor in nutrients and therefore poor in plant life.

❓ WHAT IS PAPYRUS?

Papyrus is a tall sedge that grows along rivers and in swamps. It was used in ancient Egypt from about 3000 BC to make paper, but the plant is rare there today.

❓ WHAT FOOD PLANTS COME FROM WETLANDS?

The most important wetland crop is rice, which is grown in many parts of the world, notably India and China. It grows best in flooded fields called paddies. Another aquatic grass crop is Canadian wild rice, a traditional food of Native Americans, and now a popular speciality.

❓ HOW DOES A LAKE TURN INTO LAND?

Over time, a lake will gradually turn into dry land by a process called succession. Slowly, the remains of the plants growing in the shallows accumulate, making the water more and more shallow. Eventually, the edges of the lake dry out and land plants can establish themselves.

FRESHWATER HOME
Dragonflies, water snails, frogs, fish, and diving beetles all thrive in freshwater wetlands and ponds.

IMPORTANT STAPLES

Millet and sorghum are staple crops in much of Africa. Rice is the main food crop in Asia.

❓ WHAT IS THE AMAZON COW-TREE?

The Amazon cow-tree is a tropical fig. It takes its name from the fact that it produces a milklike sap, or latex, which can be drunk just like cow's milk.

❓ WHICH TREES GIVE US A SWEET, SUGARY SYRUP?

The sugar maple has a sweet sap, which is harvested to make maple syrup. Most maple syrup comes from the province of Quebec in Canada.

What are the most important food crops?

Some 12,000 species of plant are known to have been used as food by people, and about 150 of these are in regular cultivation. The most important crops are the cereals—wheat, rice, and corn, followed by barley, sorghum, oats, millet, and rye. These form the basis of many people's diet. Root crops are also widely grown. These include potatoes, sweet potatoes, yams, and cassava or manioc. All these foods provide carbohydrates, while seeds of the pea family (known as pulses) are rich in protein. As well as peas and beans, these include soya beans, chickpeas, and lentils.

SUNFLOWERS

Sunflower seeds and olives are crushed to produce oil.

❓ WHICH FRUITS ARE GROWN FOR FOOD?

Fruits of the temperate regions include apples, pears, grapes, plums, cherries, red and black currants, strawberries, raspberries, blackberries, and gooseberries. In warmer regions, there are citrus fruits such as oranges, grapefruits, lemons, and tangerines, and also pineapples, melons, dates, figs, bananas, coconuts, mangoes, papayas, and guavas. Some fruits have a more savoury flavor. Examples are tomatoes, avocados, and peppers. They provide us with natural sugar, protein, and vital vitamins.

❓ WHICH PLANTS GIVE US OIL?

The seeds of many plants are rich in oil, which they store as a source of food and energy. We extract oil from several of these plants, including olive, sunflower, corn, soya bean, peanuts, oil-seed rape, sesame, and African oil palm.

TEA LEAVES

The fresh young leaves of the tea bush are gathered to make tea.

❓ HOW IS TEA MADE?

Tea comes from the leaves of a camellia grown on hillsides in India, Sri Lanka, Indonesia, Japan, and China. The young leaf tips are harvested, dried, and then crushed to make tea.

❓ WHERE DOES COFFEE COME FROM?

The coffee plant is a large shrub, and its berries are used to make coffee. The ripe berries are harvested, then dried to remove the flesh from the hard stones inside. These are the coffee "beans," which are then treated and often roasted.

❓ WHERE WERE POTATOES FIRST GROWN?

Potatoes grow wild in the Andes Mountains of South America and were first gathered as food by the native people of that region. All the many varieties grown today derive from that wild source.

❓ HOW IS CHOCOLATE MADE?

The cacao tree comes originally from the lowland rainforests of the Amazon and Orinoco. The fruits, called pods, develop on the sides of the trunk, and each pod contains about 20 to 60 seeds—the cocoa "beans." The beans must be fermented, roasted, and ground before they become cocoa powder, the raw material for making chocolate. Cocoa is now grown mainly in West Africa and also in the Caribbean.

❓ WHICH PLANTS ARE USED TO MAKE SUGAR?

The main source of sugar is the sweet stems of sugar cane, a tall grass that grows in tropical countries. In some temperate areas, including Europe, there are large crops of sugar beet. This plant stores sugar in its thickened roots. In some parts of the tropics, the sap of the sugar palm is made into sugar.

❓ WHERE DID WHEAT COME FROM?

Wheat is one of the oldest-known crops. It was probably first cultivated over 6,000 years ago in Mesopotamia—present-day Iraq—between the rivers Tigris and Euphrates. Many useful crop plants have their origin in the Middle East. Other examples are barley, oats, rye, peas, lentils, onions, olives, figs, apples, and pears.

CEREAL CROPS

Wheat, corn (maize) and barley are common in temperate regions.

❓ WHAT IS BREADFRUIT?

Breadfruit is a tree native to the Malay Archipelago. It grows to about 65 feet (20 m), and has large edible fruits. The fruits are up to 8 inches (20 cm) across and are cooked before being eaten as a vegetable. The related jackfruit, from India and Malaysia, also has edible fruits. These are even larger—up to 2 feet (90 cm) long.

Which countries use mainly herbal medicines?

In much of the world, especially in China and India, herbal remedies are used more than any other kind of medicine. Plants have been used as medicine for at least 100,000 years. As long ago as 3000 BC, the Chinese had identified over 350 medicinal plants. Today the Chinese use about 5,000 plant remedies, and more than 8,000 medicinal plants are in use in India and Southeast Asia.

❓ WHAT IS GINSENG?

Ginseng is a plant related to ivy, and has been used in herbal medicine for centuries. It is claimed to help many conditions, including fatigue and depression, kidney disease, heart problems, and headaches.

❓ WHAT LINKS WILLOW TREES WITH ASPIRIN?

Willow twigs were once chewed to give pain relief. A compound similar to the drug aspirin was once extracted from willow bark, as well as from the herb meadowsweet. Meadowsweet used to be known as spiraea— hence the name aspirin.

❓ HOW CAN A DEADLY OPIUM POPPY SAVE LIVES?

Many useful medicinal plants can also yield dangerous drugs, and the beautiful pink-purple opium poppy is no exception. This poppy is a source of morphine, which is widely used as an anesthetic. It is also a source of codeine, which is used in cough mixtures and many other medicines. However, addictive and dangerous substances are also made from the opium poppy, including the deadly drug heroin.

Periwinkle

Feverfew

❷ CAN PLANTS HELP FIGHT CANCER?

Several plants are known to be effective against cancer tumors. One of the most famous is the rosy periwinkle. One of its chemical extracts, vincristine, is very effective against some types of leukaemia, a cancer of the blood.

❷ WHAT ARE COCA AND COLA?

A world-famous fizzy drink originally contained extracts of two South American plants called coca and cola. The seeds of cola are chewed as a pick-me-up, because they contain caffeine. Coca is the source of the powerful anesthetic, cocaine, which is used in dentistry. It is also a dangerous drug, if abused.

❷ WHICH PLANTS HELP WITH BREATHING PROBLEMS?

Lungwort is a herb with purple flowers and spotted leaves. It is used to treat asthma and catarrh. Ephedrine, from the ephedra or joint-pine plant, is used to treat asthma and hay fever.

Foxglove

White willow

Opium poppy

VALUABLE MEDICINAL PLANTS

Plants with healing properties are still being discovered by scientists today.

❷ WHICH PLANT HELPS COMBAT MALARIA?

Quinine, from the bark of the quinine tree, which grows in the South American Andes, can cure or prevent malaria. Before the widespread use of quinine, malaria killed two million people each year.

❷ WHICH HERB IS USED TO TREAT HEADACHES?

Feverfew is a pungent plant belonging to the daisy family. It takes its name from its long use as a remedy for fevers, and has also been proven to be effective against headaches.

❷ WHAT LINKS YAMS WITH BIRTH CONTROL?

Wild yams provided the medicines for the first contraceptive pills. Both the female and male sex hormones can be prepared using extracts of yam, and the first birth-control pills were made using this natural plant extract.

❷ WHAT PLANTS AID DIGESTION?

Many plants, including the herbs and spices used in cooking, are used to help digestion. In Europe, the very bitter extract of wild gentians provides a good remedy for digestive problems. Plantain is another herb used for this purpose.

❷ WHAT MEDICINE COMES FROM DEADLY NIGHTSHADE?

Deadly nightshade has bright juicy berries, which are very poisonous. However, they can be used to prepare the chemical atropine, which is used to dilate the pupil of the eye in medical examinations.

How many things can you spot in this picture that have been made from plant materials?

We make all kinds of things from plant materials. Wood alone is used to make countless objects, big and small, from construction timbers to musical instruments. All kinds of cloth are also made from plants—and so is the paper you are looking at!

❓ HOW MANY THINGS CAN BE MADE FROM BAMBOO?

Bamboo is one of the world's most useful natural plant products. It is used for scaffolding and building houses, and for making paper, furniture, pipes and tubes, walking sticks, and (when split) for mats, hats, umbrellas, baskets, blinds, fans, and brushes. Some bamboos have young shoots that are delicious to eat in stir-fries.

❓ WHAT IS JOJOBA?

Jojoba is a low-growing bush found in Northern Mexico. The fruits have a high-grade oily wax. It is used as a lubricant, in printing inks, and in body lotions and shampoo.

❓ WHAT IS BALSA?

Balsa is the world's lightest timber—it floats high in water. Balsa trees grow in tropical America. Balsa wood is used for making models such as airplanes, and also for rafts, life-belts, and insulation.

❓ WHAT IS RAFFIA?

Raffia is a natural fiber made from the young leaves of the raphia palm, which grows in tropical Africa. Raffia is used in handicrafts such as basketry.

❓ WHAT WOOD MAKES THE BEST CRICKET BATS?

The best cricket bats are made in northern India, from the timber of the cricket-bat willow, a form of white willow. The blade (the part the ball strikes) is made from willow, and the handle usually from a different wood or cane.

❓ HOW IS CORK PRODUCED?

Cork comes from a tree called the cork oak, which grows wild around the Mediterranean Sea and has been cultivated in Portugal, Spain, and North Africa. The cork is the thick, spongy bark. It is stripped away from the lower trunk, then left to grow back for up to 10 years before the next harvest. Cork is used to make many things, from bottle corks and pin-boards to floor tiles.

❓ WHAT IS KAPOK?

Kapok is similar to cotton. It comes from the kapok tree, which is cultivated in Asia and can be as tall as 64 feet (50 m). The fluffy seed fibers are used to stuff mattresses, jackets, quilts, and sleeping bags.

❓ CAN PLANTS PRODUCE FUEL TO RUN CARS?

When tapped, the copaiba tree of the Amazon rainforest yields an oil similar to diesel, at a rate of 4 gallons (18 litres) every 2 hours. It can be used to run engines. The petroleum nut tree of southeast Asia produces a high-octane oil in its seeds that is extracted by crushing. As crude oil reserves are used up, fuel from plants may become more important.

DIVERSE USES FOR PLANTS

Plant materials are an essential part of our lives, keeping us warm, dry, safe, and even entertained!

What is the world's longest seaweed?

Giant kelp is a huge seaweed that forms underwater forests in the coastal waters of California. Its fronds can be up to 215 feet (65 m) long, making it one of the tallest plants known.

❓ WHICH PLANT HAS THE LONGEST LEAF?

The raphia palm of tropical Africa produces the longest known leaves. The stalk can be nearly 13 feet (4 m) and the leaf-blade almost 65 feet (20 m) long.

GIANT KELP

The base of the giant kelp is anchored firmly by its holdfast, but the fronds may grow up hundreds of feet through the water.

❓ HOW DEEP ARE THE DEEPEST ROOTS?

Roots of a South African fig were found to have penetrated about 400 feet (120 m) below the surface.

❓ WHAT IS THE OLDEST PLANT?

The oldest-known plant may be the creosote bush of southwestern USA and Mexico. Some of these bushes are thought to be 11,700 years old. The bristlecone pine, which grows mainly in the southwestern USA, notably in the White Mountains of California, is also very long-lived. The oldest is about 4,900 years old.

❓ WHAT PLANT CAN SPREAD ACROSS THE WIDEST AREA?

The banyan of India and Pakistan often starts life as an epiphyte—a small plant growing on another tree. As it grows, it sends down woody roots that come to resemble tree trunks. Eventually it can cover a large area and seem like a grove of separate trees, growing close together. One 200-year-old banyan covered about 500 square yards (420 sq m), had 100 separate "trunks," and 1,775 prop-roots. The quaking aspen can also form a grove of trees that look separate, but which are connected underground. One aspen grove in the USA covered 106 acres (43 ha).

❓ WHAT IS THE SMALLEST FLOWERING PLANT?

A tiny tropical floating duckweed is the world's smallest flowering plant. Some species measure less than 0.02 inch (0.5 mm) across, even when fully grown.

❓ WHAT IS THE TALLEST TREE?

The California redwood, which grows along the North American Pacific coast, is the tallest tree in the world, reaching 367 feet (112 m). Some Australian eucalyptus trees may grow almost as tall.

❓ WHICH PLANT GROWS THE SLOWEST?

The record for the slowest-growing plant probably goes to the dioon plant of Mexico. One specimen was recorded to have an average growth rate of 0.03 inch (0.76 mm) per year.

❓ WHICH PLANT GROWS THE FASTEST?

The giant bamboo of Myanmar grows up to 1 foot (12 in) a day, making it one of the fastest growing of all plants. Another species from India, the spiny bamboo, holds the record for growth in a greenhouse—it achieved 36 inches (91cm) in one day.

❓ WHAT IS THE LARGEST FLOWER?

The world's largest flower grows on the rafflesia, a plant without leaves that thrives in the tropical forests of Southeast Asia. It is a parasite, growing on the stems of lianes in the forest. Individual flowers can measure up to 3 feet (91 cm) across, making them the largest single flowers of any plant. Rafflesia's red and white flowers may look attractive, but they stink, mimicking the aroma of rotting flesh. The stench attracts flies, which then pollinate the flower.

CALIFORNIA REDWOOD SPRIG AND CONES

The cones of conifer trees are its reproductive structures.

❓ WHAT IS THE LARGEST SEED?

The coco de mer of the Seychelles has the largest seeds, each weighing up to 50 pounds (22 k). They are produced inside a large, woody fruit that takes six years to develop.

❓ WHICH PLANT HAS THE LARGEST FLOATING LEAVES?

The giant waterlily of the Amazon region has huge leaves. They grow up to 6 feet (1.8 m) across, and can support the weight of a child.

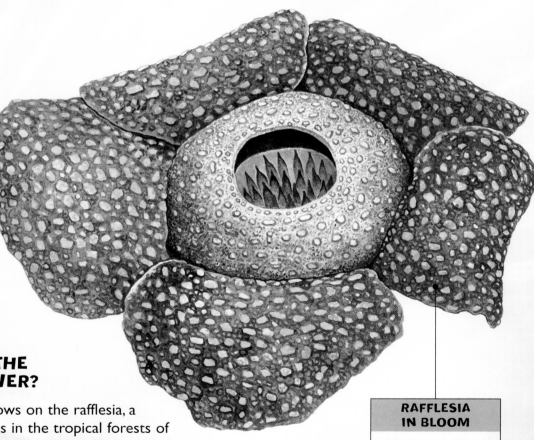

RAFFLESIA IN BLOOM

The huge rafflesia flower has blotchy red and white petals. Flies are attracted by its revolting smell.

PLANET EARTH

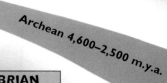

Archean 4,600–2,500 m.y.a.

EARTH'S FORMATION

The Earth was formed from a cloud of gas and dust about 4,600 million years ago.

PRECAMBRIAN

The Archean and Proterozoic eons together occupied 87% of Earth's history.

How is Earth's history divided up?

Scientists divide the last 590 million years of Earth's history into three main eras: the Paleozoic (meaning "old life") era, the Mesozoic ("middle life") era, and the Cenozoic ("new life") era. The eras are subdivided into periods, and some periods are further divided into epochs. The first period in the Paleozoic era is the Cambrian period. All of Earth's history before the Cambrian period is called the Precambrian. Scientists divide the Precambrian into two eons: the Archean and the Proterozoic. Little is known about this period, because fossils from the time are rare.

❓ WHAT WAS THE EARTH LIKE AFTER IT FORMED?

The Earth's surface was probably molten (hot and liquid) for many millions of years after its formation. The oldest-known rocks are about 3,960 million years old.

❓ WHEN DID LIVING THINGS FIRST APPEAR ON EARTH?

The oldest-known fossils (of microscopic bacteria) are about 3,500 million years old. Primitive life forms may have first appeared on Earth about 3,850 million years ago.

❓ WHEN DID PLANTS START TO GROW ON LAND?

The first land plants appeared in the Silurian period. Plants produced oxygen and provided food for the first land animals—amphibians. Amphibians first appeared in the Devonian period.

❓ WHEN DID MAMMALS FIRST APPEAR?

Mammals lived on Earth from at least the start of the Jurassic period. But they did not become common until after the extinction of the dinosaurs.

❓ WHEN DID PEOPLE FIRST LIVE ON EARTH?

Hominids (apelike creatures that walked upright) first appeared on Earth more than four million years ago. But modern humans appeared only about 100,000 years ago.

❓ WHAT WERE THE FIRST ANIMALS WITH BACKBONES?

Jawless fishes were the first animals with backbones. They appeared during the Ordovician period. Fishes with skeletons of cartilage, such as sharks, first appeared in the Devonian period.

❷ WHY DID THE DINOSAURS BECOME EXTINCT?

The dinosaurs first appeared on Earth during the Triassic period. They became the dominant animals during the Jurassic period, but at the end of the Cretaceous period, 65 million years ago, they became extinct. Scientists still argue about why they disappeared. Many experts believe that about 65 million years ago an enormous asteroid struck the Earth. The impact threw up a huge cloud of dust, which blocked out the sunlight for a long time. Land plants died and so the dinosaurs starved to death.

❷ WHY IS THE CAMBRIAN PERIOD IMPORTANT?

During the Precambrian, most living creatures were soft-bodied and left few fossils. During the Cambrian period, many creatures had hard parts, which were preserved as fossils in layers of rock.

rozoic
00–590 m.y.a.

Precambrian

590 m.y.a.

Cambrian period

505 m.y.a.

Ordovician period

438 m.y.a.

Silurian period

408 m.y.a.

Devonian period

360 m.y.a.

Paleozoic era

Carboniferous period

286 m.y.a.

Permian period

248 m.y.a.

Triassic period

213 m.y.a.

Jurassic period

144 m.y.a.

Mesozoic era

Cretaceous period

65 m.y.a.

THE GEOLOGICAL TIME SCALE

The last 590 million years of Earth history are divided into eras and periods. "M.y.a." on the diagram means "millions of years ago."

Tertiary period

Cenozoic era

Quaternary period

2 m.y.a.

Today

❓ WHAT ARE PLATES?

The Earth's hard outer layers are divided into large blocks, called plates. These consist of the Earth's crust and the top part of the mantle.

❓ HOW DEEP ARE THE PLATES?

There are about seven large plates. They are up to 90 miles (145 km) deep in places.

❓ CAN PLATES MOVE SIDEWAYS?

Plates not only move apart or push against each other, they can also move sideways along huge cracks in the ground called transform faults.

❓ WHAT HAPPENS WHEN PLATES COLLIDE?

If this happens along a deep ocean trench, one plate is pulled beneath another, and is melted and recycled. On land, when continents collide, their edges are squeezed up into new mountain ranges.

❓ HOW FAST DO PLATES MOVE?

Plates move, on average, between 2 and 3 inches (4 and 7 cm) in a year. This may sound slow. But over millions of years, these small plate movements dramatically change the face of the Earth.

❓ WHO FIRST SUGGESTED THE IDEA OF CONTINENTAL DRIFT?

In the early 1900s, an American, F.B. Taylor, and a German, Alfred Wegener, both suggested the idea of continental drift. But scientists could not explain how the plates moved until the 1960s, following studies of the ocean floor.

How do the Earth's plates move apart?

The Earth's plates float on a partly molten layer within the mantle. Currents in the partly molten rocks slowly move the plates around. Where the plates are moved apart, liquid rock, called magma, rises and plugs the gaps. When the magma hardens, it forms new crustal rock.

HOW PLATES CHANGE THE FACE OF THE EARTH
As the Earth's plates move, the continents move with them.

The ocean floor has huge ridges, where plates are moving apart. The gaps are filled with rising magma.

Plates consist of the Earth's crust and the rigid upper layer of the mantle.

Hot, liquid rock rises under the ocean ridges. It then spreads out, causing currents that pull the plates apart, as shown by the arrows.

About 280 million years ago, the world's land areas moved together to form one supercontinent named Pangaea.

Pangaea began to break apart about 180 million years ago.

About 65 million years ago, the Atlantic Ocean was opening up and India was moving toward Asia.

This map shows our world today, but plate movements are still changing the face of our planet.

CONTINENTAL DRIFT

These four maps show the extent of continental drift over the last 200 million years.

❷ HOW DO VOLCANIC ISLANDS FORM IN THE MIDDLE OF OCEANS?

Volcanic islands form when magma rises from the mantle. Lava (the name for magma when it reaches the surface) piles up until it emerges above sea level.

❷ HAVE FOSSILS HELPED TO PROVE CONTINENTAL DRIFT?

Fossils of animals that could not possibly have swum across oceans have been found in different continents. This suggests that the continents were once all joined together and the animals could walk from one continent to another.

❷ HAS THE EARTH ALWAYS LOOKED THE SAME?

If aliens had visited Earth 200 million years ago, they would have seen only one huge continent, named Pangaea, surrounded by one ocean. About 180 million years ago, Pangaea began to break up. By 135 million years ago, a plate bearing South America was drifting away from Africa, creating the South Atlantic Ocean. By 100 million years ago, plates supporting India, Australia, and Antarctica were also drifting away from Africa, and North America was moving away from Europe.

Along the deep ocean trenches, ocean plates are pushed beneath other plates. Here, the plate supports a continent.

The rocks on the edge of the continents are folded by the pressure of plate movements.

Magma from the melted plate rises. Some emerges through volcanoes.

When plates move, the land is shaken by earthquakes.

The edge of the descending plate is melted, producing huge pockets of magma.

PLATE BOUNDARIES AROUND THE WORLD
Severe earthquakes occur around the edges of the plates that form the outer, rigid layers of the Earth.

❓ WHERE ARE EARTHQUAKES LIKELY TO HAPPEN?

Earthquakes can occur anywhere, whenever rocks move along faults (cracks) in the ground. But the most violent earthquakes occur most often around the edges of the plates that make up the Earth's hard outer layers. For most of the time, the plates' edges are jammed together. But gradually currents under the plates build up, increasing pressure, and the plates move in a sharp jerk. This sudden movement shakes all the rocks around it, setting off an earthquake.

❓ WHAT INSTRUMENTS RECORD EARTHQUAKES?

Seismographs are sensitive instruments that record earthquakes. The shaking of the ground is recorded by a pen that marks the movements on a revolving drum.

❓ DO EARTHQUAKES AND VOLCANOES OCCUR IN THE SAME PLACES?

Yes, most active volcanoes occur near the edges of plates that are moving apart or colliding. Earthquakes are common in these regions too.

How do earthquakes cause damage?

Powerful earthquakes shake the ground. They make buildings sway and wobble until they collapse. The shaking sometimes breaks gas pipes or causes electrical short-circuits, starting fires. Earthquakes on high mountain slopes cause landslides that sometimes destroy towns in the valleys below. Earthquakes on the seabed trigger off waves called tsunamis. Tsunamis travel through the water at up to 500 mph (800 km/h). As they approach land, the water piles up into waves many feet high. These waves cause great damage and loss of life.

DAMAGE
Earthquakes can shake buildings to the ground and destroy roads and bridges.

Severe earthquakes occur along ocean ridges and near ocean trenches. They also occur near another kind of plate edge called a transform fault. Transform faults are long fractures in the Earth where plates move alongside each other.

❓ WHAT IS THE SAN ANDREAS FAULT?

The San Andreas fault is a long transform fault in California. Movements along this plate edge have caused huge earthquakes in the cities of San Francisco and Los Angeles.

❓ WHICH EARTHQUAKE IN MODERN TIMES CAUSED THE MOST HARM?

In 1976, an earthquake struck T'ang Shan in China. An estimated 240,000 people died. a further 500,000 were injured.

❓ CAN SCIENTISTS PREDICT EARTHQUAKES?

In 1975, Chinese scientists correctly predicted an earthquake and saved the lives of many people. But scientists have not yet found a sure way of forecasting them.

❓ CAN ANIMALS SENSE WHEN AN EARTHQUAKE IS ABOUT TO HAPPEN?

Scientists have noticed that animals often behave strangely before an earthquake. Horses rear up, dogs bark, and snakes come out of holes in the ground.

Vibrations occur when the plates move, causing violent shaking of the ground. This destroys buildings and other structures, often with loss of life.

Transform faults have ragged edges and, for most of the time, the plates are locked together. But as pressure builds up, finally the rocks break and the plates move suddenly in different directions (red arrows).

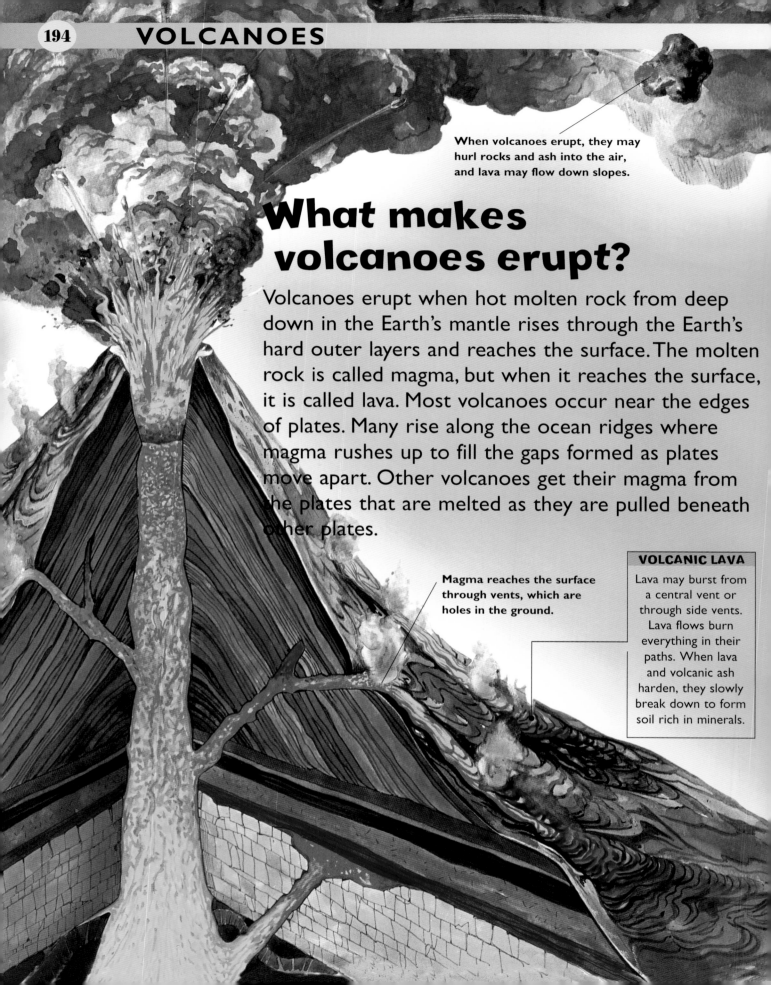

When volcanoes erupt, they may hurl rocks and ash into the air, and lava may flow down slopes.

What makes volcanoes erupt?

Volcanoes erupt when hot molten rock from deep down in the Earth's mantle rises through the Earth's hard outer layers and reaches the surface. The molten rock is called magma, but when it reaches the surface, it is called lava. Most volcanoes occur near the edges of plates. Many rise along the ocean ridges where magma rushes up to fill the gaps formed as plates move apart. Other volcanoes get their magma from the plates that are melted as they are pulled beneath other plates.

Magma reaches the surface through vents, which are holes in the ground.

VOLCANIC LAVA

Lava may burst from a central vent or through side vents. Lava flows burn everything in their paths. When lava and volcanic ash harden, they slowly break down to form soil rich in minerals.

Clouds of ash often block out the Sun. Ash falls on the land and it may bury towns. Mud flows occur when rain turns the ash into torrents of mud.

❓ WHAT ARE "HOT SPOTS"?

Some volcanoes lie far from plate edges. They form over "hot spots"—areas of great heat in the Earth's mantle. Hawaii in the Pacific Ocean is over a hot spot.

❓ WHAT ARE HOT SPRINGS AND GEYSERS?

These are places where underground water, heated by magma inside the Earth, breaks through to the surface. Warm water bubbles up at hot springs. Geysers hurl boiling water and steam into the air.

❓ WHAT IS AN EXTINCT VOLCANO?

Volcanoes that have not erupted in recorded history are said to be "extinct." This means that they are not expected to erupt ever again.

❓ WHAT IS A DORMANT VOLCANO?

Some volcanoes erupt continuously for long periods. But other active volcanoes erupt only now and then. When they are not erupting, they are said to be dormant, or sleeping.

❓ DO ALL VOLCANOES ERUPT IN THE SAME WAY?

No, they don't. Volcanoes can explode upward or sideways, or erupt "quietly." Trapped inside the magma in explosive volcanoes are lots of gases and water vapor. These gases shatter the magma and hurl columns of volcanic ash and fine volcanic dust into the air. Fragments of shattered magma are called pyroclasts. Sometimes, clouds of ash and hot gases are shot sideways out of volcanoes. They pour downhill at great speeds destroying everything in their paths. In "quietly" erupting volcanoes, the magma emerges on the surface as runny lava and flows downhill.

❓ DO VOLCANOES DO ANY GOOD?

Volcanic eruptions cause tremendous damage, but soil formed from volcanic ash is extremely fertile. Volcanic rocks are also used in building and chemical industries.

Shield volcano

Some volcanoes, shaped like upturned shields, are formed by "quiet eruptions," in which long streams of very fluid lava are emitted.

Explosive volcano

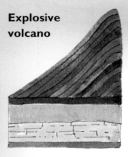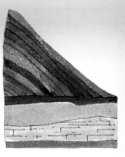

Explosive eruptions occur when the magma is thick and contains explosive gases. Explosive volcanoes are made of ash and cinders and are steep-sided.

Intermediate volcano

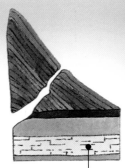

Intermediate volcanoes are cone-shaped. They are composed of alternating layers of ash and hardened lava.

KINDS OF VOLCANOES
The three main kinds are shield volcanoes, explosive volcanoes, and intermediate volcanoes.

ROCKS CHANGED BY HEAT
Earth movements and great heat turn igneous and sedimentary rocks into metamorphic rocks.

What are the three main kinds of rock?

There are igneous, sedimentary, and metamorphic rocks. Igneous rocks are formed from cooled magma. Sometimes it cools on the surface to form rocks such as basalt. Other magma cools underground to create rocks called granites. Many sedimentary rocks are made from worn fragments of other rocks. For example, sandstone is formed from sand. Sand consists mainly of quartz, a mineral found in granite. And some limestones are made from the shells of sea creatures. Metamorphic rocks are rocks changed by heat and pressure. For example, great heat turns limestone into marble.

Igneous rocks are formed from magma, which may solidify beneath or on the Earth's surface.

Surface rocks are constantly worn away, or eroded, by wind, rain, and the action of the sea.

❓ WHAT ARE ELEMENTS AND MINERALS?

The Earth's crust contains 92 elements. The two most common elements are oxygen and silicon. Also common are aluminium, iron, calcium, sodium, potassium, and magnesium. These eight elements make up 98.59% of the weight of the Earth's crust. Some elements, such as gold, occur in a pure state. But most minerals are chemical combinations of elements. For example, minerals made of oxygen and silicon, often with small amounts of other elements, are called silicates. They include feldspar, quartz, and mica—all found in granite.

GEMSTONES

Ever since the Stone Age, people have used gemstones to make jewelry.

❓ IS COAL A ROCK?

No. Rocks are inorganic (lifeless) substances. But coal, like oil and natural gas, was formed millions of years ago from the remains of once-living things. That is why coal, oil, and gas are called fossil fuels.

❓ CAN MINERALS MAKE YOU INVISIBLE?

No, although in the Middle Ages people thought that you would become invisible if you wore an opal wrapped in a bay leaf.

❓ WHAT IS THE HARDEST MINERAL?

Diamond, a pure but rare form of carbon, is formed under great pressure deep inside the Earth. It is the hardest natural substance.

❓ WHAT ARE THE MOST VALUABLE MINERALS?

Gemstones such as diamonds, rubies, sapphires, and emeralds are valuable minerals. Gold and silver are also regarded as minerals, although they occur as native, or free, elements.

Fragments of sand, silt, and mud are washed into lakes and seas. There they pile up in layers that harden into sedimentary rocks.

❓ WHAT ARE BIRTHSTONES?

Birthstones are minerals that symbolize the month of a person's birth. For example, garnet is the birthstone for January, while ruby is the stone for people born in July.

❓ WHAT ARE THE MOST COMMON ROCKS?

Sedimentary rocks cover 75% of the Earth's land surface. But igneous rocks make up 95% of the rocks in the top 10 miles (16 km) of the Earth's crust.

❓ WHAT COMMON ROCKS ARE USED FOR BUILDINGS?

Two sedimentary rocks, limestone and sandstone, and the igneous rock granite are all good building stones. The metamorphic rock marble is often used to decorate buildings.

❓ ARE SOME MINERALS MORE PLENTIFUL THAN OTHERS?

Many useful minerals are abundant. Other less common, but important, minerals are in short supply and are often recycled from scrap. Recycling saves energy, which has to be used to process metal ores.

What are fossils?

Fossils are the impressions of ancient life preserved in rocks. When dead creatures are buried on the seabed, the soft parts rot away, but the hard parts remain. Later, the mud and sand on the seabed harden into rock. Water seeping through the rock dissolves the hard parts, forming fossil molds. Minerals fill the molds to create casts, which preserve the shapes of the hard parts. Other fossils include outlines of leaves turned to stone, and insects trapped in amber.

FOSSIL TEETH
These can tell us about how extinct animals lived.

FOSSIL FOOTPRINTS
Fossil footprints are preserved in rocks. They are uncovered when overlying rocks are worn away.

TRILOBITE FOSSILS
Trilobites were common animals that lived in the sea in the Paleozoic era.

? WHAT IS AMBER?

Amber is a hard substance formed from the sticky resin of trees. Tiny animals were sometimes trapped in the resin. Their bodies were preserved when the resin hardened.

FOSSIL SPIDER
Many tiny creatures have been fossilized in amber. They are unusual fossils because they consist of the actual bodies of ancient creatures.

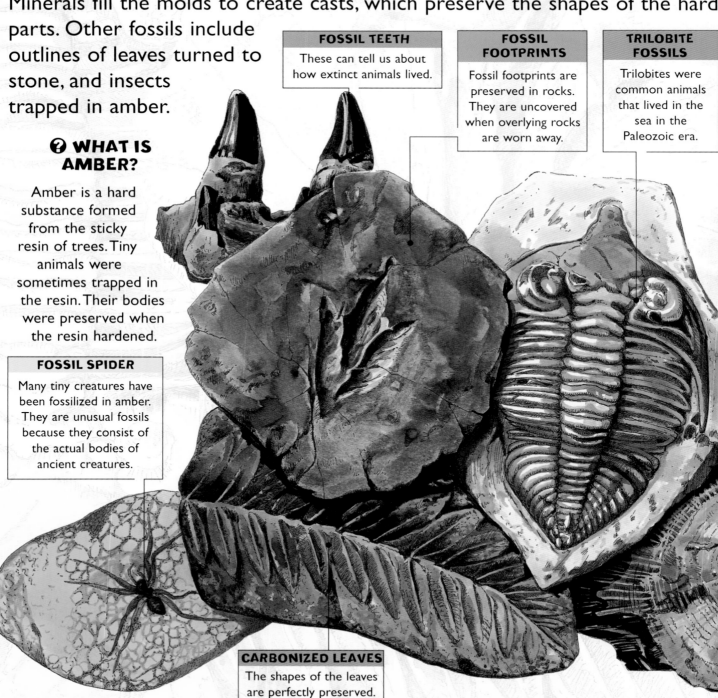

CARBONIZED LEAVES
The shapes of the leaves are perfectly preserved.

❓ HAS FLESH EVER BEEN PRESERVED AS A FOSSIL?

In Siberia, wooly mammoths, which lived more than 40,000 years ago, sank in swampy ground. When the soil froze, their complete bodies were preserved in the icy subsoil.

❓ WHAT ARE TRACE FOSSILS?

Trace fossils give information about animals that lived in ancient times. Animal burrows are sometimes preserved, giving scientists clues about the creatures that made them. Other trace fossils include footprints preserved in hardened mud and quickly buried under more mud.

PETRIFIED LOGS

Petrified logs were formed when water replaced the molecules in buried logs with minerals. Slowly, stone replicas of the logs were produced.

AMMONITE FOSSIL

Fossils of ammonites are common in rocks of the Mesozoic era. Ammonites were mollusks, related to squid.

❓ WHAT IS EOHIPPUS?

Eohippus is the name of the dog-sized ancestor of the horse, which lived about 55 million years ago. Fossil studies of eohippus and its successors have shown how the modern horse evolved.

❓ WHAT IS CARBONIZATION?

Leaves usually rot quickly after plants die. But sometimes they float to the bottom of lakes and are buried under fine mud. Sediments above and below the leaf are gradually compressed and hardened into sedimentary rocks. Over time, bacteria gradually change the chemistry of the leaf until only the carbon within it remains. The shape of the leaf is preserved in the rock as a thin carbon smear. This process is called carbonization.

❓ HOW ARE FOSSILS TURNED TO STONE?

When tree trunks or bones are buried, minerals deposited from water sometimes replace the original material. The wood or bone is then petrified, or turned to stone.

❓ HOW DO YOU DATE FOSSILS?

Sometimes, dead creatures are found buried under volcanic ash. The ash sometimes contains radioactive substances that scientists can date. Hence, they can work out the time when the animals lived.

❓ WHAT WAS PILTDOWN MAN?

Some bones, thought to be fossils of an early human ancestor, were discovered at Piltdown Common, England, between 1910 and 1912. But Piltdown man was a fake. The skull was human, but the jawbone came from an orangutan.

❓ WHAT CAN SCIENTISTS LEARN FROM FOSSILS?

From the study of fossils—known as palaeontology —scientists can learn about how living things evolved on Earth. Fossils can also help palaeontologists to date rocks. This is because some species lived for only a short period on Earth. So, if the fossils of these creatures are found in rocks in different places, the rocks must have been formed at the same time. Such fossils are called index fossils. Important index fossils include species of trilobites, graptolites, brachiopods, crinoids, ammonites, and belemnites.

❓ WHAT ARE SPRINGS?

Springs occur when ground water flows to the surface. Springs are the sources of many rivers. Hot springs often occur in volcanic areas, where the ground water is heated by magma.

How does weathering help shape the land?

Weathering is the breakdown of rocks on the Earth's surface. The wearing away of the rock limestone is an example of chemical weathering. Limestone consists mostly of calcium carbonate. This chemical reacts with rainwater, which contains carbon dioxide dissolved from the air. The rainwater is a weak acid that slowly dissolves the limestone. It opens up cracks in the surface, wearing out holes that can eventually lead down to huge caves linked by tunnels.

FREEZING
Frost action affects high mountain slopes, where water freezes at night.

CAVES
Surface water flows into layers of limestone and hollows out caves.

❓ WHAT IS GROUND WATER?

Ground water is water that seeps slowly through rocks, such as sandstones and limestones. The top level of the water in the rocks is called the water table. Wells are dug down to the water table.

SCREE
Worn rocks pile up in heaps called scree or talus.

CAN THE SUN'S HEAT CAUSE MECHANICAL WEATHERING?

In hot, dry regions, rocks are heated by the Sun, but they cool at night. These changes crack rock surfaces, which peel away like the layers of an onion.

DOES WATER REACT CHEMICALLY WITH OTHER ROCKS?

Water dissolves rock salt. It also reacts with some types of the hard rock granite, turning minerals in the rock into a clay called kaolin.

TREE ROOTS
The roots of trees can split rock apart.

WHAT ARE STALACTITES?

In limestone caves, water containing a lot of calcium carbonate drips down from the ceilings. The water gradually deposits calcium carbonate, which forms hanging, iciclelike structures called stalactites.

WHAT ARE POT HOLES?

Pot holes are holes in the ground that lead down to limestone caves. They are formed when the roofs of shallow caves collapse. People who climb down the narrow gaps to explore the caves are called pot holers.

WHAT ARE STALAGMITES?

Stalagmites, like stalactites, are columns of calcium carbonate deposited by dripping water, but stalagmites grow upward from the floors of caves, rather than hanging down from the ceilings.

WHAT IS BIOLOGICAL WEATHERING?

Biological weathering includes the splitting apart of rocks by tree roots, the exposing and consequential breaking up of rocks by burrowing animals, and the work of bacteria, which also helps to weather rocks.

CAN PLANTS CHANGE THE LAND?

Plant roots can break up the rock. When the seed of a tree falls into a crack in a rock, it develops roots that push downward. As the roots grow, they push against the sides of the crack until the rock splits apart.

WEATHERING
Weathering is rapid on sloping land, where worn rocks tumble downhill.

RIVERS
Ground water flows out of limestone caves to form the source of a river.

LIMESTONE CAVES
Limestone caves are worn out by chemical weathering. They often contain stalactites and stalagmites.

HOW QUICKLY IS THE LAND WORN AWAY?

Scientists have worked out that an average of 1.4 inches (3.5 cm) is worn away from land every 1,000 years. This sounds slow, but over millions of years, mountains are worn down to make plains.

HOW DOES THE ACTION OF FROST BREAK UP ROCKS?

At night in the mountains, people may hear sounds like gunshots. These are made by rocks being split apart by frost action (an example of mechanical weathering). As the water in cracks in the rocks freezes and turns into ice, it takes up nearly one-tenth as much space again, and so it exerts pressure, widening the cracks until they split apart.

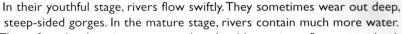

In their youthful stage, rivers flow swiftly. They sometimes wear out deep, steep-sided gorges. In the mature stage, rivers contain much more water. They often develop vigorous meanders. In old age, rivers flow more slowly. Sometimes they change course. Cut-off bends become oxbow lakes

❓ WHERE DO RIVERS START?

Some rivers start at springs, where ground water reaches the surface. Others start at the ends of melting glaciers or are the outlets of lakes.

❓ WHY DO WATERFALLS OCCUR?

Waterfalls can occur when rivers cross hard rocks. When softer rocks downstream are worn away, the hard rocks form a ledge over which the river plunges in a waterfall.

Oxbow lake

Tributary river

Tributary river

How do rivers shape the land?

Rivers sweep away weathered rocks and wear away the land. Young rivers push loose rocks down steep slopes. The rocks rub against riverbeds and deepen their valleys. They also rub against each other and break down into finer and finer pieces. Mature rivers flow down gentler slopes. They develop bends called meanders, and continue to wear away land. In old age, rivers move slowly across nearly flat plains, carrying huge loads of sand, silt, and mud toward the sea.

When heavy rains swell old-age rivers, they may overflow their banks and cause floods.

Waves can hollow out caves in rocky headlands. Blow-holes form above the caves.

When two caves in a headland meet, a natural arch occurs.

When a natural arch collapses, the tip of the headland becomes an isolated stack.

CAVES, ARCHES, AND STACKS

The sea batters continually at our coasts, changing their shape and creating dramatic natural features.

❓ CAN SEA WAVES SHAPE COASTS?

Large storm waves batter the shore. The waves pick up sand and pebbles, and hurl them at cliffs. This hollows out the bottom layers of the cliff until the top collapses and the cliff retreats. Waves hollow out bays in soft rocks, leaving hard rocks jutting into the sea as headlands. Waves then attack the headlands from both sides, wearing away the cliffs. Eventually, a natural arch is formed. When the arch collapses, all that remains is an isolated rock, called a stack.

❓ WHAT ARE SPITS?

Waves and currents transport sediments along coasts. In places where the coasts change direction, the worn sand and pebbles pile up in narrow ridges called spits.

❓ WHAT IS A BAYMOUTH BAR?

Some spits join one headland to another. They are called baymouth bars, because they cut off bays from the sea, turning them into lagoons.

❓ WHAT ARE TRIBUTARY RIVERS?

Tributary rivers are rivers that flow into a main river. They swell the amount of water in the main river and increase its load of worn material.

❓ DOES THE SEA WEAR AWAY THE LAND?

Waves wear away soft rocks to form bays, while harder rocks on either side form headlands. Parts of the coast of northeast England have been worn back by up to 3 miles (5 km) since the days when the Romans ruled the area.

❓ HOW CAN PEOPLE SLOW DOWN WAVE EROSION?

Along the beaches at many coastal resorts, structures are built at right angles to the shore. These breakwaters slow down the movement of sand on the beaches by waves and sea currents.

❓ WHAT ARE DELTAS?

Deltas are areas of sediments, made up of sand, mud, and silt, that pile up around the mouths of some rivers. In many rivers, currents sweep the sediments into the sea.

Mud carried by a river is often dumped near the river's mouth to form large mud flats. At high tide the sea often covers these areas.

A VALLEY GLACIER
Ice from mountain tops spills downhill to form glaciers. These carry worn rock, called moraine.

Snow falls on mountains. At the higher levels, the snow piles up year by year.

Snow in mountain basins, called cirques, becomes compressed into glacier ice.

❷ WHAT ARE THE WORLD'S LARGEST BODIES OF ICE?

The largest bodies of ice are the ice sheets of Antarctica and Greenland. Smaller ice caps occur in the Arctic, while mountain glaciers are found around the world.

❷ WHAT ARE ERRATICS?

Erratics are boulders made of a rock that is different from the rocks on which they rest. They were carried there by moving ice.

❷ WHEN DID THE LAST ICE AGE TAKE PLACE?

The last Ice Age began about 2 million years ago and ended 1.6 million years ago. This period saw warm spells and long periods of bitter cold.

❷ WHAT IS AN ICE AGE?

An ice age is when average temperatures fall and ice sheets spread over large areas that were once ice-free. Several ice ages have occurred in Earth's history.

Glacier carrying moraine

How does ice shape the land?

In cold mountain areas, snow piles up in hollows. Gradually the snow becomes compacted into ice. Eventually, the ice spills out of the hollows and starts to move downhill, forming a glacier. Glaciers are like conveyor belts. On the tops of glaciers are rocks shattered by frost action that have tumbled downhill. Other rocks are frozen into the sides and bottoms of glaciers. They give glaciers the power to wear away rocks and deepen the valleys through which they flow. Ice-worn valleys are U-shaped, with steep sides and flat bottoms. This distinguishes them from V-shaped river valleys.

❓ HOW CAN WE TELL THAT AN AREA WAS ONCE COVERED BY ICE?

Certain tell-tale features give this away. Mountain areas contain deep, steep-sided valleys that were worn out by glaciers. Armchair-shaped basins where glacier ice once formed are called cirques. Knife-edged ridges between cirques are called arêtes, while peaks called horns were carved when three or more cirques formed back-to-back. Boulders and other material carried by ice is called moraine. Moraine ridges show that ice sheets once reached that area.

❓ WHAT ARE FJORDS?

Fjords are deep, steep-sided valleys that wind inland along coasts. They were once river valleys that were deepened by glaciers during the last Ice Age.

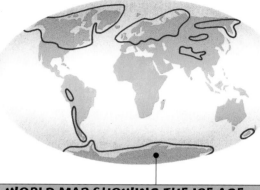

WORLD MAP SHOWING THE ICE AGE

Ice covered much of northern North America, Europe, and Asia during the Ice Age.

❓ HOW MUCH OF THE WORLD IS COVERED BY ICE?

Ice covers about 10% of the world's land area. But during the last Ice Age, it spread over much of northern North America and Europe. The same ice sheet reached what is now New York City, and covered London, England.

At the end of the glacier, the ice melts, creating streams that sweep away the glacier's rocky load.

How does wind-blown sand shape scenery?

In deserts, wind-blown sand is important in shaping the scenery. Winds lift grains of sand, which are blown and bounced forward. Sand grains are heavy and seldom rise over 6 feet (2 m) above ground level. But, at low levels, wind-blown sand acts like the sand-blasters used to clean dirty city buildings. It polishes rocks, hollows out caves in cliffs, and undercuts boulders. Boulders whose bases have been worn by wind-blown sand are top-heavy and mushroom-shaped, perched on a narrow stem.

Oases are places in deserts where water comes to the surface or where people can obtain water from wells.

❷ WHAT ARE DUST STORMS?

Desert winds sweep fine dust high into the air during choking dust storms. Wind from the Sahara in North Africa is often blown over southern Europe, carrying the pinkish dust with it.

❷ CAN WATER CHANGE DESERT SCENERY?

Thousands of years ago, many deserts were rainy areas and many land features were shaped by rivers. Flash floods sometimes occur in deserts. They sweep away much worn material.

❷ WHAT ARE OASES?

Oases are places in deserts that have water supplies. Some oases have wells tapping ground water. Sometimes, the water bubbles up to the surface in a spring.

Wind-blown sand carves top-heavy mushroom rocks that stand on thin stems.

DESERT SCENERY

Erg is the name given to sandy desert, reg is land covered with gravel and pebbles, and hammada is bare rock.

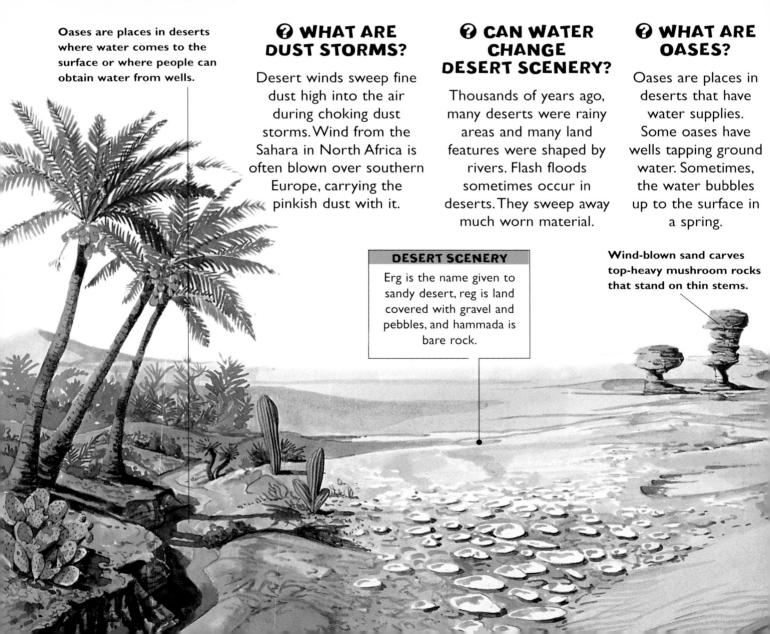

MUSHROOM ROCKS
Wind-blown sand erodes the bottoms of rocks, wearing them to a narrow stem.

BARCHANS
Crescent-shaped dunes form in sandy deserts where wind directions are constant.

❓ WHAT ARE WADIS?

Wadis are dry riverbeds in deserts. Travelers sometimes shelter in them at night. But a freak storm can soon fill them with water, and drowning in the desert can be a real, if unexpected, danger.

❓ WHY DO PEOPLE IN DESERTS WEAR HEAVY CLOTHES?

Deserts are often cold at night and heavy clothes keep people warm. Cloaks and headdresses help to keep out stinging wind-blown sand and dust, and prevent sunburn.

❓ WHAT IS DESERTIFICATION?

Human misuse of the land near deserts, caused by cutting down trees and overgrazing grasslands, may turn fertile land into desert. This is called desertification. Natural climate changes may also create deserts. This happened in the Sahara about 7,000 years ago.

❓ HOW ARE SAND DUNES FORMED?

The wind blowing across a desert piles the sand up in hills called dunes. Where the wind directions keep changing, the dunes have no particular shape. But when they blow mainly from one direction, crescent-shaped dunes called barchans form. Barchans may occur singly or in clusters. When winds drive sand dunes forward, they form seif dunes, named after an Arabic word meaning sword. Advancing dunes can bury farmland. To stop their advance, people plant trees and grasses to anchor the sand.

Why are icebergs dangerous to shipping?

Icebergs are huge chunks of ice that break off from glaciers. They float in the sea with nine-tenths of their bulk submerged, which makes them extremely dangerous to shipping. Icebergs from Greenland have sunk ships off the coasts of North America.

ICEBERGS IN THE OCEANS

Flat-topped icebergs form off the coast of Antarctica. The bulk of the ice in an iceberg is hidden beneath the waves.

❓ WHAT IT IS LIKE AROUND THE NORTH POLE?

It is bitterly cold. The North Pole lies in the middle of the Arctic Ocean, which is surrounded by northern North America, Asia, and Europe. Sea ice covers much of the ocean for most of the year. In spring, the sea ice is about 9 feet (3 m) thick in mid-ocean, and explorers can walk across it. The Arctic Ocean contains several islands, including Greenland, the world's largest. A huge ice sheet, the world's second largest, covers more than four-fifths of Greenland.

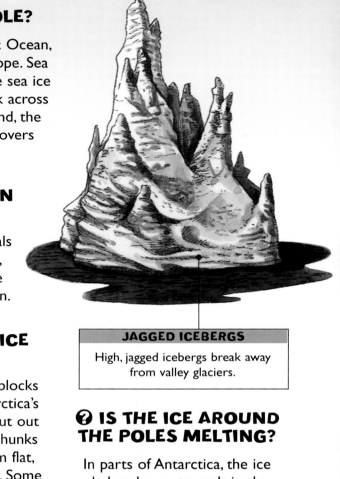

❓ WHERE ARE THE POLES?

The Earth is always spinning on its axis, giving us day and night. The points at the ends of this axis are the North and South geographic poles.

❓ WHAT ANIMALS LIVE IN POLAR REGIONS?

Penguins are the best-known animals of Antarctica. Polar bears, caribou, musk oxen, and reindeer are large animals that live in the Arctic region.

❓ WHAT ARE ICE SHELVES?

Ice shelves are large blocks of ice joined to Antarctica's ice sheet, but which jut out over the sea. When chunks break away, they form flat, table-topped icebergs. Some of them are huge. One covered an area about the size of Belgium.

JAGGED ICEBERGS

High, jagged icebergs break away from valley glaciers.

❓ IS THE ICE AROUND THE POLES MELTING?

In parts of Antarctica, the ice shelves began to melt in the 1990s. Some people think this shows that the world is getting warmer because of pollution.

Icebergs melt as they float away from polar regions and the climate becomes warmer.

Icebergs contain worn rocks that have been eroded from the land.

As icebergs melt, the rocks in the ice sink down and settle on the oceanbed.

❓ WHAT ARE THE MAGNETIC POLES?

The Earth is like a giant magnet, with two magnetic poles. They lie near the geographic North and South poles, though their positions change from time to time.

❓ HOW THICK IS THE ICE IN ANTARCTICA?

The South Pole lies in the cold and windy continent of Antarctica, which is larger than either Europe or Australia. Ice and snow cover 98% of Antarctica, although some coastal areas and high peaks are ice-free. The Antarctic ice sheet is the world's largest, and contains about seven-tenths of the world's fresh water. In places, the ice is up to 3 miles (4.8 km) thick. The world's record lowest temperature, -128.6°F (-89.2°C), was recorded at the Vostok research station in 1983.

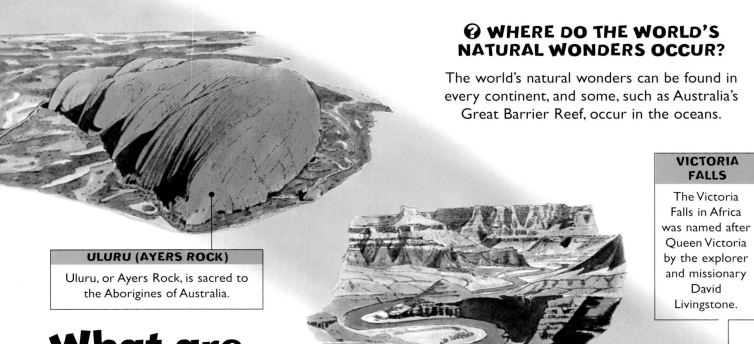

❓ WHERE DO THE WORLD'S NATURAL WONDERS OCCUR?

The world's natural wonders can be found in every continent, and some, such as Australia's Great Barrier Reef, occur in the oceans.

VICTORIA FALLS

The Victoria Falls in Africa was named after Queen Victoria by the explorer and missionary David Livingstone.

ULURU (AYERS ROCK)

Uluru, or Ayers Rock, is sacred to the Aborigines of Australia.

GRAND CANYON

The Grand Canyon is regarded as one of the seven natural wonders of the world.

What are natural wonders?

The ancient Greeks and Romans made lists of the Seven Wonders of the World. They were all made by people. But the Earth also has many natural wonders, created by the forces that continuously shape our planet. Most lists of natural wonders include the Grand Canyon in the United States. It is the world's largest canyon and the most awe-inspiring. The canyon is 277 miles (446 km) long and about 1 mile (1.6 km) deep. It was worn down by the Colorado River over the last six million years.

❓ WHERE IS THE "GREAT PEBBLE"?

The word Uluru is an Australian Aboriginal word meaning "great pebble." Also called Ayers Rock, it is the world's biggest monolith (single rock).

❓ WHICH IS THE WORLD'S HIGHEST MOUNTAIN RANGE?

The Himalayas, in Asia. It contains 96 of the world's 109 peaks over 24,000 feet (7,315 m) above sea level. One of them, Mount Everest, is the world's highest mountain.

❓ WHICH MOUNTAINS LOOK LIKE DRAGON'S TEETH?

Steep-sided hills made of limestone, found around the town of Guilin in southeastern China. Wearing away by rainwater has made them their strange shapes.

❷ HOW CAN WE PROTECT OUR NATURAL WONDERS?

Many people work to protect natural wonders so that they can be enjoyed by people in the future. One important step in protecting them was made in 1872, when the world's first national park was founded at Yellowstone, site of the famous geyser named Old Faithful, in the northwestern United States. Since then, national parks have been founded around the world.

❷ WHERE CAN YOU FIND "SMOKE THAT THUNDERS"?

The local name of the beautiful Victoria Falls on the Zambezi River, between Zambia and Zimbabwe, is Mosi oa Tunya, meaning "smoke that thunders."

❷ WHAT IS THE GREAT BARRIER REEF?

The Great Barrier Reef is the world's longest group of coral reefs. It lies off the northeast coast of Australia, and is about 1,242 miles (2,000 km) long.

❷ WHAT IS THE WORLD'S MIGHTIEST RIVER?

The Amazon River in South America contains far more water than any other river. Its river basin (the region it drains) is also the world's largest.

❷ WHAT IS METEOR CRATER?

Meteor Crater in Arizona is a circular depression. It resembles a volcanic crater, but was formed about 50,000 years ago when a meteor hit our planet. The crater is 4,180 feet (1,275 m) wide and 570 feet (175 m) deep.

❷ WHAT JAPANESE WONDER ATTRACTS PILGRIMS?

Mount Fuji in Japan is a beautiful volcanic cone. Many people regard it as a sacred mountain—a dwelling place for the gods—and they make long pilgrimages to the top.

❷ WHERE IS THE MATTERHORN?

The Matterhorn is a magnificent mountain on Switzerland's border with Italy. It was created by glaciers wearing away the mountain from opposite sides.

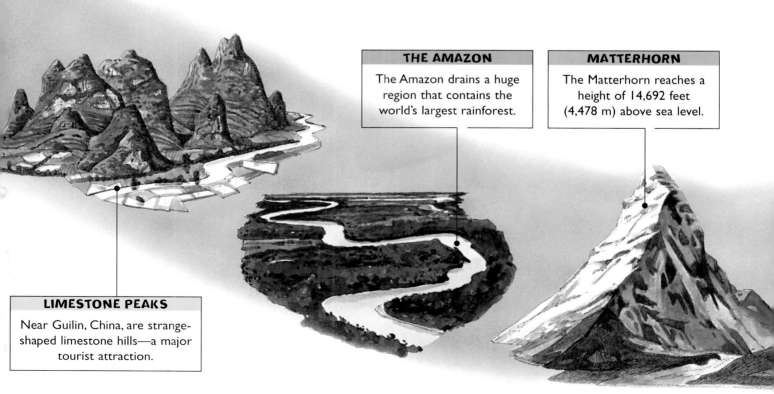

THE AMAZON

The Amazon drains a huge region that contains the world's largest rainforest.

MATTERHORN

The Matterhorn reaches a height of 14,692 feet (4,478 m) above sea level.

LIMESTONE PEAKS

Near Guilin, China, are strange-shaped limestone hills—a major tourist attraction.

What happens when people exploit the Earth?

In many areas, people are changing the Earth and causing great harm through pollution. They are cutting down forests to produce farmland. But in some places, rain and winds wear away newly exposed soil, causing soil erosion and making the land infertile. Factories, vehicles, and homes burn fuels that release gases into the air. These so-called greenhouse gases trap heat. They cause global warming and change world climates. Other kinds of pollution include the poisoning of rivers and seas by factory and household wastes.

❷ HOW HAVE PEOPLE TURNED SEA INTO LAND?

In crowded countries, people sometimes turn useless coastal land into fertile farmland. The Netherlands is a flat country and about two-fifths of it is below sea level at high tide. The Dutch have created new land, or polders, by building dykes (sea walls) around areas once under the sea. Rainwater gradually washes out the salt from the soil and the polder land eventually becomes fertile. Global warming could affect the Netherlands. Increasingly stormy weather and rises in the sea level could cause massive flooding.

❷ WHAT IS AIR POLLUTION?

Air pollution occurs when gases such as carbon dioxide are emitted into the air by factories, homes, and offices. Vehicles also cause air pollution, which produces city smogs, acid rain, and global warming.

❷ WHAT IS SOIL EROSION?

Natural erosion, caused by running water, winds, and other forces, is a slow process. Soil erosion occurs when people cut down trees and farm the land. Soil erosion on land made bare by people is a much faster process than natural erosion.

❷ WHAT IS COASTAL POLLUTION?

Coral reefs and mangrove swamps are breeding places for many fishes. The destruction or pollution of these areas is threatening the numbers of fishes in the oceans.

❷ CAN THE POLLUTION OF RIVERS HARM PEOPLE?

When factories pump poisonous wastes into rivers, creatures living near the river mouths, such as shellfish, absorb poison into their bodies. When people eat such creatures, they, too, are poisoned.

❓ WHAT IS HAPPENING TO THE WORLD'S RAINFORESTS?

The rainforests in the tropics are being destroyed. These forests contain more than half of the world's living species. Many of them are now threatened with extinction. Huge forest fires in 1997 and 1998 destroyed large areas of rainforest.

❓ WILL GLOBAL WARMING AFFECT ANY ISLAND NATIONS?

Coral islands are low-lying. If global warming melts the world's ice, then sea levels will rise. Countries such as the Maldives and Kiribati could vanish under the waves.

❓ CAN DESERTS BE FARMED?

In Israel and other countries, barren deserts have been turned into farmland by irrigation. The land is watered from wells that tap ground water, or the water is piped from far-away areas.

RAINFOREST DESTRUCTION

Rainforests are cut down by loggers who want to sell valuable hardwoods. Land stripped bare of trees is exposed to the wind and rain, which cause serious soil erosion.

What is the biggest continent?

1) Asia covers an area of 16,992,000 sq miles (44,009,000 sq km). The other continents, in order of size, are:

2) Africa (11,678,000 square miles/30,246,000 sq km)

3) North America (9,351,000 square miles/24,219,000 sq km)

4) South America (6,885,000 square miles/17,832,000 sq km)

5) Antarctica (5,400,400 square miles/14,000,000 sq km)

6) Europe (4,032,000 square miles/10,443,000 sq km)

7) Australia (2,978,000 square miles/ 7,713,000 sq km).

EARTH SEEN FROM SPACE

Viewed from space, we can see how small planet Earth is in the setting of the universe. Pictures like this have made people aware of the necessity of protecting our planet home. The patterns of cloud show how weather changes. But pollution is changing the climate and this may have serious effects on all living things on planet Earth.

❓ WHAT IS THE WORLD'S LARGEST ISLAND?

Greenland covers about 840,000 square miles (2,175,000 sq km). (Geographers regard Australia as a continent and not as an island.)

❓ WHAT IS THE WORLD'S LARGEST RIVER BASIN?

The Amazon River basin in South America covers about 2,720,000 square miles (7,045,000 sq km). The Madeira River, which flows into the Amazon, is the world's longest tributary, at 2,100 miles (3,380 km).

❓ WHICH IS THE DEEPEST LAKE?

Lake Baikal, in Siberia, eastern Russia, is the world's deepest lake. The deepest part measured so far is 5,371 feet (1,637 m).

❓ HOW MUCH OF THE WORLD IS COVERED BY LAND?

Land covers about 57,300,000 square miles (148,460,000 sq km), or 29% of the world's surface. Water covers the remaining 71%.

❓ WHAT IS THE WORLD'S HIGHEST PEAK?

Mount Everest on Nepal's border with China reaches 29,029 feet (8,848 m) above sea level. Measured from its base on the sea floor, Mauna Kea, Hawaii is 33,474 feet (10,203 m) high. But only 13,796 feet (4,205 m) appear above sea level.

❓ WHAT IS THE WORLD'S LARGEST BAY?

Hudson Bay in Canada covers an area of about 476,000 square miles (1,233,000 sq km). It is linked to the North Atlantic Ocean by the Hudson Strait.

❓ WHAT IS THE WORLD'S LARGEST HIGH PLATEAU?

The wind-swept Tibetan Plateau in China covers about 715,000 square miles (1,850,000 sq km).

❓ WHAT IS THE LARGEST INLAND BODY OF WATER, OR LAKE?

The salty Caspian Sea, which lies partly in Europe and partly in Asia, has an area of about 143,390 square miles (371,380 sq km). The largest freshwater lake is Lake Superior in North America, at 31,800 square miles (82,350 sq km).

❓ IS THERE A LAKE UNDER ANTARCTICA?

Scientists have found a lake, about the size of Lake Ontario in North America, hidden under Antarctica. It may contain creatures that lived on Earth millions of years ago.

❓ WHERE DO MOST PEOPLE LIVE?

The continent with the largest population is Asia, which has more than 3,000 million people. Europe ranks second in world population, followed by Africa, North America, South America, and Australia. The continent of Antarctica has no permanent population at all.

❓ WHICH IS THE WORLD'S LONGEST RIVER?

The River Nile in northeast Africa is 4,112 miles (6,617 km) long. The second longest river, the Amazon in South America, discharges 60 times more water than the River Nile.

❓ WHAT IS THE DEEPEST CAVE?

The Réseau Jean Bernard in France is the deepest cave system. It reaches a depth of 5,256 feet (1,602 m).

❓ WHAT IS THE WORLD'S LARGEST DESERT?

The Sahara covers an area of about 3,579,000 square miles (9,269,000 sq km). This is nearly as big as the United States.

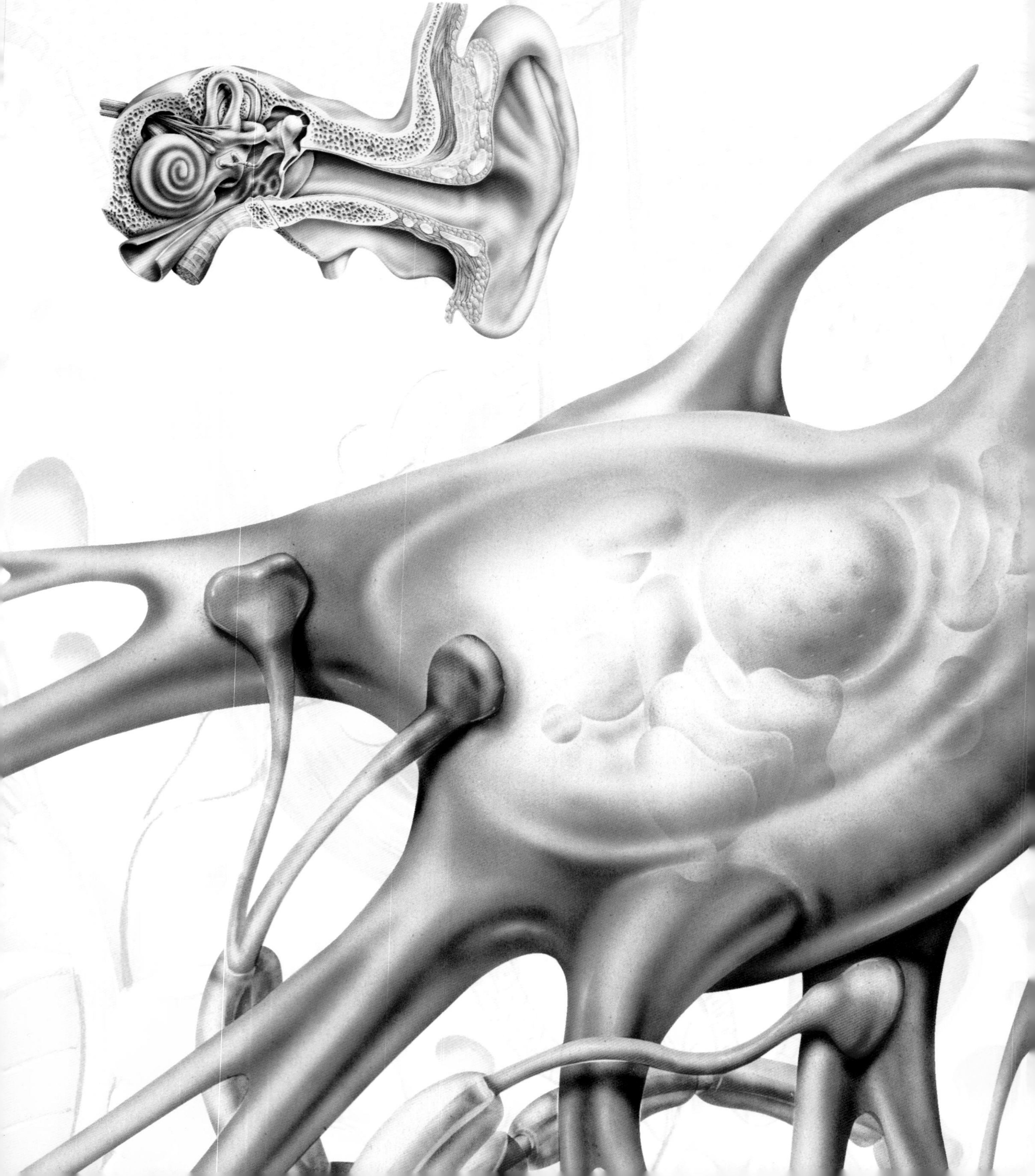

HUMAN BODY

How thick is your skin?

Skin covers the surface of the body at a thickness of just 0.006 to 0.16 inches (1.4 to 4 mm). The skin is thickest on areas such as the palms of the hands and the soles of the feet. Skin two layers. The outer skin that you see and touch is made of tough cells of dead skin and is part of the epidermis. Below this is the dermis. It contains tiny blood vessels, sweat glands, nerve endings and the roots of tiny hairs. Under the dermis is a layer of fat, which keeps you warm.

❓ WHAT DOES SKIN DO?

Skin is a tough, stretchy covering that acts as a barrier between your body and the outside world. It stops the moisture inside the body from drying out and prevents dirt and germs from getting in. Tiny particles of melanin inside the epidermis help to shield your body from the harmful rays of the Sun. The more melanin you have, the darker your skin and the better protected you are.

❓ WHAT ARE GOOSE BUMPS?

Goose bumps are bumps on your skin formed by the tiny muscles that make the hairs on your skin stand up when you are cold.

Sweat pore   Epidermis   Hair follicle

Sweat gland

❓ WHAT GIVES HAIR ITS COLOR?

The color of your hair is determined mainly by the pigments (colored substances) it contains. There are two kinds of pigment: melanin, which is very dark brown, and keratin, which is reddish-yellow. All hair color is formed by one or other or a mixture of both.

A STRAND OF HAIR

Most people have between 100,000 and 150,000 hairs growing on their head.

❓ WHY DOES SKIN HAVE PORES?

Skin has tiny holes, called sweat pores, to let out sweat and water vapor. When you are too hot, glands pump out sweat, which cools you as it dries.

❓ HOW DO NAILS GROW, AND HOW FAST DO THEY GROW?

A fingernail grows about 0.04 inch (1 mm) every 7 days. As new nail forms behind the cuticle, it pushes the older nail along.

❓ WHAT MAKES FINGERPRINTS UNIQUE?

A fingerprint is made by thin ridges of skin on the tip of each finger and thumb. The ridges form a pattern of lines, loops, or whorls, and no two people have the same pattern.

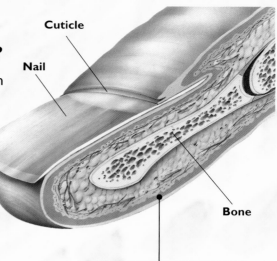

Cuticle

Nail

Bone

FINGERTIP
The pale half-moon at the base of the nail is new nail that has just grown.

Melanin

❓ WHY DOES HAIR FALL OUT?

No hair lasts more than about six years. Every day you lose about 60 hairs, but since you have about 100,000 on your scalp, you hardly notice. After a while, new hairs grow from the hair follicles.

❓ WHAT MAKES HAIR NATURALLY CURLY?

How curly your hair is depends on the shape of the follicle—the tiny pit from which it grows. Curly hair grows from flat hair follicles, wavy hair from oval follicles and straight hair from round follicles.

❓ WHY DO OLD PEOPLE HAVE GREY HAIR?

Some people's hair stops making melanin as they grow older. Fair-haired people tend to go white, while dark-haired people usually go grey. Greyness is lack of melanin plus tiny air bubbles in the hair.

A SECTION THROUGH THE SKIN
In the dermis, the deep inner layer of skin, are the blood vessels, fat, and hair roots. The thin epidermis protects the tissue beneath.

Dermis

Hair root

Fat

Blood vessel

❓ WHAT ARE FRECKLES?

Freckles are small patches of darker skin made by extra melanin. Exposure to sunshine increases the amount of melanin in the skin and the darkness of the freckles.

Why do bodies need bones?

Bones provide a strong framework that supports the rest of the body. Without bones, you would flop on the floor like an octopus! Some of the bones form a suit of internal armor, which protects the brain, the lungs, the heart, and other vital organs. All the bones together are called the skeleton. You can move and bend different parts of the body because the bones meet at joints.

❓ WHAT ARE LIGAMENTS?

They are strong, bendy straps that hold together the bones in a joint. Nearly all the body's joints have several ligaments.

❓ WHAT IS A VERTEBRA?

A vertebra is a knobbly bone in your spine. The 33 vertebrae fit together to make a strong pillar, the spine, which carries much of your weight. At the same time the vertebrae allow your back to bend and twist.

THE HUMAN SKELETON

A baby has more than 300 bones, but an adult has only about 206. This is because some of the bones fuse together as a person grows.

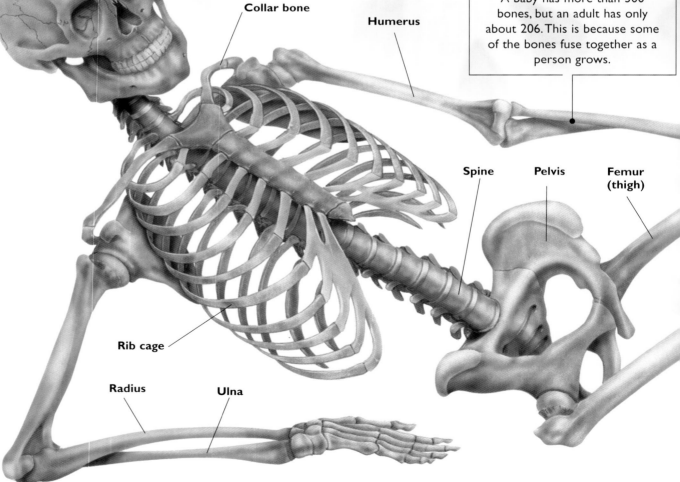

Skull

Collar bone

Humerus

Spine

Pelvis

Femur (thigh)

Rib cage

Radius

Ulna

Hinge joint

A joint that works like a hinge is found at the knee and elbow, and in the fingers and toes.

Ball and socket joint

The shoulder and hip have this joint.

Pivot joint

The pivot joint is found in the neck.

Saddle joint

This joint is found at the base of the thumb.

❓ WHAT IS A JOINT?

Where two bones meet, their ends are shaped to make different kinds of joint. Each kind of joint makes a strong connection and allows a particular kind of movement. For example, the knee is a hinge joint that lets the lower leg move only backward and forward. The hip is a ball and socket joint that allows you to move your thigh around in a circle. The saddle joint at the base of the thumb also gives a good range of movement.

❓ WHICH JOINTS MOVE LEAST?

Your skull is made up of more than 20 bones fused together in joints that allow no movement at all. These are called suture joints.

❓ WHICH JOINT MOVES THE MOST?

The shoulder joint is a ball and socket joint and it allows the greatest amount of movement in all directions.

❓ WHY DO JOINTS NOT SQUEAK?

Joints are cushioned by soft, squashy cartilage. Many joints also contain synovial fluid, which works like oil to keep them moving smoothly and painlessly.

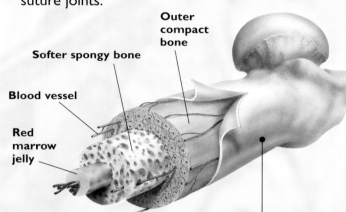

Outer compact bone

Softer spongy bone

Blood vessel

Red marrow jelly

INSIDE A BONE

At the center of some bones is a core of bone marrow.

Finger bones

Patella (knee cap)

Fibula

Tibia (shin)

Calcaneus (heel bone)

Toe bones

❓ WHICH IS THE LONGEST BONE?

The thigh bone in the upper part of the leg is the longest bone in the body. It accounts for more than a fourth of an adult's height.

❓ WHICH IS THE SMALLEST BONE?

The smallest bone is called the stirrup—it is no bigger than a grain of rice. It is deep inside your ear and its job is to pass on sounds from the outer and middle ear to the inner ear.

❓ WHAT IS INSIDE A BONE?

Inside a bone is a criss-cross honeycomb of lighter bone. Blood vessels weave in and out of the bone, keeping the cells alive.

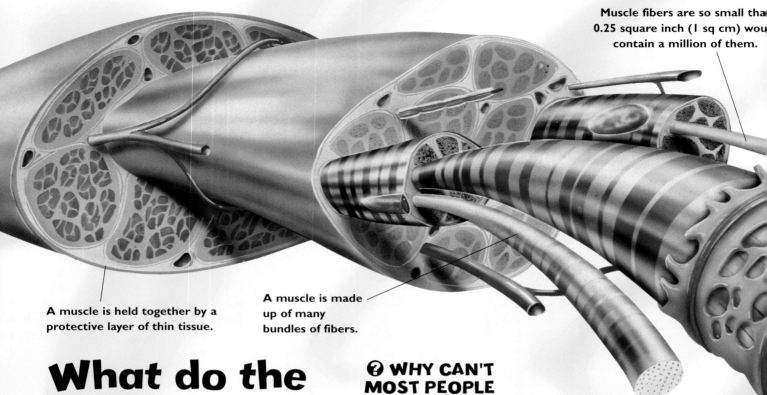

Muscle fibers are so small that 0.25 square inch (I sq cm) would contain a million of them.

A muscle is held together by a protective layer of thin tissue.

A muscle is made up of many bundles of fibers.

What do the muscles do?

Muscles make parts of your body move. The skeleton is covered with muscles that move your bones and give your body its shape. Muscles in the face move your cheeks, eyebrows, nose, mouth, tongue, and lower jaw. A different kind of muscle works in the esophagus (food pipe), stomach, and intestines to move food through your body. The heart is a third type of muscle—it never stops beating, and moves blood around your body.

❷ WHY CAN'T MOST PEOPLE MOVE THEIR EARS?

Humans, like most other animals, have a muscle behind each ear. Animals can turn their ears to hear better, but most people never learn how to use their ear muscles.

❷ HOW DO MUSCLES WORK?

Muscles work by contracting. This makes them shorter and thicker so that they pull on whatever bone or other part of the body they are attached to, thereby making it move.

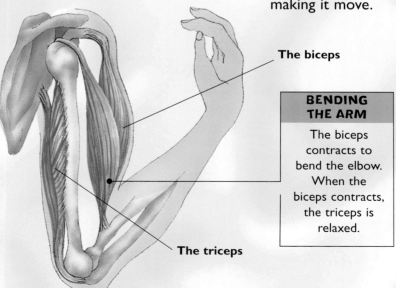

The biceps

The triceps

BENDING THE ARM

The biceps contracts to bend the elbow. When the biceps contracts, the triceps is relaxed.

❓ HOW MANY MUSCLES ARE THERE?

You have about 650 muscles that work together. Most actions—including walking, swimming, and smiling—involve dozens of muscles. Frowning uses 40 different muscles, but smiling is less energetic, using only 15.

❓ WHICH IS THE STRONGEST MUSCLE?

The strongest muscle is the one that shuts your mouth! It is called the masseter, and you use it for talking and chewing up food.

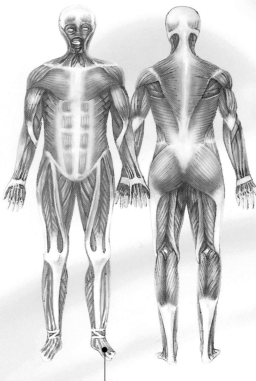

THE BODY'S MUSCLES

Here the skin is stripped away to show the muscles at the front and back of the body.

❓ WHAT IS A TENDON?

A tendon is like a tough rope that joins a muscle to a bone. If you bend and straighten your fingers, you can feel the tendons in the back of your hand. The body's strongest tendon is the Achilles tendon, which you can feel above your heel.

❓ WHY DO MUSCLES WORK IN PAIRS?

Muscles cannot push, they can only pull, and so you need two sets of muscles for many actions. For example, the biceps in your upper arm bends your elbow and you can feel it tighten when you clench your arm. To straighten the elbow again, you have to relax the biceps and tighten the triceps, which is the muscle at the back of your upper arm. In the same way, one set of muscles lifts the leg and another set of muscles straightens it.

❓ WHY DOES EXERCISE MAKE MUSCLES STRONGER?

A muscle is made of bundles of fibers that contract when you use the muscle. The more you use the muscle, the thicker the fibers become. They contract more effectively, which means the muscle is stronger.

INSIDE A MUSCLE

Each fiber is made up of hundreds of strands called fibrils.

❓ WHICH IS THE BIGGEST MUSCLE?

The biggest muscle is the gluteus maximus in the buttock. You use it to straighten your leg when you stand up, and it makes a comfortable cushion when you sit down.

❓ HOW FAST DO NERVES ACT?

A nerve signal is a tiny pulse of electricity. It travels at about 3 feet (1 m) per second in the slowest nerves to more than 300 feet (100 m) per second in the fastest ones.

❓ HOW DOES A NERVE WORK?

A chain of nerve cells carries a signal to or from the brain. The electrical impulse is received by the nerve endings and sent through the first nerve cell and along its nerve fiber to the nerve endings of the next nerve cell.

What do the nerves do?

Nerves carry information and instructions to and from the brain and from one part of the brain to the other. Sensory nerves bring information from the eyes, ears, and other sense organs to the brain, and motor nerves control the muscles. For example, if you decide to bend your knee, electrical signals move from your brain to the muscles in your leg to make them contract.

A SINGLE NERVE CELL

A nerve cell's intricate shape is suited to sending and receiving messages. The body of the cell contains the nucleus.

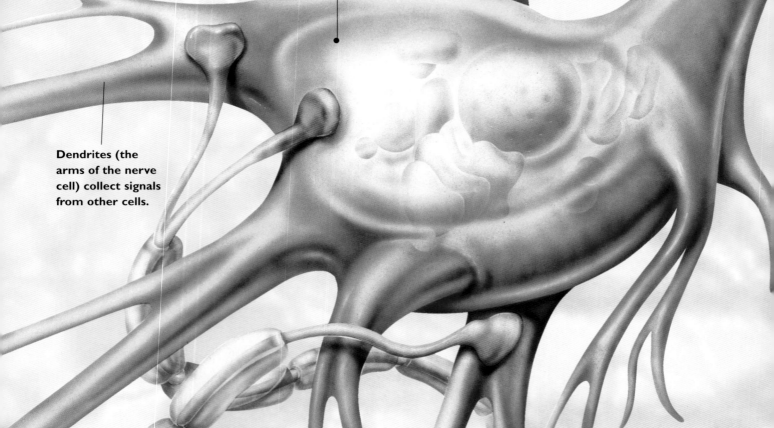

The axon carries nerve signals to the next nerve cell.

Dendrites (the arms of the nerve cell) collect signals from other cells.

❓ WHICH IS THE LONGEST NERVE?

The longest nerve is the tibial nerve. It runs alongside the shin bone, and in adults is 20 inches (50 cm) long.

JUGGLING

Juggling takes great skill. As the juggler learns to co-ordinate throwing and catching, the actions become automatic.

❓ HOW MANY NERVES DO YOU HAVE?

Thousands of millions of nerves reach out to all parts of the body.

The axon is covered with a fatty myelin sheath, which acts as an insulator to stop the signals leaking away.

❓ WHAT IS A REFLEX ACTION?

A reflex action is something you do automatically, without thinking about it. Swallowing, blinking, and choking are reflex actions. So is snatching your hand away from a hot plate.

❓ HOW DO ANESTHETICS WORK?

An anesthetic stops you feeling. A local anesthetic deadens the sensory nerves so that part of your body goes numb. A general anesthetic puts you into a deep sleep so that none of your senses is taking in information.

❓ WHAT IS THE SPINAL CORD?

The spinal cord is the largest nerve in the body. It is 0.75 inch (2 cm) wide and runs through the center of the spine. It connects the nerves in the body with the brain.

❓ WHAT ARE THE BODY'S FIVE MAIN SENSES?

The five main senses are seeing, hearing, smelling, tasting, and touching. Between them, the five senses give you all the information you have about the outside world. Each sense has a special part of the body, called a sense organ, which reacts to a particular kind of stimulus. For example, eyes react to light and ears react to sound.

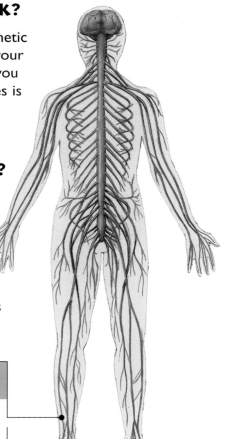

THE NERVOUS SYSTEM

Nerves link the brain and spinal cord to all parts of the body.

❓ WHAT CAUSES "PINS AND NEEDLES"?

If a nerve gets squashed, it cannot carry nerve signals. If you kneel for a long time, your leg goes numb and then, when you stretch it, it tingles as the signals begin to flow again.

SLEEPING

When you are asleep, you are not aware of what is going on around you. The brain blocks incoming signals, unless they are so strong they wake you up.

❷ WHY DO YOU NEED TO SLEEP?

A 10-year-old sleeps, on average, nine or 10 hours a night, but sleep time can vary a lot between four and 12 hours. If you sleep for eight hours a night, that's a third of your life! You need to sleep to rest your muscles and to allow your body time to repair and replace damaged cells.

❷ WHY DO SOME PEOPLE SLEEP-WALK?

People may walk in their sleep because they are worried or anxious. If someone is sleep-walking, you should gently take them back to bed.

❷ WHAT DOES THE BRAIN LOOK LIKE?

The brain looks soft and grayish pink. The top is wrinkled like a walnut and is covered with many tiny tubes of blood. The spinal cord links the brain to the rest of the body.

The front of the cortex is mainly involved with thinking and planning.

What does the brain do?

Your brain controls your body. It keeps the heart, stomach, lungs, kidneys, and other vital organs working. The information collected by the senses is processed by different parts of the brain. Some is discarded, some is stored, and some is reacted to at once, with messages being sent from the brain to the muscles and glands. The brain also gives you your sense of who you are. Memories of the past are stored in the brain and everything you think, feel, and do is controlled by the brain.

LITTLE GREY CELLS

The outer grey layer, or cerebral cortex, covers most of the brain, and is where consciousness and memory are based.

The pituitary gland controls growth and many other body processes.

The hypothalamus controls hunger, thirst, and body temperature.

❓ WHY DO YOU REMEMBER SOME THINGS AND FORGET OTHERS?

On the whole, you remember things that are important to you in some way. Some things need to be remembered for only a very short while. For instance, you might look up a telephone number, keep it in your head while you dial, and then forget it completely.

This part of the cortex deals with sight.

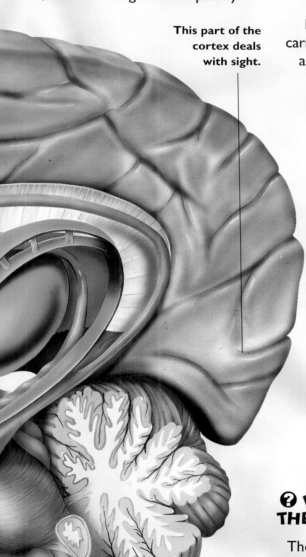

The cerebellum coordinates balance and movement.

❓ WHY ARE SOME PEOPLE MORE ARTISTIC THAN OTHERS?

One side of the brain deals more with music and artistic skills, and the other side with logical skills. How artistic or mathematical you are depends on which side of your brain is dominant (stronger).

❓ DOES THE BRAIN EVER REST?

Even while you are asleep the brain carries on controlling body activities such as breathing, heartbeat, and digestion.

❓ WHY ARE SOME PEOPLE LEFT-HANDED?

Most people are right-handed—the left side of their brain is dominant. In left-handed people, the right side of the brain is dominant. The part of the brain that controls speech is usually on the dominant side.

❓ WHAT IS THE BRAIN MADE OF?

The brain is a mass of pinkish-gray tissue made of approximately 100 billion nerve cells. It is surrounded by protective coverings called the meninges.

❓ WHAT DOES THE SKULL DO?

The skull is a hard covering of bone that protects the brain like a helmet. All the bones of the skull except the lower jaw are fused together to make them stronger.

SKIPPING
When you skip, your brain coordinates balance with the movements of your arms and legs.

❓ HOW OFTEN DO YOU DREAM?

You probably dream about five times every night, but you are only aware of dreaming if you wake up during a dream.

❓ WHAT DOES THE CEREBRAL CORTEX DO?

The cortex is the wrinkly top part of the brain. It controls all the brain activity that you are aware of—seeing, thinking, reading, feeling, and moving. Only humans have such a large and well developed cerebral cortex. Different parts of the cortex deal with different activities. The left side controls the right side of the body, while the right side of the cortex controls the left side of the body.

How do the eyes see things?

You see something when light bounces off the thing and enters your eyes. The black circle in the middle of the eye is a hole, called the pupil. Light passes through the pupil and is focused by the lens onto the retina at the back of the eye. Nerve endings in the retina send signals along the optic nerve to the brain. The picture formed on the retina is upside-down, but the brain turns it around so that you perceive things to be the right way up.

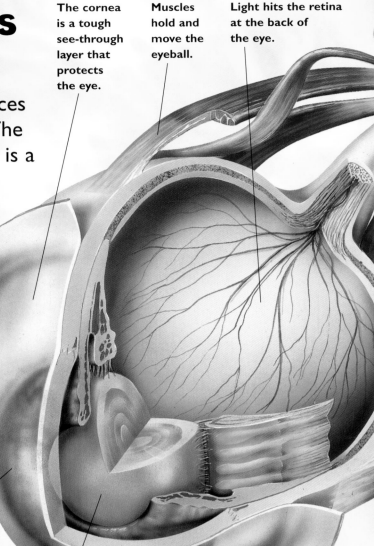

The cornea is a tough see-through layer that protects the eye.

Muscles hold and move the eyeball.

Light hits the retina at the back of the eye.

The iris is a circular muscle that controls the size of the pupil—and hence how much light enters the eye.

The lens focuses light.

❓ WHAT MAKES YOU CRY?

If dust or something gets into your eye, the tear gland above the eye releases extra tears to wash it away. Being upset can also make you cry.

❓ WHAT IS THE BLIND SPOT?

The blind spot is a spot on the retina where the optic nerve leaves the eye. There are no light-sensitive cells here, making the spot "blind."

❓ WHY DO PEOPLE HAVE DIFFERENT COLORED EYES?

The iris is the colored ring around the pupil. The color is formed by a substance called melanin. Brown-eyed people have a lot of melanin, while blue-eyed people have very little.

❓ WHAT KEEPS THE EYE IN PLACE?

The eyeball is held firmly in place by six muscles attached to the top, bottom, and each side of the eye. These muscles work together to move your eyes so that you can look around.

❓ CAN SUNSHINE DAMAGE THE EYE?

Sunshine contains ultraviolet rays, which can damage your eyes as well as your skin. You should wear sunglasses in bright sunlight and never, never look directly at the Sun.

The optic nerve takes signals from the retina to the brain.

The eyeball is filled with jelly, which keeps it in shape.

The pupil is the black hole at the center of the iris.

THE EYES
Our eyes not only detect moving images and color. They also help us to convey our moods and emotions.

The tear gland makes a constant supply of salty water.

The tear duct drains tears to the nose.

When too much water floods the eye, some spills over as tears and the rest drains into the nose.

❓ WHY DO YOU BLINK?

You blink to clean your eyes. Each eye is covered with a thin film of salty water, so every time you blink, the eyelid washes the eyeball and wipes away dust and germs. The water drains away through a narrow tube into the nose. You also blink to protect your eye when something comes too close.

❓ HOW BIG IS YOUR EYEBALL?

An adult eyeball is about the size of a golf ball, but most of the eyeball is hidden inside the head.

❓ WHY CAN'T YOU SEE COLOR WHEN IT GETS DARK?

The cells, called cones, that react to colored light only work well in bright light. Most of the eye's cells, called rods, see in black, white, and grey, and these are the ones that work at night.

❓ WHY DO YOU HAVE TWO EYES?

Two eyes help you to judge how far away something is. Each eye gets a slightly different picture, which the brain combines into a single three-dimensional (3D) picture—one that has depth as well as height and breadth.

❓ WHY DOES THE PUPIL CHANGE SIZE?

The pupil becomes smaller in bright light to stop too much light from getting in and damaging the retina. In dim light the pupil opens to let in more light.

❓ HOW DO YOU SEE COLOR?

Different nerve cells in the retina react to the colors red, blue, and green. Together they make up all the other colors.

❓ WHAT ARE EYELASHES FOR?

Your eyelashes help to protect your eyes by stopping dust and dirt getting blown into them.

HOW LIGHT ENTERS THE EYE
The image of the object projected onto the retina at the back of the eye is upside-down.

❓ WHY DO YOU GET DIZZY?

If you spin around and around and then stop, the world seems to carry on spinning. This is because the fluid in the semicircular canals of the ears is still moving as though you were spinning.

❓ HOW DO EARS HELP YOU BALANCE?

Three curved tubes in the inner ear help you to balance. They are filled with fluid and are called the semicircular canals. They are arranged at right angles to each other (like three sides of a box) so that as you move, the fluid inside them moves too. Nerves in the lining of the tubes detect changes in the fluid and send the information to the brain.

❓ WHY DO YOU HAVE TWO EARS?

Two ears help you to detect which direction sounds are coming from.

BALLET DANCER

A spinning dancer stops herself getting dizzy by turning her head quickly and keeping her eyes on a fixed point.

Outer ear (auricle or pinna)

The ear canal carries sound waves to the eardrum.

THE EAR

The ear canal carries sound waves to the eardrum. The eardrum vibrates, and passes vibrations on to the bones in the middle ear.

How do you hear?

Sound reaches your ears as vibrations in the air. The vibrations travel down the ear canal to the eardrum, which then vibrates, making the bones in the middle ear vibrate too. These three small bones make the vibrations bigger and pass them through to the fluid in the inner ear. The cochlea in the inner ear is coiled like a snail shell. As nerve endings in the lining of the cochlea detect vibrations in the fluid inside it, they send electrical signals to the brain.

❓ IS LOUD NOISE DANGEROUS?

Any noise over about 120 decibels can damage your hearing immediately. If you constantly listen to sounds of 90 decibels or more, they can damage your hearing too.

❓ WHERE DOES THE EUSTACHIAN TUBE GO?

This tube joins the middle ear to the empty spaces behind your upper throat. If mucus from a cold fills the tube, it stops you hearing as well as usual.

❓ WHAT IS EARWAX?

Yellow-brown earwax is made by glands in the skin lining the ear canal. It traps dirt and germs and is slowly pushed out of the ear.

❓ HOW LOUD IS A WHISPER?

A whisper is between 10 and 20 decibels. Some animals can detect much quieter sounds than we can.

❓ WHAT IS SOUND?

Sound is waves of energy that are carried as vibrations through air, liquid, and solid objects.

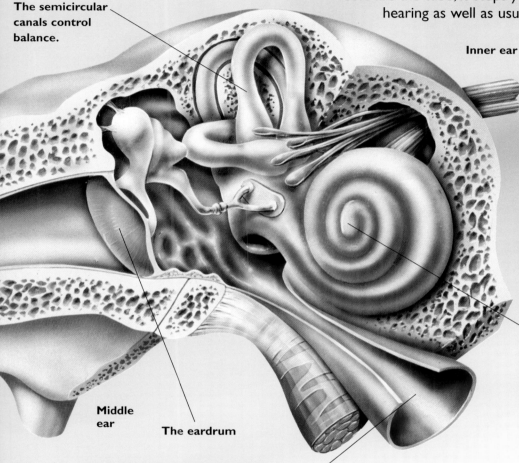

The semicircular canals control balance.

Inner ear

Middle ear

The eardrum

The Eustachian tube connects the middle ear to the top of the throat.

The cochlea is filled with fluid and lined with nerve endings.

A JET LIFTS OFF THE RUNWAY

The noise near a jet aircraft just can be as much as 120 decibels.

❓ HOW DO YOU MEASURE SOUND?

The loudness of a sound is measured in decibels. The sound of a pin dropping is less than 10 decibels, and the hum of a refrigerator is about 35 decibels. A loud personal stereo makes about 80 decibels.

❓ WHY DO YOUR EARS POP?

If you are flying in an aircraft and it changes height quickly, you may go a bit deaf, because the air inside and outside the eardrum is at different pressures. Your ears "pop" when the pressures become equal again.

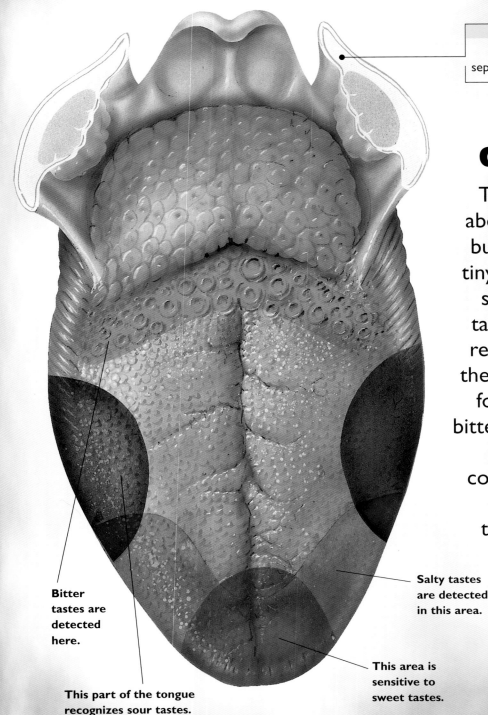

How do you detect taste?

The surface of the tongue has about 10,000 microscopic taste buds sunk into it. As you chew, tiny particles of food dissolve in saliva and trickle down to the taste buds. The taste receptors react and send messages about the taste to the brain. There are four basic tastes—sweet, salty, bitter, and sour—and every taste is made up of one or a combination of these. The taste buds in different parts of the tongue react mainly to one of these basic tastes.

Bitter tastes are detected here.

This part of the tongue recognizes sour tastes.

Salty tastes are detected in this area.

This area is sensitive to sweet tastes.

❓ DOES TASTE MATTER?

Unpleasant tastes can warn you when food has gone bad or is poisonous. Your body needs healthy food, so enjoying the taste of it encourages you to eat.

❓ WHY DO YOU LIKE SOME TASTES BETTER THAN OTHERS?

Most people prefer things that taste sweet or slightly salty, but your sense of taste can easily become used to too much sugar and salt. How you like food to taste is very much decided by your eating habits.

❓ WHY DOES A BLOCKED NOSE STOP YOU TASTING?

When you eat, you both taste and smell the food. If your nose is blocked with mucus from a cold, you can't smell properly and so food seems to have less taste too.

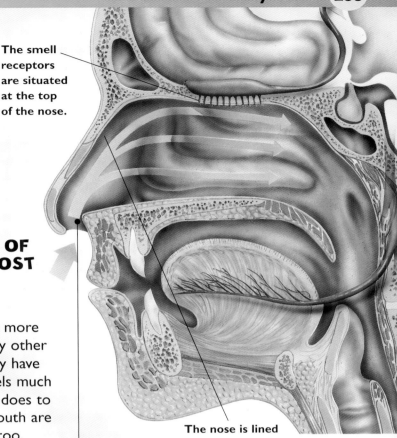

The smell receptors are situated at the top of the nose.

The nose is lined with mucus and fine hairs.

❓ WHY DO SOME ANIMALS HAVE KEENER SMELL?

So they can find food and detect the presence of attackers. The inside of their nose is lined with many smell receptors, which are situated close to their nostrils.

❓ HOW DO YOU SMELL?

A smell is made by tiny particles in the air. When you breathe in, they reach the smell receptors in your nose, which react to chemicals dissolved in the mucus inside your nose and send a message to the brain.

❓ HOW DOES TOUCH WORK?

There are many different kinds of sense receptor in the skin, which between them react to touch, heat, cold, and pain. Some touch receptors react to the slightest thing, while others need a lot of pressure to make them respond. The brain puts together all the different messages to tell you if something is rough, shiny, wet, cold, and many other things.

❓ WHY DO SOME THINGS SMELL MORE THAN OTHERS?

Things that smell strong, such as perfume or food cooking, give off more smell particles, which float through the air.

❓ WHICH PARTS OF THE BODY ARE MOST SENSITIVE TO HEAT?

Your elbows and feet are more sensitive to heat than many other parts of the body. You may have noticed that bath water feels much hotter to your feet than it does to your hand. Your lips and mouth are very sensitive to heat too.

MOUTH, NOSE, AND BRAIN

Taste and smell work independently, but often occur together and the brain associates them with one another. No one knows how the brain is able to tell one smell from another.

❓ WHY DOES SNIFFING HELP YOU DETECT SMELLS BETTER?

The smell receptors are at the top of your nose, so when you sniff you bring more smell particles up to them, which helps you detect the smell better.

A TASTE BUD

Taste cells react to chemicals dissolved in saliva.

❓ WHICH PARTS OF THE BODY ARE MOST AND LEAST SENSITIVE TO TOUCH?

Any part of the body that has lots of touch receptors is particularly sensitive to touch. These parts include the lips, tongue, fingertips, and soles of the feet. The back is one of the least sensitive areas of the body.

❓ CAN BLIND PEOPLE USE TOUCH TO SEE?

Yes. Outside, they may use a long cane to feel the way in front of them. They may also read by touch, running their fingertips over Braille—patterns of raised dots that represent different letters.

Where does food go after it is swallowed?

When you swallow, the mushy ball of food goes down the gullet or esophagus into the stomach. Here it churns around for up to four hours, while it is broken down into chyme, a soupy liquid. It is then gradually squeezed out of the stomach and through a long, coiled tube—the small intestine. The nourishing parts of the food are absorbed into the blood and the rest passes on into the large intestine. About 24 hours after swallowing, the waste, called feces, is pushed out of the body.

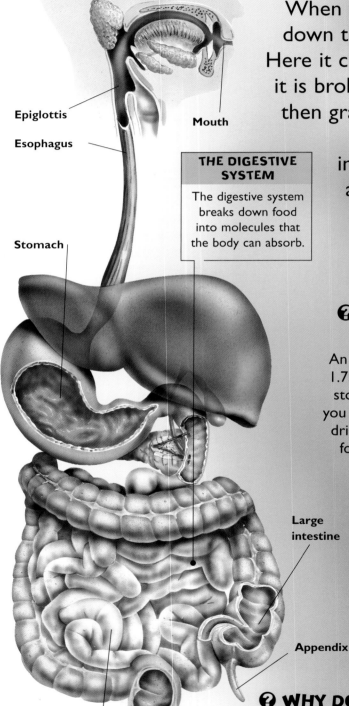

Epiglottis

Mouth

Esophagus

Stomach

Large intestine

Appendix

Small intestine

Anus

THE DIGESTIVE SYSTEM

The digestive system breaks down food into molecules that the body can absorb.

❷ HOW BIG IS YOUR STOMACH?

An adult's stomach holds about 1.75 pints (1 litre) of food. Your stomach gets bigger the more you eat. A large adult can eat and drink up to 7 pints (4 litres) of food and liquid at one meal.

❷ WHAT IS THE EPIGLOTTIS?

The epiglottis is a kind of trap door that closes off your windpipe when you swallow. It stops food going down into the lungs.

❷ WHAT IS THE APPENDIX?

The appendix is a spare part of the large intestine that plays no part in digestion. Sometimes the appendix becomes infected and has to be removed.

❷ HOW LONG ARE THE INTESTINES?

The small intestine is more than three times as long as the body! In an adult this is about 20 feet (6 m). The large intestine is a further 5 feet (1.5 m). The whole tube from mouth to anus measures about 30 feet (9 m).

❷ WHY DO FECES SMELL?

Bacteria in the large intestine help to break down waste material, but they also make it smell.

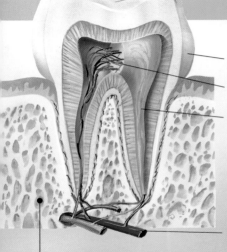

Enamel

Pulp

Dentine

Blood vessel

INSIDE A TOOTH

Teeth have long roots held in by sockets in the jaw bone and surrounded by soft gum.

❓ WHAT ARE TEETH MADE OF?

The outside of a tooth is made of enamel and is the hardest substance in the body. Underneath is dentine, which is as hard as bone, and in the center of each tooth is a tender pulpy mass of blood and nerves.

❓ HOW MANY TEETH DO YOU HAVE?

Each person has two sets of natural teeth during their life. The first set of 20 are called milk teeth and start to appear at about the age of six months. From about the age of six years, the milk teeth are gradually replaced by 32 adult teeth.

❓ WHY ARE TEETH DIFFERENT SHAPES?

Different teeth do different jobs to help you chew up food. The broad, flat teeth at the front slice through food when you take a bite. They are called incisors. The pointed canine teeth are like fangs, and grip and tear chewy food such as meat. The large, flat-topped premolars and molars grind the food between them into small pieces, which mix with saliva to make a mushy ball, ready for swallowing.

❓ WHY DOES VOMIT TASTE SOUR?

When you vomit, you bring back partly digested food into your mouth. It tastes sour because it is mixed with acid made by the lining of the stomach. The acid kills germs and helps to break the food down into smaller pieces.

❓ WHICH FOODS GIVE YOU ENERGY?

Bread, rice, potatoes, and pasta contain a lot of carbohydrates. Carbohydrates give you energy to move, work, and grow. Fats and sugars also give you energy.

❓ WHICH FOODS MAKE YOU GROW?

Milk, cheese, fish, meat, and beans contain a lot of protein, a substance that the body needs to make new cells. A varied and balanced diet provides all that the body needs to grow.

HEALTHY FOOD

Fruit, vegetables, and wholemeal bread contain plenty of fiber. Fiber makes the muscles in the intestines work better.

How do you breathe in and out?

The lungs do not have their own muscles to make you breathe in and out. The muscles between your ribs and the diaphragm—a sheet of muscle under the lungs—do the job instead. As your ribs move up and out, the diaphragm contracts and moves down. This pulls air into the lungs to fill the space. When the diaphragm and the muscles between the ribs relax, they squeeze air out of the lungs.

The windpipe is attached to loops of cartilage to make sure the airways stay open.

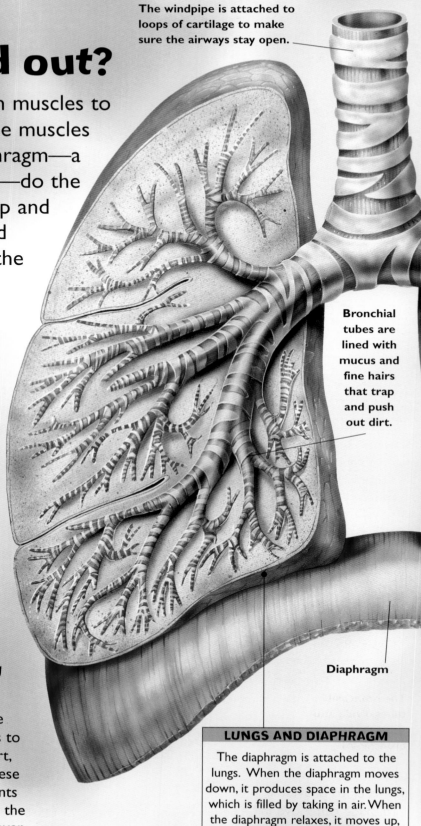

Bronchial tubes are lined with mucus and fine hairs that trap and push out dirt.

Diaphragm

❓ WHAT HAPPENS WHEN YOU SNEEZE?

When you sneeze, air rushes down your nose like a mini hurricane at 100 mph (160 km/h)—up to 20 times faster than normal. It blasts away whatever dust or pollen is irritating your nose.

❓ WHY DO YOU COUGH?

You cough when extra mucus, dust, or other particles clog the air passages between your nose and lungs. The sudden blast of air helps to clear the tubes.

❓ WHY DOES RUNNING MAKE YOU PUFF?

Muscles use up oxygen as they work. When you run, your muscles are working hard and need extra oxygen. Puffing makes you breathe in up to 20 times more air, to supply your muscles with the oxygen they need.

❓ WHAT HAPPENS WHEN YOU HICCUP?

Sometimes the diaphragm begins to contract in short, sharp spasms. These sudden movements make you "hic" as the gulps of air pass over the vocal cords.

LUNGS AND DIAPHRAGM

The diaphragm is attached to the lungs. When the diaphragm moves down, it produces space in the lungs, which is filled by taking in air. When the diaphragm relaxes, it moves up, pushing air out of the lungs.

❓ WHY DO YOU NEED TO BREATHE IN AIR?

The air contains oxygen, which the body needs to stay alive. When you breathe in, you pull air through your mouth or nose into the windpipe and through narrower and narrower tubes in the lungs. At the end of each tiny tube, or bronchiole, are hundreds of minute balloons called alveoli. As these balloons fill with air, oxygen passes from them into the blood vessels that surround them. The blood then carries the oxygen to all parts of the body. At the same time, waste carbon dioxide passes out of the blood and into the lungs. It leaves the body in the air you breathe out.

❓ HOW DO YOU TALK?

When you breathe out, the air passes over the vocal cords in the voice box or larynx in the neck. When the cords vibrate, they make a sound. Changing the shape of your lips and tongue makes different sounds, which can be put together into words.

❓ WHY CAN BREATH LOOK MISTY?

The air you breathe out contains water vapor. On a cold day this condenses into a mist of tiny water droplets.

❓ HOW MUCH AIR DO YOUR LUNGS HOLD?

An adult's lungs holds around 1.3 gallons (4.8 litres) of air, while a child's lungs hold less.

A CLUSTER OF ALVEOLI

At the end of each bronchiole is a cluster of tiny balloons called alveoli.

❓ HOW LONG CAN YOU HOLD YOUR BREATH?

You can probably hold your breath for about a minute. The longer you hold your breath, the higher the carbon dioxide level in your blood rises, and the more you feel the need to breathe out.

BREATHING IN AND OUT

To breathe in, the ribs move up and out and the diaphragm moves down. To breathe out, the ribs and diaphragm relax, pushing air out of the lungs.

The bronchial tubes divide into tiny tubes called bronchioles.

❓ WHY DO THE LUNGS HAVE SO MANY ALVEOLI?

In order to provide a huge surface across which oxygen and carbon dioxide can move in and out of the blood. In fact the lungs have over 700 million alveoli. The area of the alveolar surface in the adult human is about 100 square feet (93 sq m).

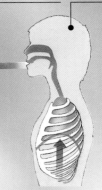

Breathing in   Breathing out

What job does your heart do?

The heart's job is to pump blood to the lungs and then all around the body. The right side of the heart takes in blood from the body and pumps it to the lungs. The left side of the heart takes blood filled with oxygen from the lungs and pumps it to the rest of the body. Valves inside the heart stop blood flowing the wrong way.

"Used" blood enters the heart from the arms and head.

"Used" blood leaves the heart for the right lung along the right pulmonary artery.

❓ WHAT IS PLASMA?

Just over half the blood is a yellowish liquid called plasma. It is mainly water with molecules of digested food and essential salts dissolved in it.

Blood stocked with oxygen enters the heart from the right lung along the right pulmonary veins.

❓ WHAT IS A BLOOD TRANSFUSION?

If a person loses a lot of blood, perhaps due to an accident or operation, the lost blood can be replaced with blood given by someone else. The new blood is dripped straight into a vein.

The right side of the heart takes in "used" blood and pumps it to the lungs.

❓ HOW MUCH BLOOD DO YOU HAVE?

An average man has 9–10 pints (5–6 litres) of blood; an average woman has about 8 pints (4–5 litres). Children have less.

Red blood cell

❓ WHAT ARE BLOOD GROUPS?

There are four main groups of blood: A, B, AB, and O. Only some groups can be mixed with others, so doctors find out which blood group a patient belongs to before giving a blood transfusion.

Plasma

White blood cell

BLOOD IN CLOSE-UP
Blood cells are a brighter red when they are carrying oxygen

"Used" blood from the lower body returns to the heart.

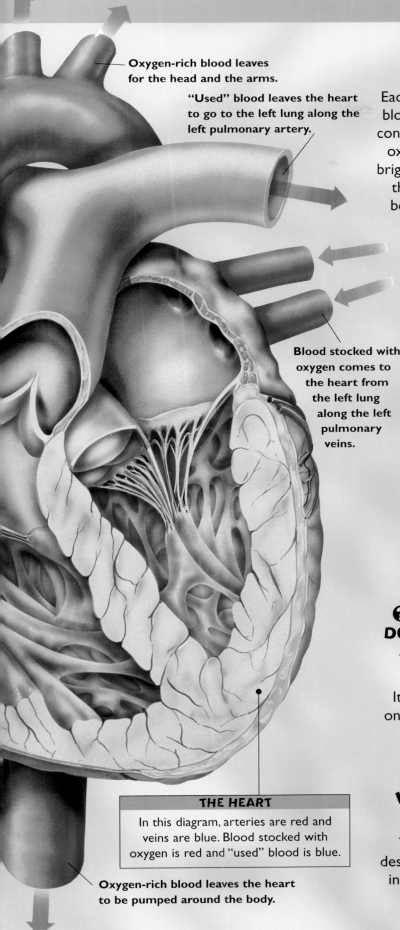

Oxygen-rich blood leaves for the head and the arms.

"Used" blood leaves the heart to go to the left lung along the left pulmonary artery.

Blood stocked with oxygen comes to the heart from the left lung along the left pulmonary veins.

THE HEART

In this diagram, arteries are red and veins are blue. Blood stocked with oxygen is red and "used" blood is blue.

Oxygen-rich blood leaves the heart to be pumped around the body.

❓ WHY IS BLOOD RED?

Each tiny drop of blood contains up to 5 million red blood cells that give blood its color. Red blood cells contain a substance called hemoglobin, which takes in oxygen in the lungs. Blood that is rich in oxygen is bright red. As this bright red blood is pumped around the body, the oxygen is gradually taken up by the body's cells. By the time the blood returns to the heart, it is a slightly darker, more rusty red.

❓ HOW OFTEN DOES THE HEART BEAT?

A child's heart usually beats about 80 times a minute, a bit faster than an adult's (70 times a minute). When you run or do something strenuous, your heart beats faster to send more blood to the muscles.

❓ WHAT IS A CAPILLARY?

Blood travels around the body through tubes called arteries and veins. These branch off into smaller and smaller tubes that reach every cell of the body. Capillaries are the tiniest blood vessels of all. Most capillaries are thinner than a single hair. If an adult's capillaries were laid end to end, they would stretch 60,000 miles (100,000 km)— nearly two and a half times around the world.

❓ HOW OFTEN DOES BLOOD GO AROUND THE BODY?

It goes around about once a minute or 1,500 times a day.

❓ HOW BIG IS THE HEART?

The heart is about the size of a clenched fist. It lies nearly in the middle of your chest and the lower end tilts toward the left side of the body.

❓ WHAT DO WHITE BLOOD CELLS DO?

They surround and destroy germs and other intruders that get into the blood.

❓ WHAT IS THE HEART MADE OF?

A special kind of muscle, called cardiac (heart) muscle, which never gets tired.

What do the kidneys do?

The kidneys filter the blood to remove wastes and extra water and salts. Each kidney has about a million tiny filters, which between them clean about a quarter of your blood every minute. The kidneys work by forcing many substances out of the blood and then taking back in only what the body needs. The unwanted substances combine with water to make urine, which trickles down to the bladder where it is stored.

A large artery called the aorta brings blood from the heart to the kidneys.

Blood is filtered in the kidneys and the waste urine is funneled into the ureters.

As urine trickles down the ureters and into the bladder, the bladder stretches.

❓ WHY DO YOU SWEAT WHEN YOU ARE HOT?

Sweating helps to cool you down. When the body becomes hot, sweat glands pump lots of salty water on to the skin. As the sweat evaporates (changes into water vapor), it takes extra heat from the body.

Cleansed blood leaves the kidneys and returns to the heart.

Urine leaves the bladder through the urethra when a circle of muscle relaxes to open the entrance to the tube.

ATHLETE SPRINTING
When muscles work hard, they produce heat as well as movement.

KIDNEYS

A kidney weighs about 5 ounces (140 g) and filters nearly 2 pints (over 1 litre) of blood a minute.

The ureter is a long tube that takes urine from the kidneys to the bladder. Muscles in the ureter help to move the urine through the tube.

❓ WHAT DOES THE LIVER DO?

The liver is a chemical factory that does more than 500 different jobs. Some of its most important functions concern the processing of digested food and the removal of waste and poisons from the blood. Digested food is taken straight from the intestines to the liver, where some nutrients may be released into the blood and the rest stored to be used later. The liver processes poisons, and changes unwanted proteins into urea. The kidneys remove poisons and urea and make them into urine.

❓ WHAT IS BILE?

Bile is a yellow-green liquid made by the liver and stored in the gall bladder. From there it passes into the small intestine, where it helps to break up fatty food.

❓ HOW MUCH URINE DOES THE BLADDER HOLD?

An adult's bladder can hold up to about 1 pint (600 ml) of urine. But you usually need to go to the bathroom as soon as your bladder is about one-fourth full.

❓ WHY DO YOU GO RED WHEN YOU ARE HOT?

As different parts of the body burn up energy they make heat. Blood carries the heat around the body. If the body becomes too hot, the tiny blood vessels near the surface of the skin expand to help the blood cool. Blood flowing near to the skin makes the skin look red.

❓ HOW MUCH LIQUID DO YOU NEED TO DRINK?

You need to drink about 2–2.5 pints (1.2–1.5 litres) of watery drinks a day. The amount of water you take in balances the amount you lose. Most water is lost in urine and feces. But sweat and the air you breathe out also contain water.

❓ WHY IS URINE YELLOW?

Urine contains traces of waste bile and this makes it yellowish. If you drink a lot of water, your urine will be diluted and less yellow, but the first urine of the morning is usually stronger and darker. Some foods affect the color of urine. Eating beetroot can turn it pinkish.

❓ WHY DO YOU NEED TO DRINK MORE IN HOT WEATHER?

When it is hot, you sweat more and so lose more water, which you then replace by drinking more.

❓ WHAT MAKES YOU URINATE?

The bladder stretches as it fills. When it contains about 0.25 pint (150 ml), nerves in the walls of the bladder send signals to the brain and you feel the need to urinate.

❓ HOW LONG CAN YOU LIVE WITHOUT WATER?

Although some people have lived for several weeks without food, you can survive only a few days without drinking water.

The umbilical cord joins the baby to the placenta.

A BABY IN THE WOMB
The placenta supplies the unborn baby with oxygen and food from the mother's blood.

❓ WHY DO CHILDREN LOOK LIKE THEIR PARENTS?

You inherit a mixture of genes from your parents, so in some ways you will look similar to your mother and in others to your father.

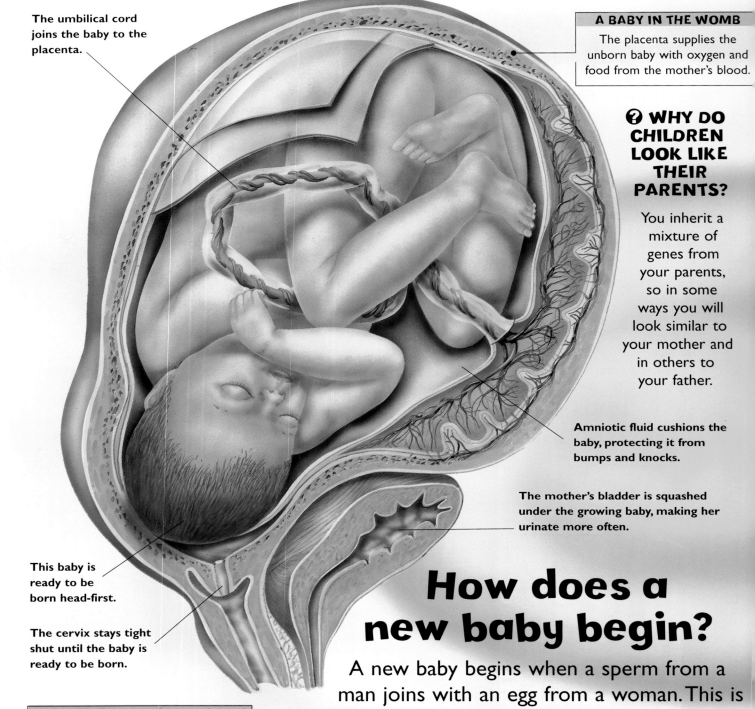

Amniotic fluid cushions the baby, protecting it from bumps and knocks.

The mother's bladder is squashed under the growing baby, making her urinate more often.

This baby is ready to be born head-first.

The cervix stays tight shut until the baby is ready to be born.

How does a new baby begin?

A new baby begins when a sperm from a man joins with an egg from a woman. This is called fertilization, and it happens after the man ejaculates sperm into the woman's vagina during sex. The cells of the fertilized egg begin to multiply into a cluster of cells, which embeds itself in the lining of the womb. There the cells continue to multiply and form the embryo of a new human being.

THE MOMENT OF FERTILIZATION
Only one sperm penetrates the egg.

WHAT IS A FETUS?

A fetus is an unborn baby from eight weeks after conception until birth. In the first seven weeks after conception it is called an embryo. By 14 weeks the fetus is fully formed, but is too small and frail to survive outside the womb. Babies of 24 weeks can survive in an incubator if they are born early, but most stay in the womb for the full 36 weeks.

WHAT IS LABOR?

Labor is the process of giving birth. The neck of the womb stretches and opens, and then the womb, which is made of strong muscle, contracts to push the baby out. Labor can take several hours.

WHERE DOES A MAN'S SPERM COME FROM?

Sperm are made in the testicles, two sacs that hang to either side of the penis. After puberty, the testicles make millions of sperm every day. Any sperm that are not ejaculated are absorbed back into the blood.

WHAT ARE GENES?

Genes are a combination of chemicals contained in each cell. They come from your mother and father and determine everything about you, including the color of your hair, how tall you will be, and even what diseases you might get in later life.

WHERE DOES THE EGG COME FROM?

When a girl is born, she already has thousands of eggs stored in her two ovaries. After puberty, one of these eggs is released every month and travels down the Fallopian tube to the womb.

WHAT IS A CONDOM?

A condom is a thin rubber sheath that fits over the man's penis. It stops sperm getting into the woman's vagina during sex, so that a baby cannot be conceived. Another contraceptive (thing that prevents pregnancy) is the Pill, which is taken by women.

HOW DOES AN UNBORN BABY FEED?

Most of the cluster of cells that embeds itself in the womb grows into an organ called the placenta. Food and oxygen from the mother's blood pass through the placenta into the blood of the growing baby.

HOW FAST DOES AN UNBORN BABY GROW?

You grow faster before you are born than at any other time in your life. Three weeks after the egg is fertilized, the embryo is no bigger than a grain of rice. Five weeks later, almost every part of the new baby has formed—the head, brain, eyes, heart, stomach, and even the fingers—yet it is only about the size of a thumb. By the time it is born, 30 weeks later, it will probably be about 20 inches (50 cm) long and weigh about 7 pounds (3.5 kg).

WHAT DO BABIES DO IN THE WOMB?

As the unborn baby gets bigger, it exercises its muscles by kicking, moving, and punching. It also sucks its thumb sometimes, opens and shuts its eyes, and goes to sleep.

WHAT IS A PERIOD?

If the egg is not fertilized by a sperm, it passes out of the woman's body through the vagina. At the same time, the lining of the womb and some blood also pass out of the body. This slow flow of blood lasts about five days every month and is called a period.

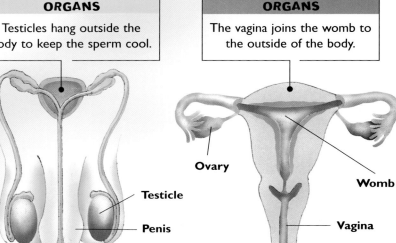

MALE REPRODUCTIVE ORGANS

Testicles hang outside the body to keep the sperm cool.

Testicle

Penis

FEMALE REPRODUCTIVE ORGANS

The vagina joins the womb to the outside of the body.

Ovary

Womb

Vagina

What is puberty?

Puberty is the time in which you grow from a child into an adult. You grow taller and your body changes shape. A girl develops breasts and her hips become broader. Her waist looks thinner. A boy's chest becomes broader and his voice grows deeper. At the same time, the sex organs develop. A girl begins to have periods and a boy begins to produce sperm. Puberty lasts several years and affects moods, feelings, and attitudes as well as bringing physical changes.

At puberty the sexual organs begin to mature.

❓ WHAT HAPPENS WHEN A BOY'S VOICE BREAKS?

A boy may be growing so fast during puberty that the muscles that control his vocal cords cannot keep up. His voice may suddenly change from high to low before finding the right pitch. The vocal cords also become thicker, making his voice deeper.

❓ WHY CAN'T YOUNG BABIES SIT UP?

Young babies cannot sit up until their back muscles have grown strong enough to support them. This happens around 6 months.

❓ WHEN ARE YOU FULLY GROWN?

Boys and girls grow quickly during puberty, then more slowly until they reach their full height some time around age 20.

❓ WHEN DO BABIES LEARN TO WALK AND TALK?

By its first birthday, a baby is usually already pulling itself up on to its feet and is nearly ready to walk. It may also be beginning to say a few words, though talking develops slowly over the next few years.

During childhood, the legs and arms grow longer and the child becomes more adept and confident.

❓ ARE NEWBORN BABIES COMPLETELY HELPLESS?

Not completely—a baby can breathe, suck, and swallow from the moment it is born.

❓ WHAT ARE HORMONES?

Hormones are chemicals released into the blood from various glands. Some glands make sex hormones that control the menstrual cycle.

A two-year-old is about half the height it will be when adult.

Babies often learn to crawl before they take their first tottering steps.

STAGES OF GROWTH

Our human development takes us through various major stages of growth and change.

❓ WHY DO PEOPLE AGE?

The cells of the body are constantly being renewed, except for brain cells and other nerve cells. As people get older, the new cells do not perform as well as the cells of younger people.

Adults are fully grown and may decide to have children of their own.

As people get older, they begin to slow down.

Very old people may become quite frail.

❓ WHAT DO ALL NEW BABIES NEED ?

All newborn babies need food, warmth, love, and protection. At first a baby can only drink liquids, so it sucks milk from its mother's breasts or from a bottle. Milk contains everything the new baby needs to grow and stay healthy. A baby also needs to be washed and have its nappy changed regularly. Babies sleep a lot of the time, but when they are awake they need plenty of smiles and cuddles. Babies and children rely on their parents for the things they need.

❓ WHAT MAKES YOU GROW?

A growth hormone tells your body to grow. This is produced in the pituitary gland in the brain and is taken all around the body in the blood. Exactly how tall you grow is determined by genes inherited from your parents.

❓ WHAT IS THE MENOPAUSE?

The menopause is when a woman's body changes so that she is no longer able to have children. As sex hormone levels drop, her ovaries stop producing eggs. The woman may experience uncomfortable hot flushes and unpredictable mood swings.

❓ WHO HAD THE MOST CHILDREN?

It is believed that a Russian woman who lived in the 1700s holds this record. She was called Madame Vassilyev and she gave birth to no fewer than 69 children.

❓ WHY DO YOU HAVE TO SUPPORT A YOUNG BABY'S HEAD?

When a baby is born, the muscles in its back and neck are very weak—too weak to hold up its own head. A baby's head is much bigger for the size of its body than a child's or an adult's.

❓ WHY DO BABIES CRY?

A baby cries when it needs something—when it is hungry or lonely. It also cries when it has a stomach ache or other pain.

❓ UNIVERSE ❓

1 When do eclipses of the Sun occur?
2 What is at the center of our solar system?
3 Why do astronauts on the Moon need to take oxygen with them?
4 Which is the Red Planet?
5 Could you land on Jupiter?
6 Which was the first artificial satellite?
7 Which planet is named after the goddess of love?
8 What is a cosmonaut?
9 What is the name for an area in space which sucks everything into itself, even light?
10 What is a meteor?

SCIENCE

1 Because hot air is lighter than cold air
2 Gravity
3 Faster than the speed of sound
4 Life
5 Iron
6 Facsimile
7 Collects television signals
8 The study of sound
9 Sir Isaac Newton
10 A chronometer

❓ LANDS AND PEOPLE ❓

1 Which is the longest and narrowest country?
2 What is the capital of Japan?
3 Who were the first people to grow potatoes corn, tomatoes, and tobacco?
4 Where is Fiji?
5 Which famous railroad crosses Russia?
6 What is a gaucho?
7 Which is Islam's most holy city?
8 Where might you find the Abominable Snowman?
9 In which city could you ride in a gondola?
10 The Caribbean Sea is part of which ocean?

HISTORY

1 Napoleon Bonaparte
2 The Colosseum
3 The first atom bomb
4 Pharaoh
5 1914
6 Berlin
7 Votes for women
8 Tutankhamun's tomb
9 Lenin
10 The Red Cross

❓ HISTORY ❓

1 Which French leader was defeated at the battle of Waterloo?

2 In which building in central Rome did the Romans hold contests between gladiators?

3 What was dropped on Hiroshima?

4 What word is used for an ancient Egyptian "king"?

5 When did World War I begin?

6 Which German city was divided by a wall?

7 What did suffragettes fight for?

8 Howard Carter discovered which Egyptian pharaoh's tomb in 1922?

9 Who led the Russian Revolution in 1917 and became the first leader of Communist Russia?

10 Which international organization was founded to care for soldiers wounded in war?

LANDS AND PEOPLE

1 Chile
2 Tokyo
3 The Native Americans
4 In the Pacific Ocean
5 The Trans Siberian Railway
6 A South American cowboy
7 Mecca in Saudi Arabia
8 In the Himalayas
9 Venice in Italy
10 The Atlantic

❓ SCIENCE ❓

1 Why do hot air balloons float in the air?

2 What is the force that pulls everything toward the Earth?

3 What does supersonic mean?

4 What is biology the science of?

5 What is produced in a blast furnace?

6 What is the word fax short for?

7 What does a television aerial do?

8 What is the study of acoustics?

9 Which scientist thought of gravity when he saw an apple fall?

10 What is an accurate sea-going clock called?

UNIVERSE

1 When the Moon hides the Sun from the Earth
2 The Sun
3 Because there is no air on the Moon
4 Mars
5 No, there is no surface to land on
6 The Russian *Sputnik*
7 Venus
8 A Russian astronaut
9 A black hole
10 A lump of rock in space

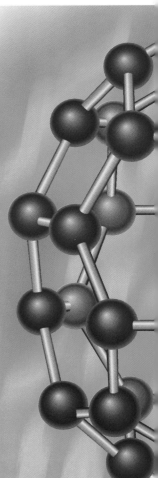

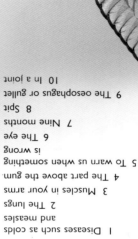

❓ ANIMALS ❓

1 Which animal lives on the sea bed, has tentacles and looks like a flower?
2 How does a marsupial carry its young?
3 What is a young swan called?
4 Which elephants have larger ears: African or Indian?
5 Why do spiders build webs?
6 How many humps does a Bactrian camel have?
7 Which insect transmits malaria?
8 Which is the largest of the apes?
9 What does a bird have that no other animal has?
10 How does a dog cool itself down?

HUMAN BODY

1 Diseases such as colds and measles
2 The lungs
3 Muscles in your arms
4 The part above the gum.
5 To warn us when something is wrong
6 The eye
7 Nine months
8 Spit
9 The oesophagus or gullet
10 In a joint

❓ PLANTS ❓

1 Which parts of a tree trap sunlight and make food for the tree?
2 Which cereal crop grows under water?
3 Why do some desert plants have very long roots?
4 Which tree is the tallest?
5 What is a word for parsley, sage and basil?
6 Lemons give us an important vitamin. Is it A, B or C?
7 What are stigma, sepals and anthers part of?
8 Where does cork come from?
9 Ginger, cloves and nutmeg are all what?
10 What do daffodils, bluebells and crocuses have in common?

PLANET EARTH

1 A fertile place in a desert
2 Clouds
3 Sandstone
4 A volcano that no longer erupts
5 366 days
6 Coal, oil and natural gas
7 A glacier
8 The South Pole
9 The Amazon basin
10 At the mouth of a river

❓ PLANET EARTH ❓

1 What is an oasis?
2 What are cirrus, cumulus and cirrostratus examples of?
3 Which rock is formed from grains of sand?
4 What is an extinct volcano?
5 How long is a leap year?
6 Which are the three most important fuels?
7 What is the name for a large, slow-moving mass of ice on the surface of the land?
8 Which is colder, the North Pole or the South Pole?
9 Where is the world's largest rainforest?
10 Where would you find a delta?

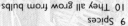

PLANTS
1 The leaves
2 Rice
3 To reach water deep underground
4 The Californian Redwood
5 Herbs
6 Vitamin C
7 Flowers
8 It is the bark of a tree (the cork oak)
9 Spices
10 They all grow from bulbs

❓ HUMAN BODY ❓

1 What do viruses cause?
2 Pneumonia affects which part of the body?
3 What are your biceps?
4 What is the crown of a tooth?
5 Why is pain useful?
6 Which part of the body is affected by conjunctivitis?
7 For how long does a baby grow inside its mother?
8 What is another word for saliva?
9 What is the name of the tube which takes food from your mouth to your stomach?
10 Where would you find a ligament?

ANIMALS
1 A sea anemone
2 In its pouch
3 A cygnet
4 African
5 To catch their prey
6 Two
7 The mosquito
8 The gorilla
9 Feathers
10 By panting